PAKISTAN INSIGHTS 2023

PAKISTAN INSIGHTS 2023

Editor

Tilak Devasher

Vivekananda International Foundation

PENTAGON PRESS LLP

First published in 2023 by
PENTAGON PRESS LLP
206, Peacock Lane, Shahpur Jat
New Delhi-110049, India
Contact: 011-26491568 • 011-26490600

Typeset in Adobe Garamond, 11 Point
Printed by Aegean Offset Printers, Greater Noida, U.P.

ISBN 978-81-951894-4-1 [HB]

www.pentagonpress.in

Contents

MAP OF PAKISTAN

Pakistan at a Glance – 2023

Aarushi Gupta

Area

Total (Land and Water): 796,095 sq km

https://www.cia.gov/the-world-factbook/countries/pakistan/

Area of Provinces

Balochistan: 347,190 sq km

Punjab 205.344 sq km

Sindh: 140.914 sq km

Khyber Pakhtunkhwa (Including Federally Administered Tribal Areas): 101,741 sq km

International Borders

Afghanistan: 2,670 km

China: 438 km

India: 3,190 km

Iran: 959 km

https://www.cia.gov/the-world-factbook/countries/pakistan/

Length of Coastline

1,046 km

ENERGY

Installed Capacity and Generation of Electricity (July-March FY2023)

Source	*Installed Capacity*		*Generation*	
	MW	*Share (%)*	*GWh*	*Share (%)*
Hydel	10,592	25.8	26,937	28.6
Thermal	24,095	58.8	43,526	46.2
Nuclear	3,530	**8.6**	19,739	21.0
Renewable	2,783	**6.8**	3,919	**4.2**
Total	**41,000**		**94,121**	

Source: Economic Survey of Pakistan 2022-23. https://www.finance.gov.pk/survey/chapters 23/ 14 Energy.pdf

Production of Crude Oil: 4.3 million metric tons (2019)

https://www.trade.gov/energy-resource-guide-pakistan-oil-and-gas

Number of Oilfields: 167 (July 2018)

Production of Natural Gas: 4 billion cubic feet (BCFT) per day

https://www.dawn.com/news/1696715#:~:text=He%20said%20Sindh%20 had% 20124,12%20years%20of%20gas%20left.

Number of Gas Fields: 181 (July 2018)

Petroleum Imports (Jul-Mar FY2023): 6,118.3 thousand tonnes

Crude Oil Imports (Jul-Mar FY2023): 5,858.4 thousand tonnes

Total Electricity Generation (Jul-Mar FY2023): 94,121 GWh

Total Electricity Consumption: 84,034 GWh

Source: Economic Survey of Pakistan 2022-23. (https://www.finance.gov.pk/ survey/chapters_23/Highlights.pdf)

DEMOGRAPHIC BASE

Population

241.49 million (2023)

Source: 7th Population and Housing Census-2023 'The Digital Census'. https:/ /www.pbs.gov.pk/sites/default/files/population/2023/Press%20Release. pdf

Population Density

295 per sq. km (2020, World Bank)

(https://data.worldbank.org/indicator/EN.POP.DNST?locations=PK)

Annual Population Growth Rate

2.55 % (2023 Census)

Human Development Index (HDI) (2021): 0.544, Rank 161 (UNDP)

(https://hdr.undp.org/data-center/specific-country-data#/countries/PAK)

Administrative Unit Population

Punjab: 127.68 million

Sindh: 55.69 million

Khyber Pakhtunkhwa: 40.85 million

Balochistan: 14.89 million

Islamabad: 2.36 million

(According to 2023 Census)

Distribution of Population

Urban Population %: 38.82

Rural Population %: 61.18

(According to 2023 Census)

Religion

Muslims: 96.47% (Sunni 85-90%, Shia 10-15%)

Hindus: (2.14%)

Christians: (1.27%)

Ahmadiyyas: (0.09%)

Others: (0.02%)

(According to 2017 Census)

(https://www.cia.gov/the-world-factbook/countries/pakistan/)

ECONOMIC PROFILE

Basic Economic Parameters

Criteria	*Values*
GDP (billion US$) (2022) [2]	376.53
Real GDP growth (2023) [3]	0.29%
Per capita income (US$) [3]	1,568
CPI national inflation avg. (Jul-May, FY 2023) [3]	29.2
Agriculture (% of GDP) [3]	22.9
Manufacturing (% of GDP) [3]	12.01
Services (% of GDP) [3]	58
Exports of goods and services (% of GDP) (2022) [2]	10.5
Imports of goods and services (% of GDP) (2022) [2]	21.9
Gross capital formation (% of GDP) (2022) [2]	15
Urban population growth (annual %) (2022) [2]	2.7
Electricity consumption (kWh million) (2022) [1]	111,263
Tax revenue (% of GDP) [1]	10.1
Personal remittances, received (billion US$) [3]	22.7
Net Foreign Direct Investment inflows (billion US$) [3]	1.2
Net official development assistance received (current US$) (million) (2021) [2]	2.6
Total public debt (end-March 2023) (billion PKR) [3]·	59,247
Domestic Debt (billion PKR) [3]·	35,076
External Public Debt (billion PKR) [3]	24,171

[1] Asian Development Bank
[2] World Bank Data
[3] Pakistan Economic Survey 2022-2023

INFRASTRUCTURE PROFILE

Infrastructure

Road Network: 263,775 km

National Highways of Pakistan: 12,131 km (39 national highways/ motorways/ expressway/ strategic routes)

Source: https://communication.gov.pk/Detail/MTAyMGFlN2ItMTc2Mi00 MjAx LTg3 MDE tZDZjYmY3NDU4N2Y1

Operating Railway Network

7,791 km (World Bank, 2019)

https://data.worldbank.org/indicator/IS.RRS.TOTL.KM?locations=PK

DEFENCE BUDGET [Pakistan Rupee (Rs)]

2018	2019	2020	2021	2022	2023
1.10 tr	1.15 tr	1.28 tr	1.37 tr	1.56 tr	1.80 tr

Budget 2018-19 https://www.finance.gov.pk/budget/Budget_in_Brief_2018_19.pdf
Budget 2019-20 https://www.finance.gov.pk/budget/Budget_in_Brief_2019_20.pdf
Budget 2020-21 https://www.finance.gov.pk/budget/Budget_in_Brief_2020_21_English.pdf
Budget 2021-22 https://www.finance.gov.pk/budget/Budget_2021_22/6_Budget_in_Brief_English_2021_22.pdf
Budget 2022-23 https://www.finance.gov.pk/budget/Budget_2022_23/Budget_in_Brief_English.pdf
Budget 2023-24 https://www.finance.gov.pk/budget/Budget_2023_24/Budget_in_Brief.pdf

MILITARY PROFILE (The Military Balance 2023, IISS)

(https://www.iiss.org/en/publications/the-military-balance/)

Force Levels

ACTIVE: 651,800

- Army: 560,000
- Navy: 21,800 (incl. ε3,200 Marines)
- Air Force: 70,000

Paramilitary: 291,000

- Airport Security Force: 9,000
- Pakistan Coast Guard: Patrol and Coastal Combatants: 5
- Frontier Corps: 70,000
- Maritime Security Agency: ε2,000
- National Guard: 185,000
- Pakistan Rangers: 25,000

Strategic Forces

Army Strategic Forces Command: 12,000-15,000 (Commands all land-based strategic nuclear forces)

Air: 1-2 sqn of F-16 A/B or Mirage 5 may be assigned a nuclear-strike role

List of Contributors

Dr. Arvind Gupta is the Director of the Vivekananda Foundation, New Delhi. He was the Deputy National Security Adviser and Secretary, National Security Council, Government of India during 2014-17. Prior to that, he was Director-General of the Institute for Defence Studies and Analyses, Ministry of Defence, New Delhi. He is a former career diplomat and has served in the Ministry of External Affairs and Indian missions abroad. Author of five books, his last book *Opportunity for India in a Changing World* was published by KW Publishers Pvt. Ltd. in 2021. Penguin India published *How India Manages Its National Security* in 2018. He has edited several books. He co-edited (with Anil Wadhwa) a volume titled *India's Foreign Policy: Surviving in a Turbulent World* (Sage, 2020) and with Arpita Mitra a volume titled *Vasudhaiva Kutumbakam: The Relevance of India's Ancient Thinking to Contemporary Strategic Reality* (Aryan International, New Delhi, 2020). He comments frequently on strategic affairs on national television, and lectures at military academies and universities.

Rana Banerji is a former officer of the Indian Administrative Services (IAS-1972, Assam-Meghalaya cadre). He retired as Special Secretary, Cabinet Secretariat, in October 2009. After retirement, Banerji headed a Task Force on Intelligence Reforms at the Institute for Defence Studies & Analyses (IDSA). He participates in the UN Human Rights Commission Privacy Rights Rapporteur's annual meetings on Accountability & Intelligence Reforms. He has participated in several Track II and Track 1.5 interactions on Indo-Pak relations, Indo-US Security Relations and Indo-Pak-Afghan Tripartite Dialogue (2010-2015). His focus area of expertise pertains to Pakistan, Afghanistan, and Islamic Terrorism.

Lt Gen (Dr.) Rakesh Sharma (retd.) was commissioned in the Indian Army in 1977, and had a career spanning forty years. He had extensive operational experience in Jammu and Kashmir, the North-East and on the western borders.

He had trained the Botswana Army for three years, attended the National College in Nigeria, and the National Defence College at New Delhi. He was a Research Fellow at the Institute for Defence Studies and Analyses (IDSA). Lt Gen Rakesh Sharma commanded the Fire and Fury Corps in Ladakh, facing both Pakistan and China. He writes regularly for newspapers, military journals and contributes chapters in books. He is currently on the Executive Council of the IDSA and Global Counter-Terrorism Council and Distinguished Fellow with the Vivekananda International Foundation and the Centre for Land Warfare Studies. He is the author of a monograph published by USI, New Delhi, titled *The Determinants of India's National Military Strategy.*

Brig Rahul K. Bhonsle (retd.) is an army veteran Brigadier with over three decades active service. He is an independent consultant on research and knowledge management in defence and security issues in Indo Asia Pacific Asia and Director Security Risks Asia, a Risk and Knowledge Management consultancy based in Delhi since 2006.

Amb. Gopalaswami Parthasarathy was born on 13 May 1940. He is a career Foreign Service Officer who retired on 31 May 2000. Prior to his entry into the Indian Foreign Service, Mr. Parthasarathy was a Commissioned Officer in the Indian Army (1963-1968), after having graduated with a B.E. Degree in Electrical Engineering from the College of Engineering, Guindy, Madras, in 1962. He has served as Ambassador of India to Myanmar, 1992-95; High Commissioner of India to Australia, 1995-98; High Commissioner of India to Pakistan, 1998-2000; and High Commissioner of India, Cyprus, 1990-92. He also served in Indian missions abroad as Second/First Secretary, Embassy of India, Moscow (1969-1973); Deputy High Commissioner to Tanzania (1974-1976); Counsellor, (Political and Press), Embassy of India, Washington D.C. (1978-1981); and Consul-General of India, Karachi (1982-1985).

In New Delhi, Mr. Parthasarathy was Deputy Secretary in the Foreign Secretary's Office (1976-1978). He has served as Spokesman, Ministry of External Affairs and Information Adviser and Spokesman in the Prime Minister's Office with Prime Minister Rajiv Gandhi (1985-90). He has been a member of Indian delegations in several international conferences including summits at the United Nations, Non-Aligned Movement, and SAARC.

Mr. Parthasarathy is a Director in the India-Sri Lanka Foundation. He is also a member of the Executive Committee of the Centre for Air Power Studies in New Delhi. He was a member of the Government of India's Task Force to Review National Security Structures in India (Naresh Chandra Committee) and till recently the Chancellor of the Central University in Jammu. He also headed the Special Committee on Documenting, Narrating and Exhibiting Sardar Patel's role in the Integration of Princely States and Unification of India, set up by Prime Minister Modi.

Amb. Sharat Sabharwal joined the Indian Foreign Service in 1975. After serving in various positions in the Permanent Mission of India to the UN in Geneva and Indian missions in Madagascar, France, and Mauritius, he was Director/Joint Secretary in the Ministry of External Affairs from 1990 to 1995. The positions held by him subsequently have been Deputy High Commissioner of India in Pakistan (1995-99), Deputy Permanent Representative of India to the UN in Geneva (1999-2002), Ambassador of India to Uzbekistan (2002-2005) and Additional Secretary/Special Secretary in the Ministry of External Affairs overseeing Administration, Consular, Passport, and Visa matters (2005-2009).

He was High Commissioner of India to Pakistan from April 2009 to June 2013. He was appointed Central Information Commissioner in November 2013 and served in this position till September 2017. He was the Deputy leader/member of Indian delegations to the UN General Assembly, the UN Commission on Human Rights, International Labour Conference, and World Health Assembly. He was also the Deputy Leader of the Indian delegation to the International Conference of the Red Cross and Red Crescent held in Geneva in October 1999 and a member of the Indian delegation to the World Conference against Racism, held in Durban in September 2001.

He is a Distinguished Visiting Fellow at the Ananta Centre, New Delhi. He has been commenting on foreign policy issues, notably concerning Pakistan and Afghanistan, in TV discussions and the print media. He is the author of the book '*India's Pakistan Conundrum – Managing a Complex Relationship*'.

Aarushi Gupta is a Research Assistant at Vivekananda International Foundation, a leading think tank in India. She graduated from Delhi University (Gargi College) with core subjects Political Science and Economics. She did Masters (MA-International Studies) from Symbiosis School of International Studies. Her dissertation was focused on National Security through a constructivist lens, titled 'Dissecting Terrorism to Uncover the Battle of Narratives'. She has previously interned at MP-IDSA and CENJOWS. She is a keen observer of Afghanistan-

Pakistan and the Indian subcontinent with themes associated with Foreign Policy and National Security.

Dr. Shalini Chawla is a Distinguished Fellow at the Centre for Air Power Studies (CAPS), New Delhi. She joined CAPS in 2006 and has published more than 100 research articles in national and international journals on a wide range of issues relating to Pakistan and Afghanistan. She has authored seven books and lectures regularly at various universities, think tanks, and leading institutions of the Indian Armed Forces and Foreign Service. She is actively engaged in India's Track 1.5 initiatives. She received a Commendation and Badge by the Chief of Air Staff in October 2020 for her praiseworthy contribution to the Service.

Amb. D.B. Venkatesh Varma served in the Indian Foreign Service from 1988 to 2021. During his diplomatic career, he worked in the Office of the External Affairs Minister and in the Prime Minister's Office. He served as India's Ambassador to the Conference on Disarmament in Geneva, to the Kingdom of Spain and to the Russian Federation, until October 2021. He has vast experience in India's Security and Defence policies and served as Joint Secretary in charge of Disarmament and International Security in the Ministry of External Affairs. He organized Prime Minister Narendra Modi's visit to Vladivostok in 2019 and contributed to India's Act Far East Policy. He was the first recipient of the S.K. Singh Award for Excellence in the Indian Foreign Service in 2011 for his contribution to the negotiations of the Civil Nuclear Initiative. He is a Distinguished Fellow at the VIF, New Delhi.

Amb. T.C.A. Raghavan retired from the Indian Foreign Service at the end of 2015 while Indian High Commissioner to Pakistan (2013-15). He had earlier served as Deputy High Commissioner in Pakistan (2003-2007) and High Commissioner to Singapore from 2009 to 2013. During his service tenure, apart from deployments in the Ministry of External Affairs, he also served in Indian embassies and high commissions in Kuwait (1983-86), Bhutan (1992-95), and the United Kingdom (1995-98).

During his last posting in New Delhi (2007-09) in the Ministry of External Affairs, Raghavan was Joint Secretary dealing with Pakistan, Afghanistan, and Iran. Posts held in the Ministry of External Affairs include Director of the Office of the External Affairs Minister (2000-2003) during the tenure of Shri Jaswant Singh as External Affairs Minister.

He was awarded a Ph.D. by the Jawaharlal Nehru University in 1992 for his dissertation relating to the economic history of India. His current interests are historical research, strategic analysis and the diplomatic and intellectual history of modern India. He writes, lectures and participates in discussions on foreign policy and diplomacy related issues and in particular those relating to Indian and South Asian diplomatic and maritime history, Pakistan, Iran, Afghanistan and South-East Asia.

He was Director-General of the Indian Council of World Affairs, New Delhi, from 2018 to 2021.

His first book was published in January 2017: *Attendant Lords, Bairam Khan and Abdur Rahim — Courtiers and Poets in Mughal India*. It was awarded the Mohammad Habib Memorial Prize by the Indian History Congress in December 2017. He is also the author of *'The People Next Door : The Curious History of India's Relations with Pakistan',* (Hurst & Co, 2017), and *History Men: Jadunath Sarkar, G.S. Sardesai, Raghubir Sinh and Their Quest for India's Past* (HarperCollins, 2020). Recently, he has co-authored *Sapru House, A Story of Institution Building in World Affairs* (ICWA, 2021) which is a history of India's first foreign policy think tank – the Indian Council of World Affairs.

Amb. Ajay Bisaria is a strategic advisor and commentator on international affairs. He is a Distinguished Fellow at the Observer Research Foundation, India's largest private sector think tank. He currently chairs a Ministry of Steel Task Force examining the international experience to inform India's pathway to manufacturing green steel.

Ambassador Bisaria has had a distinguished diplomatic career spanning 35 years, when he dealt with some of India's key economic and security relationships. He served as Indian High Commissioner to Canada from 2020 to 2022. He was earlier India's envoy in Pakistan (2017-2020), Poland and Lithuania (2015-2017). He has also represented the country at the World Bank in Washington DC and in embassies in Berlin and Moscow. He has served in various capacities in the Ministry of External Affairs, Department of Commerce and the Prime Minister's Office, where he was a key aide to Prime Minister Vajpayee from 1999 to 2004. He has dealt extensively with India's Eurasia policy, including with Russia, Ukraine and Central Asia. He has published and lectured on issues related to trade, finance and geopolitics, with a focus on South Asia, Eurasia, Central Asia and Canada. He has written a series of op-eds on Pakistan in the *Times of India* in 2022-2023. He has a Bachelor's Degree in Economics from St. Stephen's College, Delhi

University; an MBA (Finance and Marketing) from IIM, Calcutta; and a Master's Degree in Public Policy from Princeton University. He has received distinguished alumnus awards from Modern School and IIM, Calcutta. He speaks Russian, German and Urdu, apart from Hindi and English.

Amb. Jayant Prasad was India's Ambassador to Afghanistan, Algeria, Nepal, and the UN Conference on Disarmament, Geneva. At headquarters, in the Ministry of External Affairs, he served as Special Secretary (Public Diplomacy), and Head of the Americas and the Multilateral Economic Relations Division. He was Rapporteur of the U.N. Commission on Human Rights, Geneva (1986-87), Fellow at the Weatherhead Center for International Affairs, Harvard University (1998-99), member of U.N. Secretary-General's Advisory Board on Disarmament Matters (2005-07), and Visiting Scholar, Center for the Advanced Study of India, University of Pennsylvania (2014-15). Before his 37-year public service career, he was lecturer in history, St. Stephen's College, University of Delhi, after completing his studies at Modern School, St. Stephen's College, and Jawaharlal Nehru University. He was Director General, Institute for Defence Studies and Analyses, New Delhi.

Lt Gen Syed Ata Hasnain (retd.), PVSM, UYSM, AVSM, SM, VSM & BAR Through most of his 40 year illustrious career Lt General Hasnain has served in turbulent environments and hot spots. From Sri Lanka to Siachen Glacier, from the North East to Jammu & Kashmir (J&K), and in UN operations from Mozambique to Rwanda, he has seen it all in crucial appointments. He served seven tours in J&K, was decorated in almost all of them and knows the J&K conflict comprehensively. He commanded the Indian Army's Srinagar based 15 Corps and is today one of the foremost writers and analysts on J&K, Pakistan, Middle East and transnational extremist violence. He is a much sought after speaker and writes for major Indian newspapers – The Times of India, The Indian Express, The Hindu, Deccan Chronicle and The Asian Age, besides being a regular participant in television debates on mainstream television. With a strong academic background from Sherwood College, Nainital, St Stephen's College Delhi, the Royal College of Defence Studies, Kings College London and the Asia Pacific Centre for Security Studies, Hawaii, he has been at the forefront of encouraging the adoption of the US initiated Scholar Warrior concept in the Indian Army. He has spoken at the Lee Kwan Yu School for Public Policy, the Rajaratnam School for International Studies and the Indian Institute for South Asian Studies, all at Singapore. He has also spoken at the International Institute of Strategic Studies (IISS), London. He is associated with the Vivekananda International Foundation and Centre for Joint Warfare Studies, as Distinguished Fellow and is on the Governing Council of the Indian Council of World Affairs (ICWA) and Institute of Peace & Conflict Studies (IPCS). He speaks on National Security at various military, civil services and corporate institutions with a view to enhance India's strategic culture. He has recently visited Iran and was at the forefront of neutralizing Pakistani influence operations in that country. On 13 Jul 2018, the President of India appointed Lt Gen Hasnain as Chancellor of the Central University of Kashmir. Lt Gen Hasnain has six decorations awarded by the President of India and two by the Army Chief. He superannuated from the Indian Army in Jul 2013 after 40 years of active service.

Tilak Devasher is a Consultant with the Vivekananda International Foundation. He is a former Special Secretary, Cabinet Secretariat, Government of India. During his professional career Tilak specialized in security issues, especially pertaining to India's neighbourhood. He is the author of '*Pakistan: Courting the Abyss*' (December 2016), '*Pakistan: At the Helm*' (June 2018) and '*Pakistan: The Balochistan Conundrum*' and '*The Pashtuns: A Contested History*' (2022). All the books have been published by HarperCollins India. He is currently a member of the National Security Advisory Board (NSAB), Emeritus Resource Faculty at Rashtriya Raksha University and Distinguished Fellow, United Services Institution of India.

Stop Press

Tilak Devasher

While this book was going to press, major events took place in Pakistan. Politically, the key among them was the dissolution of the National Assembly, appointment of a caretaker government at the Federal level and in Sindh and Balochistan (caretaker governments already existed in Punjab and KPK), the return of Nawaz Sharif from self-imposed exile in London and the announcement of a date for the general elections. On the security front, the situation has deteriorated due to the attacks of the Tehreek-e-Taliban Pakistan (TTP) and there has been a major down-turn in Pak-Afghan relations. Pakistan's decision to evict Afghan refugees in phases, with the undocumented ones being the first, has further adversely impacted Pak-Afghan relations.

The Pakistan Democratic Movement (PDM) government headed by Shehbaz Sharif demitted office on 9 August 2023 a few days before the National Assembly completed its mandated term. A consensus was reached between the outgoing PM and the Leader of the Opposition on the appointment of a caretaker prime minister. Accordingly, Senator Anwaar-ul Haq Kakar, a Pashtun from Balochistan, was sworn in as the prime minister on14 August 2023.

As per constitutional provisions, general elections should have been held within 90 days of the dissolution of the National Assembly. However, they were delayed due to the notification of the results of the 7th Census that had to be followed by the delimitation of constituencies. The delimitation process would only completed by end November. As a result, the elections could not be held when mandated.

After much speculation, and after cases had been filed in the Supreme Court, the Election Commission of Pakistan (ECP) announced 11 February as the date for the elections. However, the Supreme Court directed the ECP to consult the president on the date, as this was a constitutional requirement. Following a meeting between the president and the chief election commissioner the date was finalized as 8 February 2024. For its part, the Supreme Court expressed the confidence that the general elections would be held on 8 February and called it a 'date carved in stone'.

As per constitutional provisions, the ECP will have to announce the election schedule in early December since a minimum of 54 days are required to conduct elections.

Three-time prime minister Nawaz Sharif returned to Pakistan on 21 October after close to four years of exile in London. Though he was a proclaimed offender in the Avenfield properties and Al-Azizia cases, the Islamabad High Court (IHC) granted him protective bail in both the cases after returning to Pakistan. In July 2018, he had been sentenced to 10 years in jail in the Avenfield properties corruption reference for owning assets beyond his known income and one year for not cooperating with the NAB, which was to be served concurrently. In the Al-Azizia Steel Mills corruption reference, he was sentenced to seven years in jail in December 2018. He was released in March 2019, following which the IHC allowed him to proceed to London in November 2019 on medical grounds. The IHC subsequently declared him a proclaimed offender in both cases in December2020.[1]

The Pakistan Muslim League (Nawaz) (PMLN) welcomed him with a large gathering at Minar-e-Pakistan in Lahore.

While Nawaz has got bail, he continues to be disqualified from contesting elections or hold any public office in the Panama case. He thus has about a month to get these convictions reversed in order to be able to contest the elections. He needs to be acquitted by the Islamabad High Court (IHC) in the Avenfield and Al-Azizia cases in addition to reversing the issue of his life-time disqualification in the Panama case handed out by the Supreme Court.

A recent verdict of the Supreme Court on The Supreme Court's Practices and Procedures Act 2023 has diminished Nawaz Sharif's chances of over-turning his lifetime disqualification. While the Supreme Court upheld the Act, it did not endorse Section 5 (2) that granted a right of appeal retrospectively, holding it ultra vires of the Constitution. Since the right of retrospective appeal has been denied, Nawaz Sharif cannot appeal against his lifetime disqualification from participation in politics.

Resultantly, the PMLN is now relying on the Election Act 2017, as amended in 2023 during the PDM government's tenure, to claim that Nawaz Sharif's disqualification for life is not relevant. The amendment of Section 232 (Qualifications and Disqualifications) of the Election Act, 2017 set the period of disqualification of a legislator under Article 62 of the Constitution at not exceeding five years. Nawaz Sharif was disqualified under Article 62(1)(f) after he was pronounced as not being Sadiq and Ameen in the Panama case by the Supreme Court. The PMLN believes the Election Act amendment is applicable to Nawaz Sharif. He would thus not be required to approach the Supreme Court since he has already completed his five-year disqualification period.

This, however, could be controversial. Some legal experts hold that without a constitutional amendment or a Supreme Court ruling, Nawaz Sharif's disqualification for life cannot be reduced to five years on the basis of an amendment in the law.[2]

Thus, the stage is set for judicial battles that could well determine Nawaz Sharif's fate.

As far as Imran Khan is concerned, he has been convicted in the Toshakhana case. Though the IHC has suspended his sentence, the conviction remains at the time of writing. To be able to contest the elections, Imran Khan would need an acquittal in the Toshakhana case. He was arrested in the Al-Qadir Trust case, while proceedings in the foreign funding case are continuing. However, the more critical cases are the ones pertaining to the Cipher and the 9 May violence.

The Cipher case should be especially worrying for Imran Khan since he is accused of mishandling state secrets, failing to ensure their safe custody and manipulating them for political gain. Crucially, a major player in the Cipher saga, the former PM's Principal Secretary Azam Khan, has already given statements against Imran Khan.[3] At the moment, Imran Khan and Shah Mehmud Qureshi stand indicted and the courts have turned down his various appeals in the case. In one such instance, the IHC held that Imran Khan, "when addressing the public gathering, was not doing so pursuant to the performance of his duties as prime minister, rather it was a political engagement". The charge sheet filed by the Federal Investigation Agency (FIA) in a special court established under the Official Secrets Act held that Imran Khan while holding the office of the prime minister, used the Cipher in a "prohibited place (*jalsa*)" and "wilfully communicated" the secret information to unauthorised persons, which was against the "interests of the State of Pakistan". Further, it noted that "The Cipher was entrusted to you in confidence by the Ministry of Foreign Affairs [but] you used the document while keeping it in your possession for the benefit of your personal political design and compromised the Cipher and the security system of Pakistan". These are very serious charges indeed.[4]

The PTI has also been faced with the wrath of the army. As a result, many leaders and supporters have been arrested and are facing trials. A host of its leaders have quit the party and either joined other parties or quit politics altogether. The PTI is also facing serious organisational problems. While many of its leaders have left the party, vice chairman Shah Mehmood Qureshi and president Chaudhry Parvez Elahi are in prison despite being granted bail in several cases. This puts in jeopardy the electoral campaign especially the issue of how candidates will be issued tickets and who will run the election campaign.[5]

Another blow for the PTI has been the emergence of the Jahangir Khan Tareen and Aleem Khan-led Istekham-e-Pakistan Party (IPP) that has resonance in south Punjab and the Pervez Khattak-led Pakistan Tehreek-e-Insaf Parliamentarians (PTIP) in KPK. The moot question is whether those who have joined these parties will be able to retain voter support and so eat into the consolidated PTI vote bank and whether the parties can win over new voters. There are also talks of alliance/seat adjustments between the PML-N and the IPP. The PML-N may well need the support of the IPP and independents to form governments, both in Punjab and at the centre. For the moment, however, alliances are up in the air and the picture would become clear over the next few weeks.[6] One sure indicator, as happens before every national election, will be politicians switching loyalties towards the party that seems to have the support of the 'establishment.' This change of political affiliations is the key pointer to which party will win the parliamentary polls.

With the announcement of the election date, there has been an uptick in political activities. To begin with, there is much talk about political alliances and seat sharing. Thus, in Sindh, there are speculations that the PML-N could form an alliance or have a seat sharing arrangement with the Mohajir Qaumi Movement (MQM) and the Grand Democratic Alliance (GDA), composed of Sindhi nationalist parties. This would act as a counter-weight to the PPP. In Punjab, the PPP has hinted at forming an electoral alliance with its hitherto rival, the Pakistan Tehreek-e-Insaf (PTI) in Punjab. Bilawal Bhutto has invited the PTI to join the Charter of Democracy (CoD) signed by the PML-N and the Pakistan People's Party (PPP). However, it may well be a huge ask to motivate the staunch PTI voters to vote for the PPP. On the other hand, the PTI is on the back foot due to the events of 9 May and will be clutching at straws. Such political moves are likely to continue till the elections and beyond as each party jockeys to get a greater share of the political pie.

There has been a steady escalation in the barbs that the PPP and the PML-N have been hurling at each other, indicating that the bonhomie of being coalition partners in the PDM government could well be a thing of the past. Thus, the PPP co-chairman Asif Ali Zardari told a gathering that he helped Shehbaz Sharif to become the prime minister but he failed to deliver the goods. He added that the previous government did not work for the people while his party had always served the masses.[7] Central leaders of the PPP have expressed reservations about a 'nexus' between the PML-N and the interim government, pointing out the affiliation of caretaker federal ministers – Ahad Cheema and Fawad Hasan Fawad – with Nawaz Sharif and Shehbaz Sharif and the Punjab governor's links with the PML-N.[8] Bilawal Bhutto has also accused the PML-N of abandoning the 'vote ko izzat do' narrative and being in cahoots with the 'selectors' that is, the 'establishment.'[9]

For its part, the PMLN has advised the PPP to stop crying over apparent lack of a level playing field and face it in the political arena.[10]

While individual leaders and parties have their vote banks and varied levels of popularity, at the end of the day what will really matter is how confident the voting public feels about a party or leader embarking on a policy of economic recovery, and building a broad-based consensus between major political parties and de facto power centres to undertake drastic structural reforms. It is well-recognised that only a consensus can address the economic challenges and polarization in the country. Nawaz Sharif and the PML-N are known for big-ticket infrastructure projects like motorways and metros but whether these will address structural economic issues and the issues of food, utility prices, etc., remains to be seen. [11]

Meanwhile, the Supreme Court in a 4-1 verdict declared the trial of civilians in military courts in the wake of the May 9 riots as ultra vires. This also calls into question Section 2 of the Pakistan Army Act of 1952 though the court made no reference to the 2015 Act of Parliament that had approved any attack on military installations and military centres as an offence that could be tried under the Army Act.[12] Unless appealed against and overturned, this would lead to the cases against those involved in the 9 May violence being put in jeopardy.

Terrorism

The resurgence of the TTP has been evident from the fact that terrorist incidents in Pakistan soared by 79 per cent in the first half of 2023 according to the Pakistan Institute for Conflict and Security Studies (PICSS).[13] According to it, the number of terrorist attacks in August – 99 – was the highest in a single month since November 2014, though the TTP had claimed 147 attacks in the same month. According to another Islamabad-based think tank, the Centre for Research and Security Studies (CRSS), almost 1,100 people, including 386 security personnel, lost their lives in militant violence in the first nine months of the year, that is, almost 42 security personnel killed per month. Furthermore, the data since 2021 indicates a consistent rise in fatalities among the security forces, raising concerns about the ongoing security challenges facing the nation.[14]

Another significant development is the emerging collaboration between the TTP and some Baloch groups. This collaboration has become a critical security issue for the Pakistani government since the combination has at its disposal thousands of combatants who are trained in carrying out high-impact assaults.[15]

As elections near, and political rallies are held all over the country, the possibility of further violence is real. This would raise serious questions about the capacity and capability of the army to fight terrorism. As Ayesha Siddiqa notes, the military must divert attention back to security matters rather than managing politics and the economy.[16]

In a media interaction on 8 November 2023, caretaker prime minister Anwaarul Haq Kakar placed the onus of the increase in terror incidents in Pakistan on the coming to power of the interim Afghan government in August 2021. He revealed that "after the establishment of the interim Afghan government, there has been a 60 per cent increase in terror incidents and 500 per cent rise in suicide attacks in Pakistan." He disclosed, "In the past two years, 2,267 innocent citizens' lives have been lost to this tragic bloodshed, for which the terrorists of the TTP who are conducting cowardly attacks on Pakistanis using Afghan soil, are responsible" Further, "During this time, 15 Afghan citizens were also among the people involved in suicide attacks. Other than this, till now, 64 Afghan citizens were killed while fighting Pakistan's law enforcement agencies during the counterterrorism campaign." However, no details were provided about the alleged involvement of Afghan nationals in any specific terror attack.[17]

Kakar's statement comes after the country witnessed a sharp rise in terror incidents in early November including on the Mianwali Training Air Base claimed by the Tehreek-e-Jihad Pakistan, an ambush in Gwadar claimed by the Balochistan Liberation Front, and attacks in Dera Ismail Khan. Soon after the Mianwali attack, four soldiers, including a lieutenant-colonel, were killed in an exchange of fire in the Tirah Valley.

Kakar accused illegal immigrants, primarily Afghan, of having a huge role in spreading unrest in Pakistan. This was the reason why Pakistan decided to send them back to their country from 1 November. He also termed the statements made by Afghan leaders criticising the deportation drive as "unnecessary, irresponsible, misleading and threatening", adding that they were "upsetting".

Pak-Afghan Relations and Afghan Refugees

There was much exultation in Pakistan over the Taliban victory in August 2021. It was seen as the crowning glory of Pakistan's two-decade long covert support to the Taliban despite being part of the US 'War on Terror'. The then Prime Minister Imran Khan claimed that the Afghans had broken the shackles of slavery, whatever that was supposed to mean. However, the relationship started souring soon thereafter. The two primary causes were the refusal of the Taliban to recognize the Durand Line. In fact, they tore down parts of it in some areas, declared that they did not accept it and that it divided brothers. The second reason was that the Taliban declined to act against the TTP as Pakistan had asked it to. Instead, they offered to facilitate Pakistan's talks with them. Against this backdrop, Pakistan's decision to expel Afghan refugees has pushed the deteriorating relations between the two countries to the edge of the abyss.

Of the more than four million Afghans living in Pakistan, the government estimates 1.7 million are undocumented, 1.4 million are registered via the 'Proof of Residence' (POR) cards while there are another 0.8 million who were registered under the 'Afghan Citizen Card' (ACC). It was clarified that the latter two categories would not be deported in the initial phase.

The plight of the refugees who are being evicted is pitiable. Many have been forced to sell all their possessions at massively reduced prices. Many have been unable to get back money they were owed with debtors refusing to pay knowing the vulnerable situation of Afghan refugees due to the crackdown. Pakistan has allowed each family to take Rs. 50,000 only with them across the border. This would be woefully inadequate to restart life in a land where many had never been to and know very little about. While Pakistan has claimed that most Afghans have left voluntarily, Kabul insists the majority have been forcibly repatriated since the 31 October deadline. According to Afghan officers from the department for refugees "Most of the refugees who are returning are sent here by force, they have been beaten, their belongings have been seized, and their money has been taken."[18]

Evicting all undocumented Afghans is clearly meant as a message to the Taliban that if they continue to host the TTP, Pakistan would use whatever levers it has. In another effort to pressurize the Taliban to act against the TTP, Pakistan has decided not to advocate the Afghan Taliban's case at the international level or extend any 'special privileges' to the interim Afghan Taliban government. This reversal of policy clearly underlines the serious deterioration in relations between the two neighbours.[19]

Afghan authorities have been overwhelmed by the scale of the exodus and are scrambling to process the returnees. A number of Taliban leaders, including the interim prime minister, and the defence and interior ministers have publicly criticised Pakistan for evicting thousands of Afghans. Afghan Interior Minister Sirajuddin Haqqani, who is supposed to be close to the ISI, in a recent video message, asked Pakistan not to punish Afghan refugees if it had any issue with the Kabul administration. He termed the Pakistani decision as un-Islamic, claiming that Islamabad could not blame Afghanistan for its own problems. Defence Minister Mullah Yaqub warned that such a decision would have consequences for Pakistan.[20] Sher Mohammad Stanikzai, Deputy Foreign Minister, warned Islamabad to treat Afghan immigrants appropriately and not to force them to react against their actions. He said that the reaction of Afghans has been recorded in history and now Afghanistan has a strong defence force and plenty of weapons. According to him, Pakistani soldiers were looting the property and assets of Afghan immigrants during their deportation from the country.[21] The Acting Taliban Foreign Minister Amir Khan Muttaqi, has accused Pakistan of using the expulsion of immigrants as a means to humiliate and pressurize Kabul, clarifying that Afghanistan will not succumb to such pressure.[22]

Several Pakistani politicians like Maulana Fazlur Rehman of the JUIF, Siraj-ul-Haq of the JI and Bilawal Bhutto of the PPP have protested at the manner in which the Afghans are being evicted and the humiliating treatment being meted out to them.

Human rights organisations like the Human Rights Commission of Pakistan (HRCP), Amnesty International, Human Rights Watch, etc., have asked Pakistan to reconsider, urged the UNHCR to ensure protection for Afghan refugees, and warned that the move to expel Afghans could "trigger a humanitarian crisis".[23]

Pakistan has, for the moment, turned down calls from the United Nations, human rights groups, and Western embassies to reconsider its decision.

Among the distraught Afghans, the worst sufferers would be the Shia Hazaras. They have faced decades of persecution by the Taliban. A Hazara was quoted as saying: "Going to Kabul would be like going to a graveyard to be buried."[24]

15 November 2023

NOTES

1. Umer Burney, "IHC restores Nawaz's appeals against conviction in Al-Azizia, Avenfield references," *Dawn*, 26 October 2023, https://www.dawn.com/news/1783887
2. https://www.thenews.com.pk/print/1125727-time-running-out-for-nawaz-imran
3. Zafar Malik, "Pakistan's political see-saw," *Daily Times*, 5 November 2023, https://dailytimes.com.pk/1145809/pakistans-political-see-saw/
4. Umer Burney, "IHC rejects Imran's bail and dismissal pleas in cipher case," *Dawn*, 27 October 2023, https://www.dawn.com/news/1784140
5. Mubasher Bukhari, "Slings and arrows of outrageous fortune?," *The Express Tribune*, 5 November 2023, https://www.thenews.com.pk/tns/detail/1125518-slings-and-arrows-of-outrageous-fortune
6. Editorial, "Season of alliances," *The News*, 4 November 2023, https://www.thenews.com.pk/print/1125588-season-of-alliances
7. "I helped Shehbaz become PM but he could not deliver: Zardari," *Dawn*, 1 November 2023, https://www.dawn.com/news/1785409/i-helped-shehbaz-become-pm-but-he-could-not-deliver-zardari
8. "PPP sounds alarms over 'caretakers-PML-N' nexus," *The Express Tribune*, 5 November 2023.
9. Azeem Samar, "PPP parted ways with PMLN after compromise on narrative: Bilawal," *The News*, 9 November 2023, https://www.thenews.com.pk/print/1127316-ppp-parted-ways-with-pmln-after-compromise-on-narrative-bilawal
10. Zulqernain Tahir, "PML-N asks PPP to 'stop crying', face it in polls," *Dawn*, 7 November 2023, https://www.dawn.com/news/1787140/n-asks-ppp-to-stop-crying-face-it-in-polls
11. Afshan Subohi, "The leadership debate," *Dawn*, 30 October 2023, https://www.dawn.com/news/1784594/the-leadership-debate
12. Dure Akram, "More Chaos?," *Daily Times*, 1 November 2023, https://dailytimes.com.pk/1144703/more-chaos-2/
13. Myra Imran, "Terrorism incidents in Pakistan soar by 79pc in first half of 2023," *The News*, 3 July 2023, https://www.thenews.com.pk/print/1086469-terrorism-incidents-in-pakistan-soar-by-79pc-in-first-half-of-2023
14. "Security forces witness highest casualties in 8 years," *The News*, 30 September 2003, https://tribune.com.pk/story/2438480/security-forces-suffer-highest-casualties-in-8-years-report
15. Imtiaz Gul, "Explaining the resurgence of terrorist violence in Pakistan," *East Asia Forum*, 29 March 2023, https://www.eastasiaforum.org/2023/03/29/explaining-the-resurgence-of-terrorist-violence-in-pakistan/

16. Ayesha Siddiqa, "Pakistan Army should leave politics and get back to security. An airbase was just attacked," *The Print,* 7 November, 2023, https://theprint.in/opinion/pakistan-army-should-leave-politics-get-back-to-security-an-airbase-was-just-attacked/1835218/
17. "Terror incidents increased since Afghan interim govt came to power in 2021: PM Kakar," *Dawn,* 8 November 2023, https://www.dawn.com/news/1787503
18. "Thousands of Afghans forcibly returned from Pakistan: Kabul," AFP report, 6 November 2023, https://timesofindia.indiatimes.com/world/south-asia/thousands-of-afghans-forcibly-returned-from-pakistan-kabul/articleshow/104990543.cms?from=mdr
19. Kamran Yousuf, "Pakistan shifts stance on Afghan Taliban," *The Express Tribune*, 9 November 2022.
20. Kamran Yousaf, "Deportation pushing Pak-Afghan ties to the edge," *Express Tribune*, 6 November 2023.
21. Bibi Amina Hakimi, "Stanikzai Warns Pakistan not to 'Force Afghans to React'," *TOLO news Online*, 6 November 2023.
22. Fidel Rahmati, "Pakistan pressuring Afghanistan with migrant deportations: Muttaqi," *Khaama Press Online*, 7 November 2023.
23. Iftikhar A. Khan, "Govt tightens noose around migrants as 'refoulement' commences," 1 November 2023, https://www.dawn.com/news/1785462/govt-tightens-noose-around-migrants-as-refoulement-commences
24. "Afghan Hazaras equate expulsion to 'going to graveyard to be buried'," *Reuters*, 30 October 2023, https://www.dawn.com/news/1784864

Editor's Note

PAKISTAN INSIGHTS 2023 is the fourth in the Pakistan Insight series brought out by the Vivekananda International Foundation (VIF) to deepen understanding of the country. Ideas for the various chapters are based on the discussions held in the Pakistan Study Group (PSG) that was set up in February 2018 in the VIF. The previous three editions of the series – Pakistan Insights 2019, Pakistan Insights 2020 and Pakistan Insight 2022-23 – had received widespread acclaim and it is hoped that this edition too will be well received.

Dr. Arvind Gupta kick-starts the discussions by pointing out how even astute observers of Pakistan affairs were taken by surprise at the rapid descent of the country into comprehensive chaos since Imran Khan was ousted as prime minister on 10 April 2022 through a no-confidence motion. Although he lost the prime ministership, he remained defiant, combative and popular in Pakistan. He holds that the 9 May incidents were a decisive moment and a lot changed in Pakistan after it. The army saw it as a well-planned controversy by Imran Khan's supporters to defy and defame the army.

Following the 9 May incident, Imran Khan and the PTI came under tremendous pressure. On 5 August 2023, he was arrested following conviction by a court in the infamous Toshakhana case and debarred from contesting elections for five years. His removal from the political scene would weaken the PTI considerably, thus changing Pakistan's political environment drastically before the next general elections. Dr. Gupta also looks at the deeper and structural issues that have made Pakistan an incomplete democracy including the political interference of the army. His conclusion is that the situation is fluid and the country can move in several possible directions. For one thing, even if the elections are held, will the Pakistan army remain politically neutral or will it back some political force or specific leader? Pakistan future politics will be deeply impacted by the stance the Pakistan army takes.

Rana Banerji takes a granular look at the internal developments in Pakistan and civil-military relations. He highlights that ever since the Pakistan Democratic Movement (PDM) government led by Prime Minister Shehbaz Sharif came to power in Pakistan (April 2022), its path was strewn by a bed of thorns. A difficult economic situation and an opposition strategy led by former Prime Minister Imran Khan, led to this predicament. Imran successfully built up populist support with a narrative of 'foreign conspiracy', 'unfair martyrdom' and 'desertion by the military establishment'. Though later exposed as false, it was fanned by an army of besotted, young social media trollers. It found support among ex-servicemen, serving officers and other ranks, even retired Generals. He identifies three major economic challenges for Pakistan: falling growth/output, continued balance of payment pressures, and strong inflation. Government intervention in restricting imports has exacerbated problems by leading to (a) reduced economic output, and (b) further pressures on the balance of payments as exports started drifting down, a situation vividly described as Pakistan's 'perfect doom loop.'

He concludes that Pakistan's polity stands at a crossroads where clashes between institutions of state have become the norm. Every organization is riven with factions that are strongly polarized. The possibilities of evolving acceptable political consensus are increasingly remote. An erosion of the state's writ seemed to have been perpetrated by state actors themselves, with lack of clarity or unity of purpose between different interest groups within the establishment, as to how they can tackle a popular leader who is increasingly becoming unacceptable from the perspective of *realpolitik*. In the interim, a new political construct with a weak civilian Prime Minister bowing before a resurgent Army Chief has come to the fore, creating 'déjà vu' for observers of Pakistan's domestic political discourse. In sum, the country's political and economic future appeared more troubled than ever, with no silver lining visible in the functioning of its flawed democratic dispensation.

Lt Gen Rakesh Sharma (retd.) examines the contemporary Pakistan Army in so far as its relationship with the politicians and the internal dynamics are concerned. He notes that Pakistan had been and is bound to remain a hybrid regime, hybridity weighted heavily in favour of the Army! The 18th Constitutional Amendment of 2010 targeted the military's interference in politics to prevent coups. To get around this, the Army decided to engineer a hybrid regime; while remaining in the proverbial shadows, allow a façade of democracy while continuing to interfere in politics. He identifies this as a root cause for many of the problems Pakistan is facing currently.

He highlights that in the last seven and a half decades, the Pakistani army's obsession with India, has suited its ambitions of being the sole power and indispensable to the nation, and it assists it in retaining the corporate control it has over businesses. To that end, the all-important Inter-Services Intelligence (ISI) and its espionage, subversion and sabotage, and public relations and propaganda division – Inter-Services Public Relations (ISPR) are foundational organisations providing the requisite support. However, for an organisation that has been at the helm of governance in Pakistan since creation, directly or behind the scenes, these are very difficult times. Though the army has stated that it would no longer engage in politics, this assertion has to be taken with many grains of salt. The institution has been entrenched in Pakistan's political fabric for so long, that it would be well-nigh impossible to engineer such a sharp shift. The army took the events of 9 May 2023 as the catalyst to launch an organized campaign to dismantle the Pakistan Tehreek-e-Insaf (PTI) and Imran Khan, by slapping over 150 cases against him with the police. His conclusion is that the Army's control of the nation and its polity can be taken as assured. In doing so, it will orchestrate events nationally and internationally. Dissensions, if any, rearing their head within the uniformed forces, will be suppressed ruthlessly, for the organisation has to ensure its prime place in Pakistan, irrespective of the government of the day.

Brig Rahul Bhonsle (retd.) argues that terrorism and Pakistan have an umbilical relationship as it has embraced terror as an instrument of state policy over decades to overcome weakness in other dimensions of national power. Thus, terror has been employed in Afghanistan for seeking influence in the West in what has been frequently referred to as, 'strategic depth,' or overcoming the geographic debility vis-a-vis India. Pakistan egged on by the USA propped up the Mujahideen in the 1980s to undermine the invasion of Kabul by the Soviet Union. As the Soviets left in 1989 and Afghanistan fell into political and security chaos of its own making, Pakistan facilitated the growth of the Taliban which took over power in Kabul in 1996. Evicted by the USA in 2001, Pakistan provided sanctuary to the Taliban and al-Qaeda – a duplicity that the USA had to swallow. Two decades later the Taliban is in power in Kabul again, but a 'triumphant' [sic] Pakistan is facing a resurgence of terror in the tribal belt of Khyber Pakhtunkhwa by the Tehreek-e-Taliban Pakistan (TTP).

He notes that episodic management of violence rather than viewing terrorism as a holistic long-term security threat has been the underlying concept adopted by the Pakistani state from time to time. Moreover, the use of a philosophy of terror as a tool for external interventions used under the 'bleeding by a thousand cuts,' strategy against India and for seeking strategic depth in Afghanistan implied that elements within the Army and the Inter Services Intelligence (ISI) retained contact with the marginalised TTP. Instead of building counter-terrorism capability and structures during the period of negotiations, the Pakistan security establishment allowed the TTP to re-establish roots within the people having learned little from experience. Thus, when negotiations were suspended in November 2022, resurgence of terrorist incidents was a given. His prognosis is that the rise of TTP violence suggests grim portents for Pakistan in the security sphere even as it grapples with a complex poly-crisis – political, economic and humanitarian.

Amb. G. Parthasarthy holds that Pakistan's main troubles today do not arise from India, but from the actions of fellow Pashtuns, affiliated with the Tehreek-e-Taliban, Pakistan, and disgruntled Baloch. This Taliban grouping has long been affiliated with and provided safe havens and support by their Pashtun Taliban cadres in Afghanistan. With the departure of the USA from Afghanistan, the Afghan and Pakistan Taliban now have a strong fraternal relationship. Pakistan made the mistake of trying to control the Taliban and determine their behaviour after the Taliban takeover, in much the same manner that they did when the ISI was arming and training them, for use against both the Russians and Americans. The Pakistan Army forgot that the Pashtuns have never yielded to foreign hegemony.

According to **Amb. Sharat Sabharwal,** of all Pakistan's problems the one that has received the least attention over the years within the country and in the international community is the adverse impact and management of environmental degradation and climate change. It has been hitting the headlines each time there was a big environment/climate change induced disaster. However, it has now emerged as a major challenge because such disasters have become recurrent and increasingly catastrophic. Seen against the backdrop of Pakistan's fragile economy, poor governance, ethnic and sectarian fault lines and extensive lawlessness, frequent climate induced hardship to the people adds significantly to the risk of instability within the country.

He identifies some of the key reasons for the environment degradation as rapid population growth; rapid urbanization; land degradation; pressure on aquatic resources; decline in per capita availability of water and also its quality; deforestation; deteriorating quality of urban air and global climate change. Paucity of funds compared to environmental and climate financial needs have been an important factor hindering the initiatives and policies of the federal and provincial governments. A major problem with Pakistan's environmental and climate-mitigating programme is the lack of consistency and continuity within the policy space. He concludes that Pakistan faces serious challenges of sustainability due to continued environmental degradation combined with climate change, which has been giving rise to extreme climate-related events, including devastating floods, with increasing frequency and intensity. This has imposed onerous costs on Pakistan's fragile economy and socio-economic fabric. Environmental degradation and climate change will continue to figure prominently among the key intractable problems that imperil Pakistan and its stability.

Aarushi Gupta notes that the perception of the inferiority of women is ingrained in the larger Pakistani fabric. Such a perception affects the personal and social life of women as well as children. As a result, women in Pakistan have a relatively lower level of participation in the economic activities with one of the lowest female workforces in South Asia and in the world and have to consistently face discrimination and disproportionately low incomes. According to estimates, women comprise about 90 per cent of the bottom one per cent of the entire labour force in Pakistan. Wage disparities not only affect women's participation in the workforce but also leads to multidimensional vulnerabilities like poor nutrition, health problems, economic vulnerability, violence against women, social justice and lack of social protection. Moreover, lack of education acts as a significant hurdle in the career aspirations of women in Pakistan. Pakistan also has one of the highest mortality rates for children under five years of age. Pakistan was ranked the fourth most dangerous country for women in 2021

Children are vulnerable to many forms of violence, exploitation, child labour, abduction and trafficking. According to Aarushi, over 2,000 child abuse cases were reported in Pakistan in just six months and 12 children were sexually abused daily in Pakistan. According to UNICEF, there are over 1.5 million street children in Pakistan. This makes them incredibly vulnerable to many forms of exploitation, violence and trafficking. A Human Rights Commission of Pakistan's report describes Pakistan as the source, transit and destination country for human trafficking. She concludes that Pakistan has the resources and functional organs to sustain gender justice but for multiple reasons, Pakistan has neglected to look at the well-being of a huge chunk of its population based on gender.

Dr. Shalini Chawla underlines that although varying degrees of intensity in tensions have been a constant feature between the two nuclear neighbours – India and Pakistan – relations are at their nadir at the moment with the complete absence of a diplomatic dialogue. The dialogue has not been revived after the Pathankot attack in January 2016. The abrogation of Article 370 by India on 5 August 2019 has intensified the tensions, and there has been massive frustration and anger expressed by the Pakistani leadership. The abrogation of Article 370 challenged the centrality of the military's positioning and actions. Pakistan's position on Kashmir, which it claimed for decades to be an *unfinished agenda of partition,* was questioned. There has been frustration, anger, and helplessness in Pakistan, and varied reactions were seen targeting the Indian leadership. Pakistan's strategic posture post revocation of Article 370 has been focused on building strong narratives and highlighting the Kashmir issue at the international level.

She identifies the following elements in Pakistan's strategic posture: *Highlighting threat perceptions; projection of victimhood; internationalizing Kashmir; highlighting Islamophobia*; *nuclear brinkmanship; trying to dominate Afghanistan; and leveraging Chinese support.* She concludes that Pakistan has shown no change in its covert war strategy. While the Kashmir Valley has been stable and the terror attacks have decreased significantly due to the heavy military presence, Pakistan's covert actions in Punjab have escalated. Narco-terrorism is the latest addition to Pakistan's covert war strategy in Punjab and Kashmir. India's growing strategic partnerships and economic development are likely to enhance Pakistan's threat perceptions, which will be dealt with by Islamabad through efforts to internationalize Kashmir, justify weapon modernization, continue propaganda against India, and maintain a narrative of victimhood.

In another chapter **Dr. Shalini Chawla** traces the background of Pak-US relations. She notes that while the focus of the previous phases of the USA-Pakistan partnership had been security, the current phase of the relationship centres more on both the USA and Pakistan attempting to reset ties and redefine common areas of interests based on cooperation in the arena of non-traditional security threats. This is a departure in the US approach from the past, where the acquisition of US equipment by Pakistan has been the defining factor of the USA-Pakistan relationship. In fact, Pakistan's foreign policy has been primarily driven by its strategic objectives, desire to modernise its military and acquire high technology equipment. Pakistan's military modernisation received a major boost as it received substantive military assistance from the USA and its Western allies.

She holds that in the past four decades, Afghanistan has been the most important factor defining USA-Pakistan relations. After the US exit from Afghanistan in August 2021, the dynamics have changed. There has been a new phase of resetting USA-Pakistan ties. The following factors have been crucial in this regard: Decrease of US interest in Afghanistan and consequent decrease of reliance on Pakistan; the USA's increasing tensions with China, Pakistan's closest ally; India's strategic and economic rise on the world stage; the USA's increasing focus on the Indo-Pacific strategy to counter China, where Pakistan does not occupy any space. She concludes that USA-Pakistan relations are currently at a relatively neutral level, where ties have not fallen to the lows of the 1990s when Pakistan struggled with US sanctions, but US policymakers have conveyed a firm message to Pakistan that the US Administration is no longer willing to provide the easy military assistance it received in the 1980s and 2000s.

Amb. Venkatesh Varma begins his chapter by tracking Pakistan's troubled relations with the Soviet Union since its creation. Coming to the present, he holds that under President Putin, Russian policy has accorded priority to India dropping any pretence of equating or balancing relations with Pakistan. Putin's coming to power also coincided with the return of US influence in Pakistan in order to tackle al-Qaeda and the Taliban threat in Afghanistan as part of the US global war on terrorism. Putin was also keen to build on the momentum in Russia's relations with India that he inherited. Russia's objective has been not to impair relations with India by crossing the redline of substantive arms transfers to Pakistan. Pakistan, for its part, keeps up the pretence of a normal relationship with Russia by submitting ambitious arms shopping lists matching the best that Russia has supplied to India, while aware that its requests have had little success.

He holds that the Russian Ministry of Foreign Affairs (MFA) and some sections of the Security Council see Pakistan as an unreliable but necessary interlocutor on matters relating to Afghanistan and Central Asia. Russia is also aware of Pakistan playing China's cat's-paw in the region especially about China's ambitious Belt and Road Initiative (BRI) projects. This, if successful, will delink Central Asia from the old Soviet era routes and relink with Chinese-dominated trade and connectivity links in which Pakistan's CPEC is a central element. Russia has thus far adopted a non-confrontational approach to the BRI with China but has its own concerns about BRI success coming at the expense of its own influence in the region. Russia has so far not endorsed any of the projects connected with the China Pakistan Economic Corridor (CPEC). Russia has long recognized that Pakistan has traded its internal weakness for borrowed strength from abroad, a pattern that was familiar during the Cold War period with external benefactors such as the USA, China, and major Gulf states. Aware that it is not in the same league as these countries having leverage within Pakistani ruling circles through various inducements, Russia's patient wait for an opening came with the decisive turn against the USA by Imran Khan in late 2021 and early 2022.

Amb. T.C.A. Raghavan highlights that India-Pakistan relations set themselves in an adversarial mould even as they emerged as independent and sovereign nation-states some seven-plus decades earlier. That mould has solidified over the years and newer issues have cemented themselves on to older points of difference and dispute. The present mould accordingly comprises layer upon layer of insecurities, suspicions and mistrust. It includes now the full spectrum of issues that comprise the negative aspects in interstate relations – geo-political and strategic rivalry, historical baggage, identity conflict, major territorial disputes and finally power asymmetries. He identifies the distinctive features of the India-Pakistan relationship as their divisions and territorial disputes, underwritten by deep religious and national identity issues, as also the nuclear weapons status, all of which have had an enduring quality to them. He underlines that in both countries the belief is strong that it is the essential nature of the other state that poses an existential threat to the other. Added to this foundational difference are other deep divisions – the two-nation theory versus secular state and Kashmir in particular. To these differences in foundational narratives over the decades additional layers of strategic dispute have accumulated – terrorism, water, 1971 and the break-up of Pakistan and others. In brief, the thesis of 'everlasting enmity' has deep roots and clearly, from conflicting perspectives, on either side, is a position of substantive content.

He points to an interesting phenomenon in that this history of failure and setback is also characterized by the consistency with which efforts to stabilize, improve and even normalize relations have been made. Equally unusual is that the full political spectrum of both countries has, at different points of time, embarked on such ventures. In Pakistan additionally the Army was directly in charge, on various occasions, for a significant extent of time through this period. He notes that the contrarian trends against the doctrine of everlasting enmity have comprised a wide spectrum of activities over the years. These include 'Talks about Talks', 'Confidence Building Measures', 'High Level Summitry', 'Restraint' even in the face of grave provocation, and on occasion attempts at 'Dispute Resolution'. With the emergence of both countries as formally declared nuclear weapon powers, a greater intensity has been evident over the past quarter century in stabilization efforts even as the basic adversarial mould has remained intact and even strengthened. He predicts that for the future such efforts will recur and the current phase of downturn and a virtual freeze in bilateral contact is no more than a phase and is by no means a new status quo or even a new normal. Realism demands seeking interim even temporary improvisations and carefully constructed regimens of stability while not being blind to their temporal nature.

Amb. Ajay Bisaria argues that Pakistan faces a wrenching dilemma: whether to continue engaging the Kabul regime, or risk estrangement by responding robustly to the terrorism challenge from the Tehreek-e-Taliban Pakistan (TTP). For Pakistan, the Taliban is soft on the TTP; for the Taliban, Pakistan's attacks on the group within Afghan territory are unacceptable. Notwithstanding these security concerns, the structural reality of Afghan dependence on Pakistan remains, as does Pakistan's perceived strategic imperative to control the Kabul regime. Lurking in the background is the traditional suspicion between the Punjabis and the Pashtuns. He adds that the Western world's attention has shifted away from Kabul; it is far too preoccupied with Russian actions in Europe and with China's global threat, particularly in the Indo-Pacific. The co-option of China in the Afghan theatre and converging interests in extending the China Pakistan Economic Corridor (CPEC) to Afghanistan marks a significant shift in Pakistan's management of the Afghan situation following the withdrawal of US forces.

Pakistan's hope that Taliban 3.0 would become a puppet regime, seeking instructions from the Pakistan Army and delivering on key Pakistani political and strategic interests, has been belied. Pakistan's *bête noir*, the TTP, continues to have close links and sympathies within the ruling Afghan Taliban. The terrorist challenge emerging from the TTP remains an existential security concern for Pakistan. The one lesson Pakistan's generals have learnt from the past is that they cannot afford to lose control over the Taliban. While Pakistan's policy makers see the TTP as the primary challenge to their approach to Afghanistan, they also try to deal with the influence of global players like the USA, China and India. One driver for Pakistan's quest for strategic depth in Afghanistan has been its paranoia about India joining hands with Afghan forces in a pincer to squeeze Pakistan.

Amb. Jayant Prasad traces the developments of Pak-China relations since the 1950s and argues that Pakistan has long relied on its close and strategic relations with China to counterbalance India, develop its nuclear weapons and, in more recent years, for obtaining development finance. Its borrowings from Chinese funding agencies outpace the loans taken from the World Bank and the International Monetary Fund. Pakistani leaders describe Sino-Pakistan relations as higher than the Himalayas, deeper than the oceans, and sweeter than honey. For China, this privileged association with Pakistan is a way to keep India busy in South Asia.

He notes that the China Pakistan Economic Corridor (CPEC) has been superimposed on the strong strategic and military tie-up between China and Pakistan that the two countries have cultivated since the early 1960s. To pretend that the CPEC is entirely about geo-economics defies credulity. Further, while the CPEC has brought benefits to Pakistan in terms of increased energy security and attracting Chinese loans and investment, it is not free from troublesome issues like growth in Pakistan's indebtedness; the terms of the Chinese debt being opaque; issues of security of the Chinese workers and projects; corruption and high costs; low actual disbursements and investments; overpromises and exaggerated expectations; political vicissitudes and instability in Pakistan; subversion of sustainable development goals; public disaffection in Pakistan, etc. His conclusion is that the CPEC has not delivered on its promises and neither has it brought the benefits expected by Pakistan's leaders.

Lt Gen Ata Hasnain (retd.) labels Pakistan as 'the survivor state'. It somehow survives every catastrophe within and bounces back before going down under, all over again. Pakistan has for long been heading towards a situation where it could be perceived as a failed state, or at least a state under immense strain. Everything that goes into the efficient functioning of a nation appears under stress. The economy, internal stability and security, political leadership and foreign affairs, all seem to drive the nation towards an abyss. He identifies five issues that have brought Pakistan to its present pass: The undue focus given to the military thus starving the allocation of resources and more importantly attention towards the well-being of its people; the lack of attention to economic planning, especially its food program and manufacturing; the inability to bring modern education to the fore and discourage radical ideological belief; the refusal to address the necessity for a social transformation among its poorly educated masses thus allowing itself to be overtaken by obscurantist ideological beliefs; the obsession with conflict and the belief that sub-conventional means would deliver it the desired results especially in dealing with its more powerful neighbour, India.

He poses the question whether India should consider Pakistan's comprehensive weakness today as an opportunity to weaken it further and let it fracture? He holds that pragmatism points at far smarter ways of victory while maintaining our silent march to such prosperity that we could secure full deterrence through a well budgeted hi-tech set of armed forces. One of these is a defensive stance with adequate scope for offensive should Pakistan decide to use the borders and its armed forces to divert internal attention.

In conclusion, the editor tries to do some crystal ball gazing to predict the future trajectory of Pakistan with the caveat that predicting Pakistan is always fraught with risk, given the number of moving parts. The trends that have dominated Pakistan in the past year are likely to continue to resonate in the year ahead – the precarious economic situation, the deteriorating security situation, the electoral scene, whether or not elections are held and when, the results they throw up, the future of Imran Khan and whether he would be allowed to contest and the fate of his PTI. What compounds these multiple crises is the fact that they are being played out against the backdrop of a completely polarised polity and society, where politics is even more bitterly contested than before, where political fragmentation and confrontation has not been amenable to resolution politically.

He notes that over the long term, Pakistan has been a crisis-prone state that has faced a political and/or an economic crisis periodically but has managed to survive them and bounce back, before the next crisis. This time, however, the situation in Pakistan is different than in the past because the objective conditions have changed. Some of these conditions include greater youth activism with over 44 per cent of the electorate, around 55 million, being between 18 and 35 years of age; the widespread use of social media to frame narratives, the limits of political engineering of the army being shown up and the widespread unrest in the population due to adverse living conditions. Compounding matters, no leader, civilian or military, has any vision on what to do and how to tackle the situation. As a result there is an element of Pakistan entering a somewhat uncharted territory and unpredictability making its future uncertain.

The editor would like to thank Ms Anuttama Ganguly and Ms Aarushi Gupta for all their support and help in bringing out this volume.

Members of the Pakistan Study Group are:

Dr. Arvind Gupta – Director, VIF

Gen N. C. Vij (retd)

Amb. Satish Chandra

Amb. G. Parthasarathy

C. D. Sahay

Lt Gen Ravi Sawhney (retd)

Lt Gen Ata Hasnain (retd)

Rana Banerji

Amb. D. P. Srivastava
Amb. T. C. A. Raghavan
Brig Rahul Bhonsle (retd)
Dr. Shalini Chawla
Sushant Sareen
Amb. Amar Sinha
Amb. Gautam Mukhopadhya
Amb. P. S. Raghavan
Amb. D B Venkatesh Varma
Tilak Devasher – Convenor

Tilak Devasher
Consultant VIF
Member, National Security Advisory Board
Editor, Pakistan Insights

New Delhi
20 September 2023

Introduction
Whither Pakistan?

Arvind Gupta

Even astute observers of Pakistan affairs were taken by surprise at the rapid descent of the country into comprehensive chaos since Imran Khan was ousted as prime minister on 10 April 2022. A year later, incredible scenes of the looting and burning of the residence of the Lahore corps commander by a furious mob following the arrest of Imran Khan, the Chairman of Pakistan Tehreek-e-Insaf (PTI), were witnessed on TV screens and social media platforms in Pakistan and around the world. The storming of the corps commander's house has become the defining image of 'new' Pakistan which is struggling to survive the various crises it currently finds itself in.

No-confidence Motion

The drama leading to the ouster of Imran Khan's government gripped the nation for several weeks. On 8 March 2022, Pakistan's opposition leaders sought to submit a no-confidence motion against Prime Minister Imran Khan. The speaker summoned a national assembly session on 25 March to take up the motion. However, the session was adjourned without the tabling of the motion. Imran Khan accused foreign powers of a 'conspiracy' to topple his regime. Eventually, on 28 March, PML (N) leader Shehbaz Sharif tabled a no-confidence motion against the government. On 3 April, the Deputy Speaker blocked the motion and abruptly ended the session. On the same day, President Arif Alvi dissolved the National Assembly on the advice of Imran Khan. Imran Khan addressed the nation and asked the people to get ready for general elections. On 7 April the Supreme Court struck down the ruling by the Deputy Speaker to block the no-trust motion, ordered the restoration of the National Assembly, and directed that the motion be taken up on 10 April. Imran Khan lost the no-confidence vote and became the first prime minister in Pakistan's history to do so. On 11 April, Shehbaz Sharif of the PML (N) was elected as the new Prime Minister. This ushered in a new phase of political instability in Pakistan.

Although Imran Khan lost the prime ministership amidst controversy and intrigue, he remained defiant and popular in Pakistan even after his ouster. He accused the USA of plotting his ouster, dubbing the Shehbaz government as an 'imported government'. To force early elections, the PTI elected representatives resigned en masse from the national and provincial assemblies. Imran Khan's strategy all along has been to force an early election. The government, in contrast, has been totally opposed to this and even went to the extent of defying the judiciary, which had directed that elections in Punjab be held before 14 May 2023. As Imran Khan upped the ante, his diehard supporters cheered him on. His popularity graph continued to rise even after his ouster. The incumbent People Democratic Movement (PDM) government, led by Shehbaz Sharif, did its best to thwart Imran Khan in every possible way.

A lot changed in Pakistan after the 9 May 2023 incidents. Several army installations including martyr's memorials were attacked by angry mobs suspected to be PTI supporters across Pakistan. The attacks on military installations on such a large scale were unprecedented in Pakistan's volatile history. The army could not tolerate its own institutions being looted and set on fire by the crowds. It saw a well-planned controversy by the supporters of Imran Khan to defy and defame the army. The furious Pakistan army launched a massive crackdown, using the Army Act as the legal foil. PTI supporters were branded as 'terrorists' and thousands, including several top leaders of the party, were arrested. Many of them were pressurised to resign from the party. They are being tried under the Army Act. No one has been convicted yet.

Following the 9 May incidents, Imran Khan and the PTI have come under tremendous pressure. The 'terrorist' tag has been attached to PTI supporters. The once mighty Imran Khan, who prided himself on having taken on the army, began to appeal for dialogue. All of sudden, the PTI, which claims a 109-million membership, began to disintegrate in front of his eyes. At the same time, invoking Allah and the Quran, he sought to arouse the masses to fight a jihad against the 'powerful' and the 'tyrants.' He even built a narrative that the 9 May incidents were 'false flag' operations by the establishment to defame him and the PTI. Allegations and counter-allegations continued to be levelled as to who was behind the 9 May violence. On Saturday, 5 August 2023, he was arrested following conviction by a court in the infamous Toshakhana case and debarred from contesting elections for five years. His removal from the political scene would weaken the PTI considerably thus changing Pakistan's political environment drastically before the next general elections.

It is not difficult to understand the reasons for Pakistan's present state of affairs. Structural weaknesses in the Pakistani polity, post 1971, have been there for all to see. Pakistan continues to remain an incomplete democracy. The 1973 constitution sought to make Pakistan a democracy, albeit an Islamic one. In a true democracy, the army is subservient to the elected civilian authority. This has never been possible in Pakistan. Gen. Zia-ul-Haq in 1977 and Gen. Pervez Musharraf in 1999 violated the constitution and imposed long spells of martial law. This damaged democracy in Pakistan seriously. Gen. Zia-ul-Haq got Prime Minister Zulfiqar Ali Bhutto, a democratically elected prime minister, hanged in 1979, and launched an aggressive policy to Islamicise the polity and society. Pakistan has some of the most stringent blasphemy laws in the world. They have been used to oppress the Ahmediyas and the minorities. Even when democratic governments came to power in the Nineties, they had to work under the thumb of the military. That position has not changed even today. Politicians who dared to challenge the army even in inconspicuous ways were ruthlessly put down. Elected prime ministers like Benazir Bhutto and Nawaz Sharif were victims of the army's wrath several times. The latest to join the list of such leaders is Imran Khan. Never in the history of Pakistan has an elected prime minister completed the stipulated five-year term.[1]

Since the end of the last martial law in 2007, successive army chiefs, including Generals Kayani, Raheel Sharif, and Bajwa have said repeatedly that the army is not interested in political interference. The fact, however, is that the army has regularly interfered in Pakistani politics by 'selecting' and 'de-selecting' political leaders at will. When the army fell out with Prime Minister Nawaz Sharif in 2018, he was implicated in a corruption case, deposed, and exiled. After doing away with the PML (N), the army bet on Imran Khan. It began to back Imran Khan and the PTI from 2011 onwards. Several deserters from other parties were brought into the PTI before the 2018 elections. The army openly helped PTI candidates to win. Imran Khan became the army's new mascot. He boasted publically that he and the army were on the 'same page'. This was an absolutely necessary condition for the prime minister to survive. Imran Khan's coming to power in 2018 was part of the 'hybrid' regime model which the army had been practicing. Like earlier, this time too the experiment failed. After the 9 May incidents in which army institutions were attacked, the army chief Gen. Asim Munir has begun to reassert to recoup the Army's loss of prestige. Surely but steadily, the army is beginning to control and guide Pakistan's political direction and its economy.

Imran Khan's Track Record

Imran Khan's launched the Pakistan Tehreek-e-Insaf in 1996. In 2002, Imran Khan became the lone member of the National Assembly from his party. In 2007, he was briefly imprisoned for criticising General Pervez Musharraf. No doubt, Imran Khan is a charismatic leader with a relatively clean image and a huge following amongst the youth. As the captain of the Pakistan cricket team, he had brought glory to the country by winning the 1992 cricket World Cup. He carefully constructed an image of being an honest, pro-poor, religious person, a fighter with an independent mind. He contrasted himself with other leaders whom he derided as rich, dynastic and highly corrupt. The PTI was built as a 'third force', an alternative to the mainstream parties. Since 2011, the army began to invest in him. In 2014, with an approving nod from the army, he led a massive march against the Nawaz Sharif government and brought the capital to a standstill. He was rapidly emerging as a national leader.

After coming to power, Imran Khan promised to build a 'Naya Pakistan' on the lines of *Riyasat-e-Madina,* an Islamic welfare state. He unveiled a highly ambitious but populist agenda, which included rooting out corruption, building a welfare state, ending the economic crisis, constructing infrastructure and following a new, bold foreign policy. The pro-poor 'Ehsas' programme was widely hailed. Imran Khan also won kudos for his efficient handling of the COVID crisis. However, Imran was fiercely vengeful. Using the anti-corruption National Accountability Board (NAB), he went after opposition party leaders with a vengeance describing them as 'dakus' and 'chors'. His rhetoric, which often invoked Allah, the Prophet, and the Quran was lapped up by the unemployed, restive, gullible youth. He was seen as a 'Messiah' for a new Pakistan with a bright future. In reality, Imran Khan was a demagogue and a deeply polarising figure. Consensus building was not his style. As a result, the traditional opposition parties got together to fight him.

All the talk of reform turned to be loud, empty rhetoric. There was nothing on the ground to show that he was capable of fulfilling the key promises he had made. Rhetorical rants could not be a substitute for good governance. The country did not have adequate resources to spend on education, health, housing and welfare schemes. Military spending and debt servicing drained most of the revenues. The mismanagement of the economy was glaring. Although he castigated the opposition as corrupt, his own record and that of his ministers and their families was no better. Imran Khan was accused of selling the expensive gifts he had received from foreign leaders for personal gain. Foreign funds were brought into the party, something that is forbidden by law. These funds disappeared without a trace. There was no accountability or transparency within the party. His family was linked to several scams and scandals. He surrounded himself with cronies, sycophants and time-servers who had their personal agendas. He was cut off from ground reality.

The economic situation in Pakistan during Imran Khan's watch became even more alarming. The common people suffered terribly from the enhanced cost of living. The prices of atta, sugar, cooking oil, fruits and vegetables increased astronomically. COVID and the unprecedented floods in 2021 that drowned a third of the country and the Russia-Ukraine war ravaged the economy. The Pakistan economy continued the downward spiral all through Imran Khan's rule. The rupee slid to historic lows losing its purchasing power drastically. Inflation continued to rise and exports continued to fall. Forex reserves plummeted.

On the foreign policy front, the country made several glaring mistakes. Imran Khan landed in Moscow on 24 February 2022, the day Russia invaded Ukraine. That was hugely embarrassing for the country. He alienated the USA big time with his trenchant criticism of its policies including accusations of regime change. China was miffed too. Pakistani security forces could not provide security to Chinese nationals who were repeatedly attacked while working on various projects of the CPEC. Before becoming the prime minister, Imran Khan was a huge critic of the CPEC. He toned it down on assuming office. But the CPEC, though generally welcomed in Pakistan, saddled the country with huge debts.

Imran and the Military

The military tolerated Imran Khan's mis-governance and his anti-army rants for some time because of the lack of a credible alternative. Matters came to a head when Imran Khan began to interfere in domains that were sacrosanct for the military. For instance, in 2019, he forced General Bajwa, the army chief, to transfer the then DG, ISI, General Asim Munir (the present Army Chief), because he did not like him. In 2021, he refused to accept the Army Chief's recommendation for a new DG, ISI and withheld approval for the new incumbent for over three weeks. He wanted Gen. Faiz Hameed to continue as the ISI chief because he was his staunch supporter in the army. Imran Khan played games with the army using the carrot of General Bajwa's extension as the army chief. Imran Khan's dangerous machinations led to differences within the army itself. Although the army has officially denied any split in its ranks, rumours of divisions in the army refuse to die down.

While the Pakistan army continues to be feared and respected, its image has been severely dented in the last few years. There was open criticism of the army in the media. Slogans that the army was supporting terrorism (*yeh jo dahshatgardi hai, iske peechche vardi hai*) were chanted by the crowds. Even politicians began to criticise the army. Imran Khan concluded that he could get the better of the army thanks to his popularity and iconic status.

As Imran Khan's run-offs with the army increased, he began to criticise it openly. He publically named an ISI official, Maj. Gen. Faisal Naseer, for plotting his assassination. He began to think himself bigger than the army. He forgot that he had become the prime minister due to its support. That was a grave miscalculation. The army had had enough of Imran Khan when he insisted that the new DG, ISI be of his choice. Such impudence on the part of a politician, who was the army's creation in the first place, was unthinkable. Their protégé had turned into a Frankenstein monster. This situation could not continue indefinitely.

Eventually, the army acted. It decided to remove Imran Khan from power. This was not difficult to do. The PTI had only a slim majority in parliament. It did not take much time for the army to pressurise a few MPs to break ranks with the PTI coalition. The opposition sensed an opportunity and moved a no-confidence motion against the Imran Khan government. Losing the vote, Imran Khan lost power on 10 April 2022 before completing his five-year term.

The establishment decided to crush Imran Khan. Over 140 FIRs were filed against him on various charges. Several unsuccessful attempts were made to arrest him. Each such attempt was played out in the media and social media. Tensions in the country built up. Not one to be cowed down, Imran Khan inflamed the passions of his supporters with incendiary speeches and staging a long march in which an unsuccessful assassination attempt on him was made. He accused specific army generals for plotting the assassination attempt. His supporters were enraged, took to the streets and indulged in rampant violence. The law and order situation in Pakistan deteriorated further.

All this drama culminated in the 9 May incidents which proved to be yet another turning point in Pakistan's history. Imran Khan was arrested on 9 May. Thanks to the crackdown, the PTI is now facing extinction. Imran's own future hangs in the balance.

Whither Pakistan?

The situation is fluid and the country can move in several possible directions. So far, the army has refrained from direct intervention. However, it is very much involved in directing the show. In the run-up to the elections, the political landscape in Pakistan is likely to change dramatically. However, the army will keep a close eye on political developments. The elections are due in October but there is uncertainty whether they will be held in time. They may be postponed on the grounds of security and 'law-and-order.' So far, the government has rejected Imran Khan's overtures for a dialogue. It thinks that the time is opportune to end Imran Khan's political career. He has been disqualified from fighting the elections. It remains to be seen how PTI supporters would react if Imran Khan is barred from contesting. This will cause a serious setback to the PTI. Jahangir Tareen, a former collaborator of Imran Khan, has set up a new party. Some of those who are leaving the PTI may join him while others may return to the parties they originally came from. The PPP is trying to strengthen its base in South Punjab.

Even if the elections are held, will the Pakistan army remain politically neutral or will it back some political force or specific leader? Pakistan's future politics will be deeply impacted by the stance the Pakistan army takes.

The judiciary has traditionally been an important player in Pakistani politics. It has seldom been neutral. Imran Khan had a sympathetic judiciary all along. This led to a major confrontation between the Shehbaz Sharif government and the Chief Justice. The Chief Justice retired in September 2023. The role of the judiciary will be critical in the shaping of Pakistan's future.

The political and constitutional crisis in Pakistan coincided with the long-standing economic crisis characterised by nearly 40 per cent annual inflation, rising unemployment, falling exports, declining growth, mounting debts and empty coffers. The foreign exchange reserves of the Central Bank and commercial banks was US$ 9.8 bn in March 2023. The Pakistani rupee fell to historic lows of Rs. 300 to one USD. The IMF, which had sanctioned a USD 6 billion loan in 2019, refused to revive the loan disbursement and release the USD 1.1 bn tranche. Instead, after hard negotiations, it agreed to a standby arrangement (SBA) for a period of nine months. Seeing the IMF's earlier reluctance, other creditors were also wary of giving fresh loans but have now opened their purses, giving Pakistan temporary relief. Ahead of the elections, the government will face the weight of incumbency. It has failed to bring any relief to the suffering masses. Ahead of the elections, a caretaker government has been installed as required by the constitution. However, whether the election will be held within 90 days of its taking over is a question mark.

Pakistan has accumulated huge debts over the years. According to State Bank of Pakistan (SBP) figures, Pakistan's total debt and liability in March 2023 was PKR 72.98 trillion (USD 256 bn at the exchange rate of 1 USD = PKR 283) amounting to 89 per cent of Pakistan's GDP. Further, official data of February 2023 indicates that Pakistan's debt repayment was $ 21.95 billion in one year; $ 19.35 billion in principal and $ 2.60 billion in interest on the total debt. It has to pay back USD 77 bn by 2026. Pakistan will find it difficult to raise fresh loans. There is no easy way out of the deep economic crises.

On the foreign policy front, Pakistan's reliance on China is increasing. Despite the much-touted multibillion dollar China-Pakistan Economic Corridor (CPEC), China has refused to bail out its all-weather friend from the deep crisis except for providing some minor sops. The CPEC has had mixed results. Several CPEC projects have been stalled and mismanagement is rampant. Reportedly, the Pakistani government has been made to accept an inflated bill of USD 3 bn for the two power plants constructed by China. It had to grant blanket tax exemptions to Chinese projects at a time when its revenue position was highly stressed. Chinese projects have done little to boost indigenous employment because of the influx of Chinese workers in Pakistan in large numbers. China is increasingly concerned about attacks against its nationals in Pakistan. It has advised Pakistan to set its house in order, restore stability, and build consensus. Pakistan is in danger of becoming a client state of China.

The government has a tough task of building relations with the USA, which were severely damaged under Imran Khan's watch. Pakistan remains in dire need of loans and investments to shore up its sinking economy. It needs US help and loans from the IMF.

During Imran Khan's tenure, Pakistan had launched with much fanfare its new foreign policy of leveraging its geostrategic location for economic gain. That policy has not paid dividends as the country has been plunged into a multidimensional crisis. Hardly any investment is coming into the country. It remains to be seen whether the newly appointed Special Facilitation Investment Council (SFIC) will succeed in directing foreign investments into the country. General Asif Munir has assured full support to the SFIC, thus indicating that the army is keeping an eye on Pakistan's economy.

Pakistan's Islamic brothers like the UAE and Saudi Arabia have barely helped to rescue the country's sinking economy. There is deep concern in Pakistan over India's growing clout in the Gulf region. Pakistan is looking towards Iran for help and assistance but there is not much on offer from the Iranian side. It is playing a double game with Russia. While it wants Russian oil at cheap rates, it also clandestinely supplies ammunition to Ukraine through Western countries.

Imran Khan had hailed the return of the Taliban to power in 2021 as a spectacular defeat of the USA and described its return as the 'liberation' of Afghanistan. For Pakistan, Afghanistan is turning out to be a major headache. Pakistan had hoped to control the Taliban when it came to power. The same Taliban is now supporting the Tehreek-e-Taliban Pakistan (TTP) which is now on the warpath against the Pakistani state. It is demanding Sharia rule, which is unacceptable to Pakistan. The TTP is closely aligned with the Afghan Taliban. In 2012, the Pakistan army launched a major operation, Zarb-e-Azb, against the TTP. After the return of the Taliban, the TTP has become active once again.[2] The border with Afghanistan has become restive. Exchange of fire between Afghan and Pak forces has become more frequent. Army and police posts have been attacked by the TTP routinely. The Pakistan Army has launched a major operation against the TTP. Under Imran Khan's watch, the government entered into a dialogue with the TTP. However, that did not stop the attacks. The army is likely to intensify its operations against the TTP.

Relations with India remain tense and deadlocked. Bereft of any new ideas, Pakistani leaders continue to rake up Kashmir. Pakistan has refused to talk with India until the abrogation of Article 370 is revoked. The Pakistani government continues to follow a hard line on India. Pakistan's foreign minister, Bilawal Bhutto Zardari, during his visit to Goa for an SCO foreign ministers meeting, took an uncompromisingly hard line on India. He repeatedly made several intemperate remarks against Indian leaders. It is unlikely that India-Pakistan relations will improve in the near future.

Pakistan is not new to crises. Instability is endemic to the country but the present crisis has distinctive features. The army has the task of restoring its image and credibility. During Imran Khan's tenure, the economy suffered grievously.

Not many are sanguine about Pakistan's politics and economy stabilising any time soon. There is more pain before the crisis subsides, if at all it does. Chronic instability and deteriorating economy may even embolden the fissiparous tendencies in the country. The country's ability to rescue itself from multiple crises will be severely tested. The future seems bleak. For the moment, with IMF loans and some help from China and the Gulf countries, Pakistan's economy has got a temporary reprieve. However, the political, economic and security crises are not over. The national assembly has been dissolved. Election date has been announced at the time of writing. Pakistan will remain turbulent in the short and medium terms. Meanwhile, the Pakistan's army is getting its act together and recovering the ground it lost during Imran Khan's rocky tenure as prime minister. India has to patiently wait and watch the evolving situation while ensuring that its interests are not harmed due to persisting instability in Pakistan.

NOTES

1. Pakistan has had 23 Prime Ministers since 14 August 1947 beginning with Liyakat Ali Khan who lasted four years and 63 days until he was assassinated. Nurul Amin lasted for 13 days (7 to 20 December 1971). Zulfiqar Ali Bhutto had three years and 325 days in office. Nawaz Sharif had three tenures, the longest being of four years 53 days until he was disqualified by the Supreme Court on 28 July 2017. Imran Khan completed only three years and 235 days as prime minister.
2. The TTP has claimed on its social media channels that it launched 367 attacks against Pakistani forces in 2022 in which 446 Pakistan's soldiers were killed and 569 injured. Of these, 348 attacks were launched in *Khyber Pakhtunkhwa* alone followed by 12 in Baluchistan, 5 in Punjab and 2 in Sindh. According to an infographic released by it, the TTP killed 164 and injured 200 persons in 117 attacks in April 2023 alone. These figures, however, cannot be independently verified. But the DG ISPR publishes from time to time reports of Pak army soldiers killed in clashes with the TTP.

1

Pakistan Politics: A Circus?

Rana Banerji

Ever since the Pakistan Democratic Movement (PDM) government led by Prime Minister Shehbaz Sharif came to power in Pakistan (April 2022), its path was strewn with a bed of thorns. A difficult economic situation and an opposition strategy led by former Prime Minister Imran Khan led to this predicament.

Imran successfully built up populist support with a narrative of 'foreign conspiracy', 'unfair martyrdom' and 'desertion by the military establishment'. Though later exposed as false, it was fanned by an army of besotted, young social media trollers. It found support among ex-servicemen, serving officers and other ranks — even retired Generals. After the Punjab by-elections, he seemed electorally invincible. In a series of public meetings, senior military officers were disparaged by name. Accusations were labelled in crass language during public discourses. Domestic politics became intensely polarized, representing a veritable political circus, aptly described as a scenario of 'dejection and despair'.[1]

Economic Difficulties Facing the New PDM Government

The Pakistani elite, comprising the civil-military ruling gentry – landlords, big businessmen, generals, judges and civil servants – have, over decades, brought the country to this pass. Living off international handouts to establish a rent-extraction, imported consumer goods-based economy, Pakistanis witnessed low rates of savings and investment, low import substitution and subsistence on low tax revenues. Perennial fiscal deficits and high, unproductive defence expenditures perpetuated domestic and international debt.

The 'Perfect Doom' Loop[2]

Facing three major challenges – falling growth/output, continued balance of payment pressures, and strong inflation, government intervention in restricting imports exacerbated problems. At one stage, the Pakistan Shipping Corporation was unable to trade as its letters of credit stopped being honoured. There was a shortage of much-needed dollars, with fluctuating rates in the 'grey market' giving birth to an illegal market in foreign currency. This ultimately forced the Exchange Companies Association of Pakistan (ECAP) to remove the cap on the US dollar. The attempt at closing the trade gap led to (a) reduced economic output, and (b) further pressures on the balance of payments as exports started drifting down, a situation vividly described as Pakistan's 'perfect doom loop.'

Deepening structural imbalances finally caught up on the perks, privileges and subsidies syndrome, fuelling inflation, currency devaluation, unsustainable expenditures and debt servicing. The solution proposed in the past by Pakistan's economists was to borrow more at home and abroad, but lenders seemed to have got wise to the financial risks involved in bailing out Pakistan without targeted guarantees of long-overdue, painful structural reforms.

Any such belt-tightening measures would adversely impact the 'have-nots rather than the haves', creating difficulties for political stakeholders locked in a battle for office and power via the ballot box. In the last four years of the Pakistan Tehreek-e-Insaf (PTI) regime, the economy went from bad to worse, accentuating structural imbalances to a breaking point. This may have forced the Opposition and the Army leadership (Miltablishment) to work together to initiate regime change.

During negotiations with IMF officials in Doha (May-July, 2022),[3] the PDM's first finance minister, Miftah Ismail, gave assurances to carry out the required 'tough' reforms. These came to naught as he was replaced by Ishaq Dar in September 2022.[4] This time, however, Dar's recipe of artificially pumping in dollars, and holding the official exchange price of currency in the international market were destined to fail.

IMF Deal Concluded Finally[5]

The International Monetary Fund (IMF) imposed tough conditions during long-drawn talks in Islamabad (2- 9 February 2023), forcing the government to enforce unpopular price hikes of petrol, diesel, cooking gas and the General Sales Tax (GST) rate, to meet an additional tax revenue demand of Rs. 170 billion.[6] Yet, the staff-level agreement (SLA) for disbursing the $ 1.17 bn second tranche seemed stuck. On 29 June, Pakistan finally signed a new nine-month stand-by agreement (SBA) with the International Monetary Fund (IMF) worth $ 3 billion.

Governance/bloated Cabinet

In public estimation, the PDM coalition came off poorly, revealing a lack of purpose or direction to take the country out of the sliding morass. Shehbaz Sharif seemed unable to make the transition from provincial to national leader. Modest communication skills laid his previous reputation bare as a 'doer'.[7] The ever increasing size of his Cabinet, with 34 ministers and a plethora of special assistants (continuing to mount, touching 50!) did not inspire confidence.[8] The government tried hard to give an impression of 'business as usual', without letting the economic crisis inhibit either the PM's frequent foreign tours or peregrinations of other Cabinet members, notably, Foreign Minister Bilawal Bhutto Zardari. To the latter's credit though, it must be acknowledged that he made a good impression in his interactions with his counterparts of Western countries, showing an unflappable countenance and a reasonable grip over Pakistan's difficult foreign policy challenges.

In contrast, Finance Minister Ishaq Dar made heavy weather of his charge. Much was made of the success in getting a commitment of $ 9 billion flood relief funds at the Geneva 'International conference on climate resilient Pakistan' (9 January 2023), but evidence on ground of implementation of rehabilitation projects in Sindh and Baluchistan remained unsatisfactory.[9]

On the domestic law and order front, Interior Minister Rana Sanaullah was left to do the heavy lifting to counter Imran's ever escalating agitational agenda, aimed to put pressure for early elections and build on his populist support.

Supreme Court's 'controversial' Verdict on Art. 63-A of 1973 Constitution

On 17 May 2022, on a Presidential reference seeking interpretation of Art 63-A of the 1973 Constitution, the Supreme Court held that votes of defecting lawmakers, cast against the whip of the party leader in the House, could not be counted during any vote of confidence or no-confidence against prime ministers or chief ministers.[10] This verdict seemed to run counter to provisions of Art. 95. Review petitions moved by the Shehbaz government and the Supreme Court Bar Association (SCBA) in the Supreme Court were not taken up for consideration.[11]

Violence during Imran Khan's 25 May 'Long March'

Demanding early elections, Imran Khan announced a long march towards Islamabad, starting on 25 May 2022. He gave a six-day ultimatum to the government to declare elections and dissolve the assemblies. Khan led the march from Peshawar, Khyber Pakhtunkhwa (KP), while other senior PTI members joined from Lahore. Though it was expected that the protest would be large, a crackdown in Lahore saw a much smaller gathering. The aim initially was to hold a sit-in at D-Chowk in Islamabad. Later, the venue was shifted to a park in I-9 locality. To prevent protestors from reaching the Red Zone (Islamabad) and entering the capital, hundreds of containers were installed by the Islamabad Police and a ban was placed on gatherings. The entrance towards the D-Chowk (Islamabad) was blocked by personnel from the Capital Territory Police. Some PTI cadres nevertheless breached the barricades to reach D-Chowk and vandalized trees and plants laid across the VIP boulevards there. On 26 May, Imran Khan called off the March, ostensibly to avoid a large bloodshed. Cases were filed against Imran Khan and his supporters for violating assurances given earlier regarding the venue of the gathering but the Supreme Court dragged its feet over meting out any punishment.

The July '22 By-elections

In what turned out to be 'a watershed moment',[12] by-elections to eight National Assembly (NA) and three Punjab Provincial Assembly (PA) seats were held on 17 July 2022, of which the PTI won seven NA and two PA seats.[13] This trend has continued with PTI winning in 30 out of 35 by-elections held in the last year.

Changes in Punjab

Hamza Shehbaz had earlier won a vote of confidence in the Punjab Provincial Assembly (16 April 022) to become Chief Minister, getting 197 votes in the 381-member House, but this included 25 dissident PTI MPAs. After the Supreme Court's order on Art. 63-A of the Constitution (25 July), the Supreme Court struck down the vote and installed former Speaker Chaudhry Pervez Elahi as CM.[14]

In an increasingly polarized atmosphere, this order signified an indirect boost for ousted Prime Minister Imran Khan and a setback to the PDM government at the Centre.

The PML (N) Huddle in London

Former Prime Minister Nawaz Sharif called senior PML (N) leaders, including PM Shehbaz and Defence Minister Khwaja Asif to London in September 2022 in an attempt to find a way out of this economic and political dilemma.[15]

ECP Disqualifies Imran Khan

On 21 October the Election Commission of Pakistan (ECP) disqualified PTI chief Imran Khan as MNA, in the Toshakhana reference case. By selling the gifts obtained from the Toshakhana in the open market, the order ruled that the action violated Article 63(1)(p) of the 1973 Constitution and section 137 of the Elections Act (EA), for making "false statements and incorrect declaration", "intentionally and deliberately". It also held that Imran had indulged in "corrupt practices", under sections 167 and 173 of the EA, which would be punishable under Section 174 thereof.[16] The verdict led to spontaneous outbreaks of protest by PTI supporters outside the ECP office in Islamabad and several other cities in Pakistan. Though small in number, they resorted to burning tyres on streets, jamming traffic and shouting slogans. In an address to the nation later, Imran disparaged the decision as 'collusive vendetta by a mafia'. He asked his supporters to call off their protests but prepare for another 'Long March'. [17]

Arshad Sharif murder[18]

On 23 October 23, a journalist supporting the PTI, Arshad Sharif, was killed, ostensibly in an accident at a road block set up by the Kenyan police in Kajiado, near Nairobi while travelling in a car which apparently did not stop at the checkpoint. His dead body had gunshot wounds in the head and chest, shot from behind. Even as his corpse arrived in Pakistan for a largely attended funeral on October 27 the PTI started making political capital of his death, implying that it was a planned political murder in which the military establishment may have been complicit.

Joint Press Conference of DG, ISPR & DG, ISI[19]

In an unprecedented, even historic, joint press conference in Islamabad (27 October 2022), the Director-General, Inter Services Public Relations (DG, ISPR), Lt-Gen Babar Iftikhar, and Director-General, Inter-Services Intelligence (ISI), Lt-Gen Nadeem Ahmed Anjum, read out a veritable riot act to Imran Khan. In the first ever public appearance by an ISI Chief, Lt.-Gen Anjum said he had decided to break his silence as he was seeing 'lies' being perpetuated and 'the youth accepting them'! He negated the PTI leadership's attempts to extract mileage from the deceased journalist's murder. Emphasizing that he was not there for himself but for 'his institution and officers, who were sacrificing their lives', but 'were being targeted for no reason', he clarified that Arshad Sharif faced no threat in Pakistan and the military establishment 'had no personal enmity' against him. Officers martyred recently in Lasbela (1 August 2022 helicopter accident in which XII Corps Commander, Lt-Gen Sarfraz Ali died) 'were mocked' by social media trolls, words like 'neutral and janwar', or 'betrayers' were bandied about to suggest that the institution (Army) was 'indulging in sedition'. Anjum said it was condemnable to speak without any proof in this manner, merely because the establishment had 'refused to bend' before 'unconstitutional and illegal' demands.

Bajwa Rejected Imran's Open-ended Extension Offer

Anjum further disclosed he was present at a meeting in March 2022 in which Imran had offered Gen Bajwa another extension in tenure as COAS, if only the threat to his government from the no-confidence motion moved by the opposition could be prevented. Bajwa rejected this offer outright, as he wanted 'the institution (Army) to move forward from a controversial to a constitutional role'. The DG ISI sharply castigated Imran for holding 'quiet meetings at night' with the Army Chief, even while calling him 'a traitor in daylight', which was 'quite unacceptable'.[20]

Imran Khan's October 2022 Long March

Imran's long-threatened 'Long March 2' finally got underway from Lahore on 28 October 2022, this time without any hindrance from the provincial government in Punjab, now under the stewardship of PTI ally, Chaudhry Pervez Elahi of the Pakistan Muslim League (Quaid-e-Azam). The movement of the caravan was deliberately slowed to coincide its arrival in Rawalpindi/Islamabad with the retirement of Army Chief Gen Bajwa (29 November). In his speeches during rallies at different venues of the Long March, Imran focused on making the issue of the Army Chief's succession controversial.

Assassination Attempt on Imran Khan

On 3 November 2022, even as the PTI's 'Long March' reached Wazirabad, a 'lone wolf' gunman, Naveed Mohd Basheer shot at and wounded Imran Khan in the leg. He was immediately apprehended by a PTI supporter and handed over to the Gujrat Police. In his confession he claimed to have acted on his own ostensibly because his religious sensibilities had been offended by the festive, non-Islamic atmosphere accompanying PTI supporters at their rallies.

Refusing to undertake a mandatory medical examination at the nearest government facility, Imran underwent minor surgery after travelling to the Shaukat Khanum hospital, Lahore. Recovering from his injuries, he alleged a conspiracy had been hatched to eliminate him, in which both the army and civilian leadership were involved.[21] Bitter recrimination ensued subsequently over filing of a First Information Report (FIR) over the incident as Imran Khan wanted the names of the Prime Minister, Home Minister and a senior Inter-Services Intelligence (ISI) official, Maj-Gen Faisal Naseer to be included. Despite the Punjab police being under control of PTI's ally, police officials baulked at acquiescing to this demand, leading to transfers of some senior officers.[22]

Meanwhile, the remaining part of the Long March was temporarily suspended, to be resumed later, arriving in Rawalpindi on 26 November 2022 just after it was announced that Gen Syed Asim Munir would be Pakistan's new Army Chief.[23]

Gen Bajwa's Farewell Speech: Army to Stay Away from Politics

Addressing the delayed Defence and Martyrs' Day ceremony at Rawalpindi (23 November 2022), retiring Army Chief Gen Bajwa lamented the continuing criticism against the Army, acknowledging that 'a major reason for this is the army's interference in politics for the last 70 years, which is unconstitutional'. He went on to say, 'that is why, the Army decided in February last year (2021) not to interfere in politics'. Yet, instead of welcoming the military's decision, "many sectors used very inappropriate and undignified language while making the army the target of severe criticism," and a "false narrative was created", from which "an escape is now being attempted."[24]

The Army Succession[25]

After a seemingly inordinate delay, Lt-Gen Syed Asim Munir Shah, Frontier Force Regiment, was appointed Pakistan's new Army Chief on 24 November. A lingering 'technical issue' had been complicating the appointment, as Munir was slated to retire on 27 November, two days before Gen Bajwa. PM Shehbaz Sharif tackled this glitch during a Cabinet meeting on 24 November where the relevant Rules of Business relating to the Army Act, 1952, were suitably tinkered with, authorizing the PM to retain Lt-Gen Munir's services in an elevated rank until he took over formally as COAS.

Art. 243(4) of the 1973 Constitution prescribes that the advice of the PM is binding on the President. However, under Art. 48(1) thereof, the President has the option to delay accepting the PM's advice. Former PM Imran Khan told a private TV channel on 23 November that President Alvi was in touch with him and would definitely consult him on the appointment. After receiving the summary from the Prime Minister's office (24 November), Alvi made a big show of proceeding to Lahore by road, where he met Imran at his Zaman Park house. However, he came back to Islamabad and signed the summary rather meekly, without forcing a constitutional impasse.

Alongside, the appointment of Gen Sahir Shamshad Mirza, Sindh Regiment, was also announced to Pakistan's other 4-star general's post, as Chairman, Joint Chiefs of Staff Committee (CJCSC).

PML (Q) split – Pervez Elahi Merges his Faction with PTI

In January 2023, Punjab CM Pervez Elahi carried out Imran's bidding to dissolve the Punjab Assembly. The Pakistan Muslim League (Quaid-e-Azam) split with Pervez Elahi joining PTI with 10 MPAs. He was expelled from the PML (Q) by Chaudhry Shujaat Hussain but Imran made him the PTI party president.[26]

Opposition Leaders Implicated in Legal Wrangles

A deliberate process of subjecting opposition leaders to accountability was now initiated, apparently with the backing of the military establishment. Shehbaz Gill, Imran's Special Assistant (10 August 2022) and Senator Azam Swati (27 November 2022) were arrested for alleged sedition and inflammatory statements against the Army leadership. Both claimed to have been subjected to brutal custodial torture, provoking Imran to indulge in nasty name-calling against senior army officers working in the ISI ('Dirty Harry').[27]

On 25 January 2023 (PTI)'s former Information Minister, Fawad Chaudhry, was arrested from Lahore by the Islamabad police. Efforts to stymie this move through a sympathetic Lahore High Court judge failed. Having threatened violence against ECP officials, Chaudhry was charged under sections 124-A (sedition), 153-A (promoting enmity between different groups, etc.), 505 (statements conducive to public mischief) and 506 (punishment for criminal intimidation) of the Pakistan Penal Code (PPC).[28] Though a longer incarceration seemed on the cards initially, he was released on bail from Adiala Jail, Rawalpindi, on 1 February 2023. Another prominent PTI supporter, Sheikh Rasheed Ahmed was arrested briefly (2 February 2023) but released on bail. After Imran announced the 'Jail Bharo Tehrik' (courting arrests voluntarily) in March 2023, Shah Mehmood Quereshi and Asad Umar went to jail.

In a carefully considered rap on the knuckles, eighty-year old Lt-Gen (retd.) Amjad Shoaib, who runs his own TV site, 'Defence, Diplomacy & Politics', was arrested on 27 February 2003, for statements conducive to public mischief (Sec. 505 Pakistan Penal Code), inciting revolt against institutions and promoting enmity (Sec. 153 PPC). Shoaib's telephone records revealed he was in touch with prominent pro-Imran Khan television show anchors. As head of an ex-servicemen's organization (PESS), he enjoyed some support within a section of retired and serving Army personnel, though he had dabbled in defence housing scams in the past in league with estate dealer Malik Riaz. He was discharged by a court on 4 March 2023.

These arrests played out almost in replica, the cases launched against the families of Nawaz and Shehbaz Sharif during the Imran Khan regime, then under a pliant National Accountability Bureau (NAB) headed by Justice (retd.) Javed Iqbal (who was apparently blackmailed as well over alleged overtures to a lady, Tayyaba Gul).[29] Now the wheel of arrests of political opponents appeared to be turning full circle.

The Election Commission of Pakistan (ECP) directed the Federal Investigation agency to start the process for Imran's arrest in the Toshakhana (false declaration/concealment of assets) and illegal foreign funding cases. A petition was also filed in court to rake up the issue of Imran's undeclared parenthood in the Tyrian White case. However, Imran has been stalling progress by avoiding appearing in courts, citing security considerations.

Retired General Appointed to Head NAB[30]

On 4 March 2023 Lt- Gen (retd.) Nazir Ahmed Butt was appointed Chairman, NAB for a three-year term. He is the third Army officer to head the NAB, after Lt-Gen Syed Mohd Amjad and Lt-Gen Shaukat Aziz. The post fell vacant after the unexpected resignation of Aftab Sultan, former Intelligence Bureau Chief under Nawaz Sharif (2013- 2018), who became head of the NAB only in August last year.

The appointment indicated, for the moment, continuing support of the military establishment for the beleaguered Shehbaz Sharif government.

The Zaman Park standoff (13-16 March 2023)

After the non-appearance of Imran Khan and several deferments, non-bailable warrants of arrest were issued by an Islamabad sessions court (13 March) at the indictment stage of hearings in the Toshakhana case. The police authorities of Islamabad and Lahore were unable to execute the warrant of arrest. Police contingents approaching Imran's Zaman Park, Lahore, residence were attacked by stone-pelting PTI supporters. A posse of police from Gilgit Baltistan was also present. The stand-off continued for over two days even while Imran Khan remained closeted inside.[31] PTI supporters hurled 'petrol bombs' against the police. The Lahore High Court asked the police to temporarily stop their operation (15 March).[32] The Federal Government transferred Gilgit-Baltistan IGP, Muhd Saeed and replaced him with an officer from KP, Dar Ali Khan Khattak.[33]

Audio Leaks of High Dignitaries

In conversations between senior government functionaries and politicians, leaked to social media (15 March), PTI's Yasmin Rashid was heard urging President Alvi to counsel Imran to surrender to avoid further bloodshed.[34] Audio leaks also surfaced (23 April 2023) of abusive anti-Asim Munir conversations between the Lahore Corps Commander's wife and the spouse of former Punjab Governor Khwaja Tariq Rahim.

Lahore IGP Holds Press Conference

Addressing a press conference (Lahore, 16 March) along with Punjab caretaker Information Minister Amir Mir, Punjab's IGP Usman Anwer explained that the Lahore police deployed to execute the warrant of arrest at Zaman Park was unarmed and had strict orders to exercise restraint. He mentioned that PTI supporters present inside Imran Khan's house included members of sectarian and terrorist outfits like the Tehrik-e-Nifaz Fiqh Jaffria (TNFJ) and Tehreek-e-Taliban (TTP).[35]

On 18 March even as Imran's convoy left to attend court in Islamabad, the Lahore police raided Imran's house through a court authorized search warrant, clearing road blocks in Zaman Park area, arrested over 60 armed PTI cadres and recovered a cache of arms, incendiary explosives from inside.

Indictment in Toshakhana Case Stalled

The Islamabad High Court initially rejected attempts by Imran Khan's legal team to suspend the warrant (16 March) despite furnishing a surety bond.[36] However, sure enough, the next day (17 March), Chief Justice Amir Farooq provided relief, suspending the warrant and accepting the surety. Imran's demand to change the venue of the court hearing to the Federal Court complex, Islamabad, was also accepted.

Vandalism outside Islamabad Court Complex by PTI Supporters

The indictment process could not start on March 18 as Imran Khan again came to Islamabad from Lahore with a crowd of unruly supporters, who clashed with police and disrupted law and order near the court precincts. Imran was allowed to sign his attendance from his car and the warrant of arrest was cancelled.[37] Imran claimed later, he escaped as there was a plan to kill him in the court premises.

This entire imbroglio seemed to strengthen Imran's popularity. A *Dawn* editorial alleged the PDM government had 'shot itself in the foot'.[38]

A Divided Judiciary

Imran Khan successfully kept evading arrest, stalling progress in indictment in courts. His legal teams approached different courts in different jurisdictions. The Lahore High Court granted (17 March) Imran Khan protective bail in nine cases. A variety of orders were issued that ended up contradicting each other. Judgments in these cases revealed confusion in the ranks of the lower and superior courts, underlining their fast-eroding credibility as a fair and non-partisan arbiter of legal and political disputes.[39]

Schisms within Pakistan's higher judiciary had come into the open even earlier, over promotions of judges from high courts to the Supreme Court (SC). Chief Justice Umar Ata Bandial, slated to retire on 16 September 2023, was forced to eat humble pie at deliberations of the Supreme Judicial Council, as Bar associations and government representatives objected to the panel of high court judges he wanted to promote.

Selective assignment of judges to benches also caused discontent.[40] Bandial seemed over reliant on comparatively junior judges, especially Justice Ijazul Ahsan, repeatedly excluding or isolating senior judges Justices Qazi Faiz Isa and Tariq Masood from benches dealing with important cases. Allegations of complicity in bench fixing and other corruption of some Supreme Court judges emerged in audio leaks of former Punjab CM Pervez Elahi, and his Private Secretary Mohd. Khan Bhatti. The latter was arrested from Quetta on 3 March.[41]

On 27 March, Justices Syed Mansoor Ali Shah and Jamal Khan Mandokhail issued a 27-page order questioning the Supreme Court's earlier suo moto order regarding the date of Punjab Provincial Assembly in which they questioned the power of a 'one-man show' by the Chief Justice.[42] Another three-judge bench headed by Qazi Faiz Isa ruled (March 29) against the powers of the Supreme Court to initiate suo moto proceedings at this juncture. However, CJ Bandial deemed this judgment irrelevant to the current case.[43] Justice Aminuddin Khan also recused himself from the Punjab poll timing case, reducing the Bandial bench to three, widely believed to be his henchman issuing one-sided judgments.[44] On 7 April, Justice Athar Minallah also issued his dissenting note, questioning CJ Bandial's dubious position on the suo moto issue.[45]

Among the common public, an impression grew strongly that both the Umar Ata Bandial-led Supreme Court and judges of the Lahore High Court were being partial to Imran.[46] While historically, the permanent establishment, that is, the military and judiciary had worked in unison, this time a divergence seemed evident.

Elections When?[47]

The Punjab and Khyber Pakhtunkhwa assemblies were dissolved in January 2023 but the PDM government, which installed caretaker administrations in the two provinces, prevented their governors from fixing a poll date. In the face of this reluctance, the Supreme Court took up the issue suo moto [under Art. 184 (3) of the Constitution]. Two controversial judges, Mazahar Ali Naqvi and Izharul Ahsan, were forced to recuse themselves, along with two others from the nine-member bench constituted to decide the matter. On 1 March 2023, a truncated five-member bench ruled in a 3-2 judgment that elections should be held within the constitutionally stipulated 90-day period, with deviations "to the barest minimum" on account of administrative or logistic constraints.[48] President Alvi thereafter approved 30 April as the election date for Punjab. KP Governor Ghulam Ali procrastinated about giving any date for the KP Assembly election.

Confusion and legal uncertainty continued to prevail about the holding of these elections. Art. 224 (A) of the Constitution requires appointment of caretaker administrations before elections. In the past, these elections were held on the same date. If two provincial assembly elections were to be held earlier, an incongruous situation would emerge, with regular elected governments in two provinces, as also in the Centre, while caretakers would function in others.

The ongoing 2023 Census, being conducted by the Pakistan Bureau of Statistics (PBS), added to the uncertainty. Detailed results, which were due to become public on 30 April 2023, could have a bearing on the position of National Assembly seats, their inter-province distribution, as well as on the timing of the next general elections.[49] This issue may have been deliberately left vague.

ECP Postpones Punjab Elections to 8 October 2023

Meanwhile, the Defence Ministry indicated that Army officers would not be spared for security tasks during the elections.[50] Citing security considerations and shortage of personnel for deployment in election duties, the ECP withdrew its earlier notification, resorting to its powers under Art. 218 (3) of the Constitution, read with Sec. 58 and 8 (c) of the Elections Act, 2017. Fresh dates were announced for the Punjab Provincial Assembly elections, to be held now on 8 October 2023.[51] Legal opinion in Pakistan was divided about the legality of the ECP order on postponement of elections to 8 October. The PTI filed a legal challenge in the Supreme Court (25 March).

Efforts to Defuse Polarized Atmosphere/President Alvi Acting as Emissary

President Arif Alvi had claimed earlier that back-channel contacts were initiated to defuse the political confrontation between the ruling PDM government and the PTI.[52] While Imran Khan did not deny these reports, the efforts did not make much headway.

Addressing the golden jubilee session of the Pakistan Senate (16 March 2023) PM Shehbaz Sharif called for 'unity to face difficult economic challenges facing the nation'.[53] In the past, Imran had shown willingness to talk only to the military establishment, not the civilian political leadership, that too conditionally, confining discussion only to fixing of election dates. This time, he tweeted he was ready to 'talk to anyone' for the sake of the country's 'uplift, interest and democracy'.[54]

A group of well-meaning journalists, intellectuals, and lawyers led by Imtiaz Alam and Mujibur Rehman Shami met Imran Khan (Lahore, 22 March 2023) and urged him to participate in an all-party meeting under the aegis of the Supreme Court Bar Association, to arrive at some sort of consensus to defuse the political tension and agree to a date for elections.[55] Imran Khan seemed agreeable to participate.

However, tumultuous developments relating to the police raid on Imran's house in Lahore and clashes outside the federal judicial complex in Islamabad (18 March) seemed to have overtaken this fleeting moment of détente.[56]

A joint investigation team (JIT) of senior police officials was set up, with representatives also from the ISI, Military Intelligence (MI) and the Intelligence Bureau (IB), to report within a fortnight on those responsible for the vandalism in Islamabad court premises.[57] Seasoned observers in the Pakistani media said this 'vicious twist' 'to the ongoing power struggle' had diminished 'any hopes of resolving the deadlock between the two sides'.[58] Predictably, Imran stayed away from questioning the summons of this JIT.

Summarising the country's predicament with unusual candour, Foreign Minister Bilawal Bhutto Zardari told an American TV audience (15 March), 'Unfortunately, Pakistan is facing a perfect storm. Not only do we have heightened partisanship to the extent that political parties or political stakeholders aren't even in a position to sit in a room and discuss issues amongst themselves, we are also facing an economic crisis'.[59]

Joint Session of Parliament

After a meeting with PDM allies (21 March), a joint session of the National Assembly and Senate was convened on 22 March, which was boycotted by opposition senators of the PTI.[60] PM Shehbaz Sharif decried Imran's 'disgusting smear campaign against Chief of the Army Staff, General Asim Munir'.[61] On his part, Imran alleged, the PDM was 'attempting to incite a quarrel between the PTI and the army'.[62] He reiterated allegations about a plan to assassinate him.[63]

Exchange of Accusatory Missives

On 24 March, President Alvi sent a strongly-worded letter to PM Shehbaz Sharif alleging constitutional violation in deferring the provincial assembly polls.[64] Reflecting perhaps desperation as his controversial five-year presidential term draws to an end on 9 September 2023, the letter included a litany of other allegations, seemingly setting the ground to justify a possible dismissal of the PM. Shehbaz responded firmly in kind, denying charges of malgovernance and accusing the President of writing a 'blatantly partisan' missive, which read more like 'a press release of the PTI'![65]

Clash between Legislature and Judiciary

On 28 March, in an obvious attempt to curb the powers of Chief Justice Bandial, a bill {Supreme Court (Practice and Procedure) Bill, 2023} was introduced in the National Assembly to prevent constitution of benches or take suo moto notice of cases, without consulting an empowered committee of two senior-most judges. A resolution was also passed cautioning against 'judicial interference in political matters'.[66] The bill was passed in both the NA and Senate but it languished for want of Presidential approval. On 8 April, President Alvi sent it back for reconsideration, 'citing concerns that it went beyond the parliament's competence' and hence, could be deemed as 'a colourable legislation'.[67]

Supreme Court Rules ECP Order Invalid

On 4 April, a three-judge bench of the Supreme Court (SC), headed by CJ Umar Ata Bandial, declared the ECP order deferring the Punjab and KP elections invalid and unconstitutional. It further declared that the Punjab Assembly polls would be held on 14 May. Detailed stages of the fresh election nomination process were also specified, leaving little scope for the ECP to delineate these dates.

After holding discussions in party and alliance conclaves of the ruling PDM, Interior Minister Rana Sanaullah suggested they were considering filing a reference (before the Supreme Judicial Council) against these three judges, including the CJ (apart from Justices Izharul Ahsan and Munib Akhtar).[68]

Resolution in National Assembly against Supreme Court Judgment on Polls only in Punjab and KP

On 6 April, the National Assembly passed a resolution against the SC verdict. It was moved by Baloch Awami Party leader Khalid Magsi stressing the need to hold general elections all over the country simultaneously, not merely in two provinces.[69] Most legal experts in Pakistan held this step to be 'an exercise in futility', acknowledging though, that the real threat 'came from within' the hopelessly divided apex court, with 'judicial politics' converting now into 'a judicial war.'[70] On 9 April, after another hastily convened Cabinet meeting, the Shehbaz Sharif government decided to refer the matter of allocating Rs. 2 billion funds to hold the polls as per the Supreme Court's orders again to the National Assembly.[71]

Meanwhile, caretaker regimes in Punjab and KP, under Chief Ministers Mohsin Naqvi and Muhd Azam Khan, respectively, continued to function beyond their constitutionally mandated 90-day tenures.

Efforts to Discredit Army Chief's Religious Antecedents

New facts came to light suggesting that low-level officials of some institutions like the National Data Registration Authority (NADRA) were involved in Oct,-Nov. 2022 to find out travel details of Gen Munir's family to Iran. The aim was to impute allegations that these may have been connected to some family members having converted recently to the Shia 'ahle tashi' sect. Complaints in this regard were apparently brought before the Saudi monarch by parties close to Lt-Gen Faiz Hameed and Imran Khan, despite which Munir's appointment as the new Army Chief came through, albeit, after a slight delay.[72]

This incident only confirmed the strategy of pro- Imran supporters in social media, persisting in their efforts to sow dissensions within the Army, possibly under guidance, still, of retired former DG, ISI, Lt-Gen Faiz Hameed. In fact, Pakistan's new Army Chief, Gen Asim Munir seemed aware of these machinations. He set up a special investigation bureau (SIB) in GHQ, under his direct control, to try and keep in check Army officers indulging in unauthorized political contacts.[73]

PART II

Cataclysmic Events of 9 May 2023[74]

In what came to be since referred to as 'Pakistan's own 9/11' (a parallel reference to the twin tower bombings of September 2001 in New York, USA), fast paced developments severely shook up the domestic political situation in the country.

Imran seemed to have crossed a red line during his Lahore public meeting a few days earlier, accusing DG, Counter Intelligence (DG-C) in the Inter Services Intelligence Directorate (ISI), Maj-Gen Faisal Naseer of plotting to kill him. This statement elicited an angry response from the DG, Inter-Services Public Relations (ISPR), Maj-Gen Ahmed Sharif Chaudhry.

The ISPR's press release No. PR-55/2023-ISPR of 8 May accused Imran of levelling "highly irresponsible and baseless allegations against a serving senior military officer without any evidence." It emphasized, "this has been a consistent pattern (of Imran and other PTI leaders) for the last one year wherein military and intelligence agencies officials" were targeted "for the furtherance of political objectives."

Imran was arrested from the premises of Islamabad High Court on the afternoon of 9 May by a team of Pakistan Rangers called in by the Islamabad

Inspector General of Police, Dr. Akbar Nazir Khan, to help execute a warrant of arrest issued by the National Accountability Bureau (NAB) implicating Imran and his wife for corrupt practices by a holder of public office, under Sec. 9 of the NAB Ordinance, 1999.

The Offence

Nearly 458 kanals of land in Mouza Bakrala, Tehsil Sohawa, Jhelum district, and 240 kanals in Bani Gala, Islamabad (in the name of absconding business lady associate, Farah Gogi) were gifted by notorious property dealer Malik Riaz to Imran, ostensibly for setting up a university in the name of the Al Qadir Trust, of which both Imran and his wife, Bushra Bibi, are the only trustees.

Malik Riaz had sold a property in Britain (purchased ironically, from the son of Nawaz Sharif). The National Crimes Office (NCA, UK) had frozen these funds. Later, after an out-of-court settlement, 190 mn pounds sterling were released for refund to the Government of Pakistan. Part of this money was adjusted in the Supreme Court of Pakistan's account, against Malik Riaz's dues. The balance was apparently set off, in violation of money laundering laws, for these land grants to Imran's family and friends. These transactions happened in 2019, when Imran was PM. Imran tried to stall appearing before the NAB Rawalpindi but the stratagem did not work after awhile.

Spontaneous Protests Nationwide[75]

Soon after Imran's arrest on 9 May, Pakistan Tehreek-e-Insaf (PTI) cadres resorted to slogan shouting, arson and violence, holding protest demonstrations in Lahore, Islamabad, Karachi and other cities. The Lahore Corps Commander's residential compound, also known as the iconic 'Jinnah House' was stormed by an unruly armed mob of PTI supporters, who indulged in looting and burning property there. Surprisingly enough, IV Corps Commander, Lt-Gen Salman Fayyaz Ghani appeared before the rioters in civvies and tried to reason with them. He then managed to leave the premises, with his family. No military guards were deployed or tried to prevent the rioters. Several prominently placed women supporters of Imran, having connections with retired army generals were involved in instigating these mobs. PTI supporters, including women, gathered outside and broke through the gates of the General Headquarters cantonment boundary fencing in Rawalpindi. This was only the second time this had happened, after the TTP attack in October 2009. Two PTI protestors in Faislabad and one at Askari checkpoint in Quetta were killed in police firings. The demonstrators tried to attack the Mianwali and Sargodha air bases as well as the Multan and Gujranwala cantonments. A pillar at Chaghi, Khyber Pakhtunkhwa, commemorating Pakistan's nuclear explosions of 1998 was damaged. The direction of public ire witnessed in these uprisings was rather unprecedented, focusing singularly against the military establishment.

Higher Judiciary Reacts

On 11 May 2023 the Supreme Court extended 'extraordinary' relief to Imran Khan, with CJ Bandial greeting him with 'a good to see you' remark, and his three-member bench terming his arrest on the premises of the Islamabad High Court "invalid and unlawful".[76] This order was later formalized by Chief Justice (CJI) Amir Farooq of the Islamabad High Court.

Lahore Corps Commander Disciplined[77]

A lot of rumours swirled in Pakistan over what happened after the unprecedented storming of Jinnah House and the virtual laying down of arms by the incumbent corps commander, Lt-Gen Ghani.

Pakistan Army chief General Asim Munir, who was on an official visit to the UAE, visited the ravaged Jinnah House on his return. He addressed officers and other ranks of the Lahore garrison on 20 May. Mystery prevailed for awhile about who would be in command at IV Corps, Lahore. Contrary to usual practice, the Inter Services Public Relations press release covering the visit tersely mentioned that General Munir was received by the corps commander. No name was given. Later, it became evident that Lt-Gen Ghani was being court-martialled, along with several other officers under him.

Reports indicated that initially Lt-Gen Muhammad Asim Malik, 12 Baloch, a sword of honour winner from the 80th Pakistan Military Academy (PMA) long course, currently Adjutant-General, was sounded to go as the new IV Corps Commander but he reportedly declined. The next offer was made to Lt-Gen Fayyaz Hussain Shah, Sindh Regiment, also of the 80th PMA, who was serving as Inspector-General, Arms, at General Headquarters. He was reported to have taken over. However, subsequently COAS Gen Asim Munir sent Lt- Gen Syed Aamer Raza, Armoured Corps (6 Lancers), 80th PMA, erstwhile Chairman, Heavy Industries, Taxila, as the new IV Corps Commander, Lahore. These developments indicated Asim Munir was still feeling his way among the coterie of senior-three star Generals, to ascertain the extent of support Imran Khan enjoyed within the Army.

However, the vandalism by PTI supporters on 9 May directed, especially against long venerated martyrs' memorials all over the country saw the ambience of public outrage change gradually. The ISPR lost no time in exploiting this changing mood.

Asim Munir Tightens his Grip on Army

After some delay, the first formation commander's conference after Gen Munir became Army Chief was held in early June (Rawalpindi, 5-7 June 2023). It saw Gen Munir asserting his control over Pakistan's top military commanders.

According to the ISPR, it was decided therein to tighten the noose around the "planners and masterminds" of those who had mounted "the hate ripened and politically driven rebellion against the state and state institutions". It was stressed that endeavours by any quarter to create obstructions and stymie the conclusive defeat of the ill design of inimical forces would be dealt with an iron hand. "Unfounded and baseless allegations on law enforcement agencies and security forces for custodial torture, human rights abuses and stifling of political activities are meant to mislead the people and malign the Armed Forces in order to achieve trivial vested political interests". The ISPR release added, "Hostile forces and their abettors have been trying hard to create societal division and confusion through fake news and propaganda but all such designs will continue to be defeated with the full support of the nation, Insha'Allah," adding for good measure that, 'efforts to create distortions and attempts to take refuge' behind an 'imaginary mirage of human rights violations to create a smoke screen' would be absolutely futile in the face of 'abundantly collected irrefutable evidences'.[78]

DG, ISPR's 26 June Disclosures

In another press conference (26 June, Islamabad) Director General, ISPR, Maj-Gen Ahmed Sharif Chaudhry conveyed a firm message to Pakistan's higher judiciary that military courts were there to stay and had been dealing with the culpability of civilians in the past as well. Talking about trials under the Army Act, Maj-Gen Sharif said standing military courts were functioning in which "trial of 102 miscreants is underway and this process will continue". In response to a question, the DG ISPR said the suspects being tried in military courts had complete legal rights, including the right of appeal in high courts and the Supreme Court. These suspects would be penalised according to their crime, adding that the "Pakistan Army has resolved time and again that the Constitution is sacred for us and a reflection of the nation's wishes". In particular, these actions were necessary as there was tremendous pressure from the families of Army martyrs who had not taken kindly to the desecration of monuments for the 'shushed' (martyrs) by the violent mobs of the Pakistan Tehreek-e-Insaf (PTI) on 9 May 2023.

CJ Bandial's Infructuous Manoeuvres

This 'warning' from the DG (ISPR) came in the wake of three lawyers' petitions filed before Pakistan's Supreme Court challenging the trial of civilians in military courts. These petitions were expeditiously rushed through the Supreme Court case roster and put up for hearing after senior lawyers Aitzaz Ahsan, Latif Khosa (former Punjab Governor) and another counsel representing former Chief Justice Khwaja, met CJ Umar Ata Bandial in his chamber (19 June).

In an apparently clever tactical move aimed to somehow patch up divisions within the Supreme Court, Chief Justice Bandial constituted a nine-member bench to hear the petitions on the trial of civilians in military courts, this time including long-ignored senior judges, CJ-designate Qazi Faiz Isa and the next senior judge, Justice Sardar Tariq Masood.

However, this move boomeranged as Qazi Faiz Isa did not join this bench, pointing out that he did not consider it a bench at all, as the CJ had avoided issuing a verdict on the Supreme Court Practice and Procedure Bill, 2023, which had taken away the CJ's unilateral discretion to constitute new benches. "If I hear the cases now, I will violate my constitutional and legal position," said Justice Isa, adding that the Chief Justice had put him in a state of uncertainty, which could only be resolved if a decision was made regarding the petitions against this law or the stay order is withdrawn.

The DG, ISPR, also disclosed that the Army's accountability process against its own officers and other ranks, for lapses or dereliction of duty during the countrywide violence on 9 May 2023 was proceeding apace. Three army officers, including a lieutenant general, were sacked from their jobs as a part of this "self-accountability process". They included Lt-Gen Salman Fayyaz Ghani, then IV Corps Commander, Lahore, his Chief of Staff and several other senior officers. Disciplinary proceedings against three major generals and seven brigadiers had been completed. Among those arrested were a granddaughter of a retired four-star general (noted fashion designer, Ms. Khadija Shah), son-in-law of a retired four-star star general (Rizwan, son-in-law of Gen Yousuf), wife of a retired three-star general (Shabnam Jehangir), and wife and son-in-law of a retired two-star general (Rubina Jameel and Mehboob), all of whom "are facing this process of accountability due to irrefutable evidence." These penalties showed that accountability in the Pakistan Army was carried out without discrimination, irrespective of rank or social status.[79]

The DG, ISPR, emphasized that investigations had proven that the events of 9 May 2023 had been planned for several months, creating a conducive environment first and instigating people against the army. A diabolical narrative 'based on lies and exaggeration' was spread on social media inside and outside the country. Confirming what had already been pointed out by Army Chief Gen Asim Munir at the recently concluded 81st Formation Commanders' conference (Rawalpindi, 7 June) about 'tightening the noose around the planners and masterminds', Maj-Gen Sharif added that the authorities had obtained clear evidence against those involved. Though not naming Imran Khan, the DG ISPR was clearly hinting that the trail traced back directly to the former PM.

The Dismantling of Pakistan Tehreek-e-Insaf [80]

Soon thereafter, Defence Minister Khwaja Asif issued statements to media indicating that the government may be contemplating banning the Pakistan Tehreek-e-Insaf (PTI) after the violence by its cadres. This intensified speculation about its imminent implosion and possible disqualification of its members and leader, before the next general elections. Dozens of PTI leaders hastened to resign, including former Ministers Shireen Mazari and Fawad Chaudhry, who said they were taking a break from politics. 'Electables' earlier herded into the party at the Army's nod – the likes of Faiz Ullah Kamoka, Chaudhry Wajahat Hussain, Aftab Siddiqui, Dost Muhammad Mazari, Hisham Inamullah Khan, Syed Zulfiqar Ali Shah, Usman Khan Tarakai, and Mahmood Moulvi needed no second urging to desert the sinking ship. Prominent ex- military scion, Asad Umar (son of the late Gen Umar, of 1971 purges notoriety) announced he was quitting as Secretary-General though not leaving the party (yet). These were obviously not 'organic' desertions but brought about under intense military pressure. It seemed as if the party was being dismantled the same way it was brought into power!

Political Isolation of Imran Khan

There was talk of a new faction of erstwhile PTI politicians emerging under the umbrella of Jehangir Tareen, sugar baron-cum-industrialist who was instrumental in providing a bridge to Imran in 2017-18. He fell out with Imran later and distanced himself on health grounds. He was still on a good wicket with the military establishment. Sure enough, the formation of a new party, Ishtekam-e-Pakistan Party (IPP), was announced on 8 June 2023.[81] In KP, former CM and Imran's Defence Minister, Pervez Khattak, who was expelled from the PTI only a few days earlier, announced the formation of his own PTI Parliamentarians party on July 17.[82]

While there was no indication of these splinter groups emerging as popular political forces at this stage that could erode or challenge Imran Khan's popularity, in a scenario of the latter's disqualification or arrest, they could be facilitated to win enough seats in the ensuing elections to establish a semblance of credibility and create a 'hung parliament'.

Knowing well that his personal charisma had not ebbed, an increasingly isolated Imran described these events as threats 'at the point of the gun', claiming that while he had no problem with the new Army leadership, Gen Munir apparently did.[83]. He indicated in a televised address (24 May) that he was ready to hold a dialogue 'for the sake of democracy and Pakistan'. There was no response from Gen Munir.

Even as the tortuous judicial process continued in almost cast-iron cases against him, Imran also changed his strategy of non-appearance in courts. The establishment appeared to be more cautious this time, leaving no loopholes before finally arresting or disqualifying him. The process of snaring Imran gathered pace, especially in the Toshakhana watch sale, and Al-Qadir Trust land allotment cases. After his Principal Secretary, Azam Khan, turned approver, the Cipher revelation involving alleged US complicity to oust him and his claimed misplacement of the document became a fresh issue with the Federal Investigation Agency (FIA) poised to haul Imran over the coals for violating the Official Secrets Act.

Qazi Faiz Isa Appointed new Chief Justice of Pakistan

An increasingly beleaguered Chief Justice Bandial sought to hold out against the recent amendments curbing his powers by reserving judgments or deferring hearings on instigated petitions. Counter attacking, the Shehbaz government announced (21 June 2023) that Qazi Faez Isa was being appointed the new Chief Justice of Pakistan. President Alvi, another Imran acolyte, whose own term of office was drawing to a close (10 September) meekly threw in the towel, approving this appointment almost three months before CJ Bandial's term ends on 16 September.[84]

After sitting on the government's recommended withdrawal of the 2022 Supreme Judicial Council reference against Justice Isa, Bandial finally allowed it to lapse (21 July 2023).[85]

Formation of Special Investment Facilitation Council (SIFC): Army's Foray into Agricultural Development[86]

On 21 June, PM Shehbaz Sharif and Army Chief Gen Asim Munir shared a podium to announce the setting up of a new body, the Special Investment Facilitation Council (SIFC) to provide an impetus to efforts for Pakistan's economic revival, with regard, especially, to attract investment from GCC countries in the fields of defence, agriculture, minerals, IT and energy. In an impassioned speech, the Army Chief held forth on the Army's potential to engage in agricultural development projects, and its capacity to deliver Pakistan out of its impending economic slide.

Consensus Eludes on 'Caretaker' Regime and Duration of Tenure

Meanwhile, consensus eluded deliberations between PDM allies and also with the military establishment, on who should become the caretaker prime minister after 13 August 13 or for how long the caretakers should function before elections to the National and Provincial assemblies, either in mid-October or early November, as the Constitution mandates. In particular, the name of incumbent Finance Minister, Ishaq Dar, did the rumour rounds, suggesting a longer duration.

Actually, this difficulty related directly to Imran's persisting popularity and the delays in the judicial process, which were affecting the credibility of the intention to finally bar him from the electoral process. For the Army establishment especially, it seemed a classic dilemma of 'failing to push the genie back' into the magician's bottle!

Though three times former PM Nawaz Sharif seemed to be calling the shots from exile in London, there was no certainty on when he would return to Pakistan, whether his lifetime disqualification would now end or whether he would be allowed to participate fully in the ensuing elections. Meanwhile, his brother, current PM Shehbaz Sharif enhanced his acceptability to the powers that be in Pakistan's powerful military establishment, emerging as a docile yet competent civilian face.

Amendments to Pakistan Army Act, 1952[87]

On 29 July, a new Pakistan Army Act amendment bill was introduced in and passed by the Senate, without PTI Senators opposing it.

A new clause, 4-A (convening authority) has been proposed, which refers to an officer who is empowered to convene a 'court martial' under the Act. Under Section 26-A(1) (unauthorised disclosure), the amendment has proposed that "If any person, who is or has been subject to this Act, discloses or causes to be disclosed any information, acquired in an official capacity, which is or may be prejudicial to the security and interest of Pakistan or the Armed Forces of Pakistan, shall be guilty of an offence, and on conviction by the court constituted under this Act, be punished with rigorous imprisonment for a term which may extend to five years."

Section 18 (retirement, resignation, release or discharge) gives powers to the competent authority to "accept or reject resignation" of a person, in addition to "retirement, release or discharge from the service". It also empowers the federal government to "retain" compulsorily in service, up to 60 years of age, other officers with the recommendation of the chief of army staff (COAS) owing to exigencies, extraordinary circumstances or if war is imminent.

These changes seemed intended to strengthen the Army Chief's hand to curb dissent within the Army.

They also fuelled rumours that the stage was being set for the extension of DG, ISI, Lt-Gen Nadeem Anjum's tenure, slated to retire otherwise, with three other Lieutenant Generals in September 2023.

Concluding Thoughts

The long stalemate between the country's two main political factions—the PDM versus Imran Khan's PTI—has benefited neither.[88] Pakistan's polity stands at the crossroads where clashes between institutions of state have become the norm. Every organization is riven with factions who are strongly polarized. The possibilities of evolving acceptable political consensus are increasingly remote. An erosion of the state's writ seemed to have been perpetrated by state actors themselves, with lack of clarity or unity of purpose between different interest groups within the establishment, as to how they can tackle a popular leader who is increasingly becoming unacceptable from the perspective of *realpolitik*.[89] In the interim, a new political construct with a weak civilian Prime Minister bowing before a resurgent Army Chief has come to the fore, creating 'déjà vu' for observers of Pakistan's domestic political discourse.

In sum, the country's political and economic future appeared more troubled than ever, with no silver lining visible on the functioning of its flawed democratic dispensation.

NOTES

1. Najam Sethi, "Dejection & Despair," *The Friday Times*, 13 July 2022, www.thefridaytimes.com
2. Atif Mian (currently Professor of Economics, Princeton University, USA), "Perfect doom loop: Pakistan's current policies", *Business Recorder*, 24 January 2023, www.brecorder.com
3. Tahir Sherani, "In talks with IMF, Miftah agrees to take tough decisions," *Dawn*, 18 May 2022, www.dawn.com
4. *The Express Tribune*, News Report, 28 March 2022, www.expresstribune.com.pk.
5. Dr. Muhd Abdul Kamal, "Beyond the IMF deal," *The News*, 12 July 2023, www.thenews.com.pk
6. Shehbaz Rana, "Rs. 170 b mini-budget on cards," *The Express Tribune*, 11 February 2023, www.expresstribune.com.pk
7. Maleeha Lodhi, "A year of lost opportunity," *Dawn*, 13 March 2023, www.dawn.com
8. Rizwan Shehzad, "Federal Cabinet swells," *The Express Tribune*, 13 September 2022, www.tribune.com.pk
9. UN report, 9 January 2023, https://www.un.org>content.note&MSF, 9 January 2023, https/ /:www.msf.org>flood-emergency
10. Mohd Omer Hayat, "After SC opinion, what is status of Punjab CM," *Dawn*, 17 May 2022, www.dawn.com
11. Asif Shehzad, "Pakistan police fire teargas, round up supporters of ousted PM, Imran Khan," *Reuters*, www.reuters.com
12. Najam Sethi, n 1, *The Friday Times*, 13 July 2022, www.thefridaytimes.com
13. Mansoor Malik, "PTI stuns PML-N with thumping win," *Dawn*, 18 July 2022, www.dawn.com
14. Rana Yasif, "SC's Art 63-A not applicable," *The Express Tribune*, www.expresstribune.com.pk
15. News Report, "Polls to be held on time – PML-N leaders agree to steer country out of multiple crises," 18 September 2022, www.thenews.com
16. Saqib Virk, "Imran disqualified," *The Express Tribune*, 22 July 2022, www.tribune.com.pk.
17. Tahir Naseer and Imtiaz Ali, "Imran tells RTI supporters to prepare for long march," *Dawn*, 21 October 2022, www.dawn.com
18. Emmanuel Igunza, "Mystery over killing of Pakistani journalist in Kenya," *BBC News*, Nairobi, 29 October 2022, www.bbc.com.
19. "Burnt Bridges," *Dawn* Editorial, 29 October 2022, www.dawn.com.
20. Staff report, "Army claims PTI offered Bajwa 'indefinite extension' in return for trust vote help," *Pakistan Today*, 27 October 2022, www.pakistantoday.com.pk
21. Wikipedia, https://en.m.wikipedia.org, accessed on 7 March 2023.
22. Rameez Khan, "Punjab top cop seeks transfer amid FIR row," *The Express Tribune*, 6 November 2022, www.express.com.pk
23. Mansoor Malik, "Imran heads to Pindi today for 'climax' of long march," *Dawn*, 26 November 2022, www.dawn.com
24. News report, *Dawn*, 23 November 2023, www.dawn.com
25. Rana Banerji, "Will Gen Munir take on Imran Khan?", *Rediff.com*, 24 November 2022, https://www.rediff.com/news/column/rana-banerji-will-general-munir-take-on-imran-khan/

20221124.htm

26. Adnan Sheikh, "Elahi camp removes Shujaat as PML-Q President," *Dawn*, 26 January 2023, www.dawn.com
27. News report, "Gill arrested on sedition charges" and "Pakistan's Dark Age," *The Express Tribune*, 10 August 2022 & 27 November 2022, www.tribune.com.pk
28. "Will former Pak PM Imran Khan go to jail after Fawad Chaudhry's dramatic arrest?", *India Narrative*, 28 January 2023, https://www.indianarrative.com/opinion-news/will-former-pak-pm-imran-khan-go-to-jail-after-fawad-chaudhrys-dramatic-arrest-101181.html
29. Correspondent report, "Imran fraudulently acquired 'objectionable videos' to blackmail NAB chief: Maryam," *The Express Tribune*, 21 June 2022, www.tribune.com.pk
30. Rana Banerji, "Pak Army Chief is in no mood to forgive Imran Khan," *Rediff.com*, 6 March 2023, https://www.rediff.com/news/column/rana-banerji-why-asim-munir-is-in-no-mood-to-forgive-imran-khan/20230306.htm
31. M. Shahzad, "Law enforcers withdraw from around Imran Khan's Zaman Park residence," *The Express Tribune*, 15 March 2023, www.tribune.com.pk
32. Rana Yasif, "LHC order stopping police action extended till today," *The Express Tribune*, 16 March 2023, www.tribune.com.pk
33. *Daily Times* News Desk, 16 March 2023, https://dailytimes.com.pk
34. Web desk, "Another audio leak surfaces online," 15 March 2023, https://en.dailypakistan.com.pk
35. *Geo TV*, 16 March, https://live.geo.tv
36. Umer Burney, "Islamabad court rejects Imran's plea seeking suspension of arrest warrants in Toshakhana case," *Dawn*, 16 March 2023, www.dawn.com
37. Umer Burney, Abdullah Mohamad, and Nauman Liaquat, "Toshakhana case: Imran's arrest warrants cancelled after PTI chief marks attendance amid chaos, clashes," *Dawn*, 19 March 2023, www.dawn.com
38. *Dawn* Editorial, 20 March 2023, www.dawn.com
39. Raza Rumi, "Imran Khan vs Military Establishment: final showdown?," *The Friday Times*, 16 March 2023, https://www.thefridaytimes.com/2023/03/16/imran-khan-vs-military-establishment-the-final-showdown-begins
40. Hasnaat Malik, "Justice Isa questions provisions of 'special bench' constitution," *The Express Tribune*, 15 March, www.tribune.com.pk and Sherry Rehman, Minister, Climate Change, *Dunya News*, 27 February 2023, https://dunyanews.tv>Pakistan>
41. www.nation.com.pk, 17 March 2023, https://www.unewstv.com, accessed on 21 March 2023.
42. Sohail Khan, "Two apex court judges' dissenting order," *The News*, 28 March 2023, www.thenews.com.pk
43. *ARY News*, https:/arynews.tv/sc-office-sets-aside-justice-qazi-faez-isa-observation/, accessed on 2 April 2023.
44. *Pakistan News*, Staff Report, https://www.pakistanstandard.com/justice-aminud-din-recuses-himself-from-punjab-election-delay-case/, accessed on 30 March 2023.
45. "Justice Minallah wades into suo moto row," *The Express Tribune*, 7 April 2023, www.tribune.com.pk
46. Hasnaat Malik, "Judiciary on Imran's side, unlike Nawaz," *The Express Tribune*, 19 March 2023, www.tribune.com.pk.
47. Maleeha Lodhi, "The only way out?," *Dawn*, 7 March 2023, www.dawn.com
48. Haseeb Bhatti, "Closely watched SC suo moto hearing to wrap up tomorrow," *Dawn*, 28 February 2023, www.dawn.com
49. "Pakistan Bureau of Statistics-Census Story," census.pbs.gov.pk, accessed on 19 March 2023.

50. "Pakistan Army not available for election duty," *Daily Times* Web Desk, 15 March 2023, https://dailytimes.com.pk
51. Mohd Anis, Mumtaz Alvi and Nausheen Yousaf, "ECP postpones Punjab polls," *The News*, 23 March 2023, www.thenews.com.pk
52. Najam Sethi, "Pindi Plan," *The Friday Times*, 9 September 2022, www.thefridaytimes.com
53. "Economic stability links to politics," *The Express Tribune*, 16 March 2023, www.tribune.com.pk
54. *Dawn*, 16 March 2023, www.dawn.com
55. *Naya Daur TV*, 22 March 2023, https://nayadaurtv
56. Abbas Nasir, "A test of leadership," *Dawn*, 19 March 2023, www.dawn.com
57. News Desk, *Dawn*, 23 March 2023, www.dawn.com
58. Zahid Hussain, "The clock is ticking," *Dawn*, 22 March 2023. www.dawn.com
59. "We are in the perfect storm," *The News*, Web Desk, 15 March 2023, www.thenews.com.pk
60. *The Express Tribune*, News Desk, 23 March, www.tribune.com.pk
61. Ali Raza, Muhd Anis and Muhd Saleh Zaafir, "Six-hour long PDM meeting: PM orders nailing anti-COAS campaigners," *The News*, 21 March 2023, www.thenews.com.pk
62. *The Express Tribune,* News Desk, 20 March 2023, www.tribun.com.pk
63. News Report, 22 March 2023, www.dawn.com
64. Nausheen Yusuf, "Letter to PM," 24 March 2023, www.thenews.com.pk
65. Tahir Sherani, "'A PTI press release': In strongly worded reply to president, PM Shehbaz calls out Alvi's 'partisan attitude'," *Dawn*, 26 March 2023,www.dawn.com
66. Sanaullah Khan, "Cabinet approves bill aimed at curbing CJP's powers to take suo motu notice, constitute benches," *Dawn*, 28 March 2023, www.dawn.com
67. Staff Report, "'Beyond parliament's competence': President Alvi returns bill 'clipping' CJP's suo motu powers to parliament," *Pakistan Today*, 8 April 2023, www.pakistantoday.com.pk
68. Rehman Azhar, "Govt threatens SC judges with references," *The Express Tribune*, 1 April 2023, www.tribune.com.pk
69. Staff Report, *Pakistan Today*, 7 April 2023, www.pakistantoday.com.pk
70. Hasnaat Malik, "NA resolution rejecting SC poll order: An exercise in futility," *The Express Tribune*, 7 April, www.tribune.com.pk
71. AAP, "Bill to discuss fund allocation for K-P, Punjab polls tabled in NA," *The Express Tribune*, 10 April 2023, www.tribune.com.pk
72. Azaz Syed, "COAS data accessed with illegitimate motives," *The News*, 2 April 2023, www.thenews.com.pk
73. Rana Banerji, "Is Pakistan headed towards martial law as political turmoil persists despite Supreme Court verdict?," *First Post*, 6 April 2023, https://www.firstpost.com/opinion/is-pakistan-headed-towards-martial-law-as-political-turmoil-persists-despite-supreme-court-verdict-12414592.html
74. Rana Banerji, "Will Pakistan military stay united after Imran Khan's dramatic arrest?", *India Narrative*, 10 May 2023, https://www.indianarrative.com/opinion-news/ -141511.html
75. Rana Banerji, n 74, *India Narrative*, https://www.indianarrative.com/opinion-news/will-Pakistan-military-stay-united-after-Imran-Khan's-dramatic-arrest-141511.html
76. Nasir Iqbal, "CJP 'pleased' to release Imran," www.dawn.com, accessed on 12 May 2023.
77. Rana Banerji, "How will Pakistan Army deal with Imran Khan?", *Rediff.com*, 22 May 2023, www.rediff.com
78. Inter Services Public Relations Press release extracts, *Dawn*, 7 June 2023, www.dawn.com
79. Rana Banerji, "DG, ISPR's warning and the way forward," *India Narrative*, 27 June 2023, https://www.indianarrative.com/opinion-news/pakistan-dg-isprs-warning-and-the-way-forward-146341.html

80. Rana Banerji, "Is Imran Khan's PTI imploding?", *Rediff.com*, 25 May 2023, https://www.rediff.com/news/column/20230525.htm
81. Dr. Qaisar Rashid, "And now the Istehkam-e-Pakistan Party," *Pakistan Today*, 10 June 2023, www. pakistantoday.com
82. *The Express Tribune*, 17 July 2023, www.tribune.com.pk
83. Staff reporter, *Al Jazeera*, 17 May 2023, www.aljazeera.com
84. Nadir Guramani, *Dawn*, 21 June 2023, www.dawn.com
85. Haseeb Bhatti, *Dawn*, 21 July 2023, www.dawn.com
86. "Army Chief included in body formed for economic revival," Siasat.com, 21 June 2023, www.Siasat.com
87. Rizwan Sehzad, "Bill ratifies Army role in development," *The Express Tribune*, 29 July 2023, www.tribune.com.pk
88. *Dawn* Editorial, "Some softening," 18 March 2023, www.dawn.com
89. Raza Rumi, "Imran Khan vs Military Establishment – the final showdown begins," *The Friday Times*, 16 March 2023, www.thefridaytimes.com

2

The Pakistan Army: The Wars Within

Lt-Gen Rakesh Sharma

Background

At his maiden press conference as the Director-General of the Inter-Services Public Relations (ISPR), Maj-Gen Ahmed Sharif Chaudhry said on 23 April 2023 that the "...Pakistan Army was a "national army" and that all politicians and parties were "respectable". The army will not want to go to any one ideology or party. Every region is represented in the army. Political leaders should strengthen our thinking. The army and the politicians have a non-political relationship; it will not be appropriate to give it a political colour."

The truth is historically converse. Pakistan had been and is bound to remain a hybrid regime, hybridism weighted heavily in favour of the Army! This term 'Hybrid regime' was used to describe the communist regime of János Kádár in Hungary. Kádár treaded a fine line between the democratic aspirations of the people and Soviet-style authoritarianism. Hybrid regime in the context of Pakistan indicates control by a powerful institution, the Army, backed by powerful Chiefs of Army Staff and the hierarchy, acting in unison! Naturally, the Army allowed certain democratic traditions, such as elections to be held and the judiciary to function, to legitimise their extraordinary power as part and parcel of a democratic dispensation.

The central theme of this paper is to examine the contemporary Pakistan Army in so far as its relationship with the politicians and internal dynamics are concerned.

Pakistan Post Gen Musharraf

Gen Pervez Musharraf, in 2008, allowed elections that permitted the transition of Pakistan to a democracy and fled the country. His imprint on the constitutional framework was to leave the state in disarray. In the quest for absolute power, President Musharraf drastically rewrote Pakistan's 1973 Constitution, concentrating power with the executive branch of government, weakened the Parliament and subdued the judiciary. Musharraf also reintroduced Article 58 2(b) of the Constitution which endowed the President with the power to dissolve the National Assembly at his discretion.

In 2010, Prime Minister Yusuf Raza Gillani pushed Pakistan's Parliament to pass the 18th Constitutional Amendment, which literally changed almost 40 per cent of the Constitution. While reversing some of the changes made previously by Pervez Musharraf (in the 17th amendment), the 18th amendment also abolished the Concurrent Legislative List, which had given parallel powers to federal government and provincial governments, making the provinces autonomous. The amendment made Parliament supreme, even giving it a role in appointing Supreme Court judges. The 19th amendment, passed later the same year, took these powers away from Parliament and vested them in the chief justice. This made the judicial system fully independent, which heralded an era of judicial activism in Pakistan's politics. The amended Article 6 took away the judiciary's power to legitimise military coups, though it did not nationalise the multibillion-dollar industrial empire controlled by the military establishment.

The 2010 reforms targeted the military's interference in politics in terms of preventing coups. As the Constitutional conditions were not suited for another coup, the Army decided to shape a hybrid regime to remain in the proverbial shadows, allow a façade of democracy and continue as a state within the state. Hence, the environment was of continued military interference in politics, and that is a root cause for many of the problems Pakistan is facing currently.

The elections of 2013 led to a peaceful democratic transition, with Nawaz Sharif's Pakistan Muslim League (PML-N) taking the reins, though the Government soon realised the limits of civilian supremacy in the hybrid democracy! In the 2018 general election, running on a populist platform, the Pakistan Tehreek-e-Insaf (PTI) became the largest party in the National Assembly, and formed a coalition government with independents with Imran Khan as Prime Minister. By the time PM Imran Khan and the PTI were propped up in 2018, the Army had broken away from the Pakistan People's Party (PPP) and the PML-

N. In the 2018 elections, the PTI led by Imran Khan, was chosen by the Army to become the recipient of this military vote bank that had been cultivated by Musharraf. The Army used its resources to bolster Imran Khan through the manipulation of mainstream electronic media, social media, and the induction of electable candidates in the PTI taken from other mainstream parties.

Imran Khan's tenure turned out to be a disaster for Pakistan, ending in disrupting Pakistan's relationship with the USA and the EU, and even Saudi Arabia, the UAE and China. The PTI had a narrow four-vote majority, and the Government's power was severely constrained in the hybrid democracy, largely by the Army!

While ostensibly it was often stated that the Government and the Army were on the same page, and even Gen Qamar Javed Bajwa's tenure as Chief of the Army Staff (COAS) was extended, the divide was apparent soon, and grew steadily. By 2021 the delay in the change of leadership at the Inter-Services Intelligence (ISI) and Imran Khan's insistence of retaining Gen Faiz Hameed as DG, ISI, against the wishes of Gen Bajwa, the COAS, was the last straw. It became apparent that in the hybrid democracy, the Pakistan Army was the prima donna, and firmly in the saddle.

The ousting of Imran Khan in Pakistan's first no-confidence vote raised the pitch many notches higher with his statement that his political opponents "...want to bring in an Army Chief of their choice..." The DG ISPR responded characteristically that the military was "aghast at the defamatory and uncalled for remarks by Imran Khan."

Woes of the Pakistan Army: Internal and External

The mass following of Imran Khan evident in political rallies has put the hybrid democracy –civilian and military – both, under tremendous strain. Added to the woes are the economic conditions and pulling back of external guarantors including the IMF, Saudi Arabia, the UAE and China, which has further discredited the military establishment. The election scenario is in a quandary and the PTI-PDM talks that were to bring some sanity are floundering. The Supreme Court, though having allowed some time to arrive at a consensus, is breathing down the politicians' necks.

Further complicating the situation is that the popularity of Imran Khan and his anti-Army tirade has propelled an anti-military social media campaign. Just to recollect, Nawaz Sharif as PM too had his strong angst against the Army!

Despite the plethora of FIRs and cases against him, Imran Khan is scenting blood, riding on the popularity wave.

Historically, the Pakistan military sees itself as a breed apart, and devotes great effort to inculcating in new recruits the feeling that they belong to a military family different from and vastly superior to Pakistani civilian society.[1] Its professionalism, discipline, efficiency and solidarity have repeatedly enabled it to take over the state, and dominate it from behind the scenes with a civilian government at the helm.

Pakistan military's success as an institution and power over the state comes from its immunity from kinship interests and the corruption they bring with them.[2] Pakistan's economy is controlled by a ruthless business conglomerate – the army that owns everything in the country, from factories and bakeries to farmland and golf courses. Many of Pakistan's largest corporations are also controlled by the military, thanks largely to an opaque network of powerful 'foundations'. The largest three – the Fauji Foundation under the Pakistan Army, Shaheen with the Pakistan Air Force and Bahria with the Navy, control more than 100 separate commercial entities involved in everything from cement to cereal production.[3] The pervasiveness of the Fauji Foundation is exemplified by the quote "...it's early morning in Islamabad, and a middle-class child sits down for breakfast. He pours sugar refined from Fauji Sugar Mills into a bowl of Fauji oatmeal, which his mother cooked using gas bottled by Fauji LPG. In the next room his father logs onto his computer running on electricity produced by the Fauji Kabirwala power plant and clicks onto a program that uses Fauji software. The house they all live in was, of course, built with Fauji cement."[4]

The military leadership justified its power and privileges and ever-increasing perquisites as just rewards for its labour in the course of building a Pakistani nation and state. Many of Pakistan's intellectuals accuse the Army of being more interested in making money than in defending the state. They describe the military as parasitical, insisting it grabs the best land – both agricultural and commercial – monopolises large areas of the country's economy and seizes the most lucrative state contracts. They argue that the ills that beset Pakistan are the result of a corrupt and predatory Army.[5] Closer scrutiny reveals a pattern of careful planning including disorder on the streets orchestrated with the help of the reliable street power of Islamist political power.[6]

The Pakistan Army is the greatest organisation for social advancement in the country with officers recruited from the lower middle classes moving into the educated middle classes. In this context, the organisation is changing, and is changing faster than the rest of the nation. These days many generals are the sons of clerks and shopkeepers, or if they come from military families they are sons of *havildars.*[7] Indeed, the Pakistan Army has been a nationalist army with an Islamic look.[8] It neither runs Pakistan effectively nor allows any other organization to do so. The Pak Army, in dominating the polity, has eroded the capacity of the Pakistan State. The Pakistani political pattern has been, hence, an alternation between weak, unstable democratic governments and a benign authority, usually led by the Army. The military's role has been central, in which one province, Punjab, is grossly over-represented.

Officers and men of the Pak Army speculate endlessly on Indian intentions and capabilities. India, most men in uniform believe, is implacably hostile to the country's existence and intent on absorbing Pak territories into its own republic. When terrorist groups attack India...their actions enjoy a degree of instinctive, gut sympathy from a majority of Pakistanis...[9] However, between 2004 and 2007, there were a number of instances of mass desertion and refusal to fight against militants, albeit more so in the Frontier Corps units.

In the last seven and a half decades, the Pakistani army's obsession with India, has suited its ambitions of being the sole power and indispensable to the nation, and it assists it in retaining the corporate control it has over businesses. To that end, the all-important Inter-Services Intelligence (ISI) and its espionage, subversion and sabotage, and public relations and propaganda division – Inter-Services Public Relations (ISPR) – are foundational organisations providing the requisite support. The Pakistan Army is the largest and most powerful political party in Pakistan and the de facto government, and the biggest and most diverse business conglomerate and land owner in the country.

The Pakistan Army hierarchy has often been reported for corruption, Corps Commanders have been called 'crore' (crore implies ten million) commanders! It is obvious that in the higher ranks corruption is institutionalised, and hence any internal differences of opinions, remain buried or muted, lest their constituency gets challenged. In fact, in November 2022, a week prior to his retirement, an online investigative news portal *Fact Focus* published a story about the accumulation of wealth and property worth nearly $ 56 million by the family of Gen Qamar Javed Bajwa, the army chief. The news outlet shared confidential tax documents to substantiate its claims. It was alleged that the General's relatives had exponentially expanded their domestic and foreign property as well as businesses.

These internal dissensions, consequent to the Imran Khan phenomenon, have come to the fore, in open domain. The noted author, Ayesha Siddiqa, in her article in the online magazine *The Wire* in August 2022, stated: "If the current (till Nov 2022) army chief Qamar Javed Bajwa, widely viewed as the most powerful man in the country, has shown signs of weakness in taking on the PTI leader (reference to Imran Khan), it is not because his respect for democratic principles is greater than that of his predecessors. Rather, there are divisions within his own fraternity, which is comprised of serving and retired military personnel. Military sources with whom I spoke even suggested that there might be a rebellion of some kind against the army chief if there were any adverse action again Khan. A number of senior officers, including one former head of the Inter-Services Intelligence (ISI), retired lieutenant general Zaheer-ul-Islam, have come out in support of the PTI. This does not mean that there will be a coup initiated by army colonels against the leadership. But this level of internal dissent within the armed forces is already unprecedented."

A case in point is of former DG ISI Lt-Gen (retd.) Faiz Hameed, who first rose to prominence when he was heading the counter-intelligence wing of the ISI, known as DG-C. His name surfaced on the agreement the government had signed with the Tehreek-e-Labaik (TLP) to end the 21-day-long sit-in at Faizabad in November 2017. He had developed close links (read relationship) with PM Imran Khan, and his posting out from DG ISI by the COAS became intensely disputed. It was openly stated that if Imran Khan was the PM, Lt-Gen Hameed would have become the COAS, a brazen manner of being in cahoots. General Asim Munir's appointment as COAS did lead to two of his peers, Lieutenant Generals Azhar Abbas and Faiz Hameed, seeking premature retirement going out protesting. Though in a functional manner, it needs to be stated that both supersession or pure ambition are reasons enough for resignation.

The PML-N has, since his resignation, repeatedly accused Gen Hameed of influencing the courts to ensure convictions against its leadership. Currently there are allegations of his involvement in political matters when he was in command, not in line with the Constitution and the oath of the armed forces. The PML-N top leaders, particularly Maryam Nawaz, have demanded court martial of former DG ISI Lt-Gen (retd.) Faiz Hameed for his alleged involvement in political matters. Recently, the PMLN leadership has been continuously demanding action against the retired general.

What Next for the Pakistan Army?

For an organisation that has been at the helm of governance in Pakistan since Independence, directly or behind the scenes, these are very difficult times. This is not to decry the professionalism, training and modernisation of the organisation at the tactical and operational levels. The Pakistan Army is also a much respected institution internally, an important choice as a profession. Dissent can also be loyal, and is present to varying degrees inside every army organization all the time. It will occur in military organizations whether it is acknowledged or not. The existence of some dissent does not mean an organization is broken or badly led. The only peculiar consideration is the political nature of the Pakistani military hierarchy, and this politicization may trickle down. In the instant case there is an apparent following that Imran Khan would have in even the Army rank and file, as it is a microcosm of society.

In a self-serving statement, Gen Bajwa had recently stated that "Our army, which is busy serving the nation day and night, is subjected to criticism from time to time. I believe the major reason has been the military's interference in politics for the past 70 years, which is unconstitutional. Therefore, in February last year (2022) the military decided after a lot of deliberation that it would never again interfere in any political matter in future. I assure you we are strictly committed to it."

Indeed, this 2022 formal commitment of Gen Bajwa to disengage the military from politics in Pakistan is path-breaking, where four military coups against elected governments led to more than three decades of dictatorial rule in 75 years. However, this assertion for the Army to get out of politics must be taken with a grain of salt. The institution has been entrenched in Pakistan's political fabric for so long that it would be well-nigh impossible to engineer such a sharp shift. It also depends on the current army chief, and the course of events that politics and the judiciary will take in 2023 and thereafter. The Army Chief may still be a key actor to help reduce the tensions between the government and Imran Khan, in order to reduce political instability. The military hierarchy would still feel that it has a very potent role to play. The politicians also tend to run to the Army hierarchy for support as this perception persists that to gain power, the support of the Pakistan Army is a great facilitator.

The Army (and military's) dabbling in politics which is currently so divisive, and the atmosphere so charred, that invariably divisions in the Army will be evident on support for Imran Khan or otherwise. The presence of dissent is inevitable because it is a normal human reaction to frustration even among highly disciplined soldiers. Complaining within the organisation is not dissent, and real dissent is not about a subordinate's fear of change, for example the new Government withdrawing the perks and privileges that the military-folk enjoy! This, however, at the sake of repetition, needs be stated, need not be taken as grave dissensions in the Pakistan Army, and may be short lived till the crescendo of the electoral politics is quietened! Samuel Huntington had noted over five decades ago, "loyalty and obedience" are the cardinal military virtues of professional militaries. This precept, it is argued, has seemingly remained embedded in the Pakistan Army's professional ethos at the tactical and operational levels.

However, it must be stated that Imran Khan sought to influence the appointment of the army chief, seemingly in favour of a 'loyal' general who would have extended behind-the-scenes support to help him regain power. Imran Khan did not want Gen Asim Munir, the current COAS, who he had removed as ISI chief in 2019. If Imran Khan were to be elected as PM later in 2023, the chemistry between him and Gen Munir will need watching. This is more so as it is unlikely that Gen Munir will change course and concede to Imran Khan's demands.

Contextually, the events in Pakistan in the first half of 2023 are instructive, as they prove continuity in the roles adopted by the Pakistan Army since Independence and the subservience of the Pak polity. The agitation of the PTI following the arrest of Imran Khan got out of control, leading to damage to Jinnah House, the official residence of 4 Corps Commander in Lahore, and other military and civilian establishments on 9 May 2023. As Husain Haqqani, former Pakistani ambassador to the USA put it, "The Pakistan army has a history of reacting harshly against real or perceived attacks on its pre-eminence. The 9 May attacks on military facilities and installations were larger than anything the army has ever faced before. The crackdown in response has also been disproportionate and heavy-handed."

Indeed, the Pakistan Army, which had in 2022, promised to stop meddling in the country's political affairs, took the events of 9 May 2023 as the catalyst to launch an organized campaign to dismantle the PTI and Imran Khan, by slapping over 150 cases against him with the police. Islamabad and the adjoining city of Rawalpindi were smattered with posters glorifying the Pakistan army and denouncing the perpetrators of 9 May – a day the army has termed 'Pakistan's 9/

11.' Imran Khan and the PTI seen to have popular support for the forthcoming general elections, have been systematically and in a well-orchestrated manner, denigrated in public eyes by the Pakistan Army.

Pakistan though bailed out economically by the IMF and some other nations, stands at the cusp of elections to the National Assembly. Whatever the result might be, the Pakistan Army and the COAS will remain at the helm even if in the hybrid mode. As is evident in the sacking of the Lahore Corps Commander and other officers, dissensions if any within the Services are unlikely to rear their head, or will be suppressed firmly!

Conclusion

If Gen Munir were to explore a more hawkish India policy – such as by stepping back from the LoC cease-fire or by changing Pakistan's approach to the India-China border conflict – this would increase the risk of military escalation between India and Pakistan in times of crisis. The obsession of the Pak Army with India and J&K as national identity issues, are unlikely to be shelved. The main near-term challenge for Gen Munir will however be dealing with increasing Pakistani losses at the hands of the Tehreek-e-Taliban Pakistan operating often from Afghan soil, and of course husbanding the conduct of the national elections.

Gen Munir represents continuity in Pakistan's military establishment and will likely deal with the USA as many other army chiefs have done – in view of what they believe is in Pakistan's national interest. There is no doubt that the army played a major role in Imran Khan's ouster, even if the Shehbaz Sharif Government claims that the success of the no-confidence motion, later endorsed by Pakistan's highest court, was their own work. Post events of 9 May 2023, the army's top brass will deny Imran Khan by having him imprisoned or exiled, and hence denied any opportunity to upset the hustings. Gen Munir will use his range of powers as army chief to check internal challenges to the military's cohesion. Civil-military relations have been greatly tarnished under Gen Bajwa's six-year tenure, and Gen Munir may try to telegraph an ostensible "back to the barracks" approach, post the general elections to shield the military from criticism and restore its public image. This is not to say that in any which way, the Pak Army will loosen its control on the national governance.

Pakistan has a strong military and economic partnership with China, but Pakistan's military (and other elites) want a relationship with the USA – and some may argue the need to balance their ties with Beijing. US-Pakistan ties have deteriorated over the past many years due to Pakistan's support for the Taliban, its growing alignment with China and indeed the diatribes of Imran Khan. In sum, though it is not easy to predict the future journey of Pakistan, the Army's control of the nation and its polity can be taken as assured. In doing so, it will orchestrate events nationally and internationally. Dissensions, if any, rearing their head within the uniformed forces will be suppressed ruthlessly, for the organisation has to ensure it prime place in Pakistan, irrespective of the government of the day.

NOTES

1. Anatol Lieven, *Pakistan: A Hard Country* (Penguin Group, 2011), p. 163 C.
2. Ibid., p. 167.
3. "Pakistan's economy controlled by a ruthless conglomerate – the army," *The Times of India*, New Delhi, 12 November 2020.
4. Bloomberg Businessweek, https://www.bloomberg.com/news/articles/2001-11-11/pakistan-armed-forces-inc-dot
5. Carey Schofield, *Inside the Pakistan Army* (New Delhi: Pentagon Press, 2011), p. 2.
6. Husain Haqqani, *Pakistan Between Mosque and Military* (The Brookings Institution Press, 2005), p. 255.
7. Anatol Lieven, *Pakistan: A Hard Country* (Penguin Group, 2011), p. 182.
8. Ibid., p. 184.
9. Ibid., p. 5.

3

Environment and Floods in Pakistan

Sharat Sabharwal

Pakistan has been frequently on the edge of a precipice owing to its dysfunctionality, years of misgovernance and policies driven by elites headed by the security establishment. It is beset with multiple intractable crises. Of all its problems, the one that has received the least attention over the years within the country and in the international community is the adverse impact and management of environmental degradation and climate change. It has been hitting the headlines each time there was a big environment/climate change-induced disaster. However, it has now emerged as a major challenge because such disasters have become recurrent and increasingly catastrophic.

According to the Global Climate Risk Index 2021 of GERMANWATCH,[1] Pakistan was among the 10 most affected countries from 2000 to 2019, with 173 climate-related events. They caused over 10,000 fatalities and resulted in an annual average loss of 3.7 billion US dollars PPP,[2] thereby resulting in widespread human misery. Freak climate-related events have included water shortages, drought, floods, heat waves, forest fires, melting glaciers, winter smog, landslides, and population displacement, etc. Seen against the backdrop of Pakistan's fragile economy, poor governance, ethnic and sectarian fault lines, and extensive lawlessness, frequent climate-induced hardship to the people adds significantly to the risk of instability within the country.

Pakistan's Environmental and Climate Challenges

Pakistan faces multiple environmental and climate challenges. According to a report[3] of the UN Environment Programme (UNEP), the situation has deteriorated over the years due to an emphasis on quantitative growth at the expense of quality; lack of integration of environmental factors in planning and decision making; dependence on expediencies without regard to their impact on environment; failure of institutions to consider environment in its totality; and lack of realisation of fundamental interdependence of men, resources, environment and development. The same report lists some key reasons of environmental degradation.

A major factor is rapid population growth. The western wing of Pakistan, which constitutes today's Pakistan, had a population of 33 million as per the 1951 census. This had grown to nearly 208 million as per the 2017 census, with a population growth rate of 2.4 per cent from 1998 to 2017, and is reported to have increased by another 27 million since then. The growth rate continues to be close to 2 per cent. For various reasons, including lack of political will, Pakistan's population control measures have remained inadequate. The rapidly growing population places an enormous burden on Pakistan's resources and environment.

Rapid population growth has been accompanied by rapid urbanisation. Pakistan's urban population multiplied more than tenfold during 1950-2012, while the total population increased over fivefold only. Urban population has gravitated towards a few major cities. Karachi, the largest city of Pakistan, has around 20 per cent of the urban population, with Lahore and Faisalabad accounting for another 20 per cent. The eight largest cities of Pakistan have been growing at over 3 per cent per year.[4] Growth of infrastructure and other amenities in these cities has not kept pace with the population growth, resulting in environmental degradation.

The pressure on all types of ecosystems is growing rapidly in Pakistan. For example, in the terrestrial ecosystem, cropped area is under high pressure and per capita availability of cropped land is only about a quarter hectare. Land degradation has adversely impacted a large part of Pakistan's agricultural land. The suspended sediment load per square kilometre of drainage basin is one of the highest in the world. It indicates the intensity of soil erosion, which has impacted about 18 million hectares of land; salt affected land area is estimated to be over 5 million hectares; and another 2 million hectares is believed to be waterlogged.[5] In spite of land reclamation efforts, a large area of irrigated land is lying waste as a result of water logging and salinity.

Pakistan's aquatic resources are also under pressure. The Indus River irrigates around 80 per cent of the agricultural land. According to the International Union for Conservation of Nature, because of diversion of water for irrigation, the amount of water in the Indus River downstream declined sharply from 1,85,000 million cubic metres per annum in 1892 to 12,300 million cubic metres per annum in the 1990s.[6] As a consequence, the natural ecosystem of the Indus Delta has been seriously impacted by saltwater intrusion due to backwash from the sea, resulting in loss of millions of dollars. Sub-optimum use of water in the country's badly managed irrigation system has caused water logging and salinity and average water delivery efficiency of canals has reduced from 35 to 40 per cent from the canal head to the root zone due to their overuse and poor maintenance.

Pakistan's per capita availability of water has fallen below 1,000 cubic metres, placing it in the category of 'high water stress' countries. It is estimated that water shortage in Pakistan will grow to over 30 per cent of its needs by 2025. This requires judicious management and use; as well as conservation of water resources, but efforts in this regard have remained highly inadequate. Due to inefficient management and extremely deficient water storage capacity (Pakistan's storage capacity is around 10 per cent of average annual flows compared to the world average of 40 per cent), over 40 billion cubic metres of water flows into the sea during the flood season; floods causes extensive damage, while there is water scarcity in the lean season. Aquifers are getting depleted and underground water tables going down as a result of overuse of groundwater. The quality of available water has deteriorated due to silt, salinity and municipal and industrial wastes. Only about one per cent of urban wastewater is treated in Pakistan and the rest flows into streams and rivers.

Deforestation is another important factor impacting the environment and climate in Pakistan. According to data put out by the World Bank, forest area in Pakistan as percentage of land area dropped from 6.4 in 1991 to 4.8 per cent in 2020,[7] though some other estimates peg it even lower. In any case, this area is quite low as compared to the desired level of 20 to 30 per cent. Pakistan's deforestation rate is said to be the second highest in Asia, next only to Afghanistan. Rapid deforestation results in increased greenhouse gas emissions, disruption of water cycles, increased soil erosion and disrupted livelihoods.

The atmospheric ecosystem has suffered due to the deteriorating quality of urban air and global climate change. Deterioration of urban air quality has been caused by growing industrialisation, enhanced use of chemicals, fast-growing vehicular traffic, increased energy consumption, and excessive dependence on fossil fuels. Around 86 per cent of Pakistan's energy comes from fossil fuels.[8] Brick kilns, tobacco curing, cement, fertiliser, sugar units, and power plants are the most air polluting industries of Pakistan. The use of low-grade coal and old tyres in brick kilns generates considerable air pollution. The other air pollutants are particulate matter; and sulphur and nitrogen-oxides that are emitted by burning fuel. The government ordered a switch to the Euro 5 emissions standard for all new vehicle approvals from January 2021, but this is work in progress. A World Bank report of 2006 pegged the health costs of air pollution-related diseases at about 1 per cent of GDP.[9]

As for climate change, the average annual temperature over Pakistan increased by 0.6 degree Centigrade during the last century. Studies based on the ensemble output of several global circulation models project that the average temperature over Pakistan will increase progressively corresponding to an increase in average global surface temperature by 2.8 to 3.4 degrees Centigrade by the turn of this century.[10] Pakistan contributes very little to global greenhouse gas (GHG) emissions, only about one-third of the world average. In 2018, its total GHG emissions were estimated at 499 million metric tons of carbon dioxide equivalent, with Agriculture, Forestry, other Land use, and Energy contributing 46 and 45 per cent, respectively.[11] It is one of the major methane emitters, primarily through its agriculture sector. However, in view of its large population, high energy intensity and growth aspirations, its future GHG emissions could become globally material in the absence of effective action to curb their growth. Pakistan is one of the countries that are most vulnerable to climate change, which has a serious impact on all aspects of sustainable development, besides climate change-related disasters. It adversely impacts health, water security, food security, agriculture, forests, livestock and fisheries and causes events such as floods, drought, and sea level rises. The Pakistan Country Climate and Development Report (November 2022)[12] issued by the World Bank notes that the combined risks of intensification of climate change and environmental degradation, unless addressed, could reduce the country's annual GDP by 18 to 20 per cent by 2050, thereby stalling progress on economic development and poverty reduction.

Efforts to Manage and Mitigate Environmental and Climate Change Challenges

According to the aforementioned report[13] of the UN Environment Programme, Pakistan's policy response to environmental problems can be divided into four phases: environmental neglect till 1957; ad-hocism and piecemeal action from

1958 to the UN Conference on Human Environment in 1972; a period of evolution of institutions, policies and legislation from 1972 to 2000; and the current phase from 2000 onwards, characterised by maturing of environmental institutions and development of a number of policies as well as an environmental management system.

The first significant measure was issuance of the Pakistan Environmental Protection Ordinance in 1983, which resulted in the setting up of the Pakistan Environmental Protection Council and an Environmental Protection Agency in 1984. The Pakistan Environmental Protection Act of 1997 superseded the above ordinance and provided, inter alia, a framework for pollution control and promotion of sustainable development. In recognition of the link between development and environment, environment sections were set up in the federal and provincial planning commissions in the Eighties and Nineties. Pakistan also ratified important multilateral environmental agreements/conventions during these decades. The National Conservation Strategy was adopted in 1992 as the guiding environmental policy.

The turn of the century registered considerable progress in environmental policy making, including the Biodiversity Action Plan 2000, National Environmental Action Plan 2001, National Action Programme to Combat Desertification 2002, National Environment Policy 2005, National Energy Conservation Policy 2006, Pakistan Wetland Programme 2007, National Forest Policy and National Climate Change Policy. Pakistan also finalised its National Sustainable Development Strategy, which emphasised priorities in three dimensions of sustainable development: environmental, economic, and social.

In terms of the institutional framework to deal with climate change and environmental issues, Pakistan has the Ministry of Climate Change (MoCC) at the federal level, which is responsible for climate change policymaking and environmental issues; and acts as a coordinator for mainstreaming climate change and environmental policies at the federal and provincial level. It also monitors progress on international climate change agreements and accessing funding from the international community. However, in practice, its performance has left much to be desired due to capacity and resource constraints as well as devolution of policy implementation to the provinces. The 18th amendment to the Pakistan constitution in 2010 devolved a number of functions to provinces, including education, health, water, sanitation and solid waste management; as well as support to major economic activities and responsibility for environmental and climate change issues. However, the process of devolution is still work in progress. There has been no effective devolution of functions or budgets to local governments, thereby leaving critical services at the city and village level without adequate resources or direction. Provinces rely primarily on federal handouts as per a revenue transfer formula decided by the National Finance Commission and are invariably short of funds for various services, including climate change and environmental programmes. Further, climate change and environmental challenges are multi-sectoral and require coordination across provincial boundaries and with the federal departments. However, coordination of policies between the federation and provinces and among provinces remains beset with problems. The capacity problem at the provincial level is far worse than at the federal level and hinders the work of the Environmental Protection Agency, which looks after environment and climate change-related work in each province. This often results in action only when a problem becomes serious. Balochistan lags far behind other provinces in this area, as indeed in many other areas.

In 2012, Pakistan adopted the National Climate Change Policy (NCCP)[14] to comprehensively address all possible challenges of climate change adaptation and mitigation and provide a framework for climate change action plans and programmes. The policy provided for its updating every five years and was last updated in October 2021. Steering Pakistan towards climate resilient and low carbon development has been described as the main goal of the NCCP; other major objectives being: to pursue sustained economic growth by appropriately addressing the climate change challenges; to integrate climate change policy with other national policies; to build climate resilient infrastructure; to track the impact of climate change on water, food and energy security of the country; to minimize the risks from extreme weather events; and to accelerate policy coherence and integration to achieve the UN Sustainable Development Goals. The NCCP, which is primarily an aspirational document, mentions detailed policy measures in various areas. These include: improvement of water storage and infrastructure, water conservation and integrated water management; agricultural research including developing high yield crop varieties resistant, inter alia, to climate extremes; development of adaptive strategies for projected impact of climate change on agriculture; development of health-related strategies in areas prone to adverse impact of climate change; afforestation and forest management; preservation and protection of biodiversity from climate change; management of climate change and environmental problems in mountain areas as well as arid and hyper-arid areas; preservation and protection of coastal and marine ecosystems; disaster preparedness; development of hydro power generation and

Alternate and Renewable Energy resources; energy efficiency and energy conservation; urban planning and waste management; emissions reduction; and carbon sequestration and forestry. Particular emphasis has been placed on capacity building and institutional strengthening as well as securing financing and technology from the international community to meet environmental and climate change challenges. Some recent initiatives taken by the Government of Pakistan under this policy are: The 'Clean Green Pakistan' programme to make Pakistan pollution-free and counter the effects of climate change; 'Recharge Pakistan' project to, inter alia, utilise flood waters for restoring and recharging ground water; 'Ten Billion Tree Tsunami', a five-year across the country programme for afforestation; and the National Electric Vehicle Policy, which aims at boosting the share of electric vehicles by having 30 to 50 per cent electric vehicles in new sales of vehicles of various categories by 2030 and 90 per cent by 2040.

Paucity of funds compared to environmental and climate financial needs has been an important factor hindering the initiatives and policies of the federal and provincial governments. According to Pakistan's Updated Nationally Determined Contributions (NDC) 2021[15] as a party to the Paris Agreement of the United Nations Framework Convention on Climate Change (UNFCCC), the total cost of NDC implementation will be close to \$ 200 billion by 2030. The cost of clean energy transition alone would be \$ 101 billion by then. In 2016, Pakistan's adaptation needs were placed in the range of \$ 7 to 14 billion per annum to 2050, 70 per cent of it primarily due to infrastructure cost. Overall public spending on environmental and climate actions has been low and Pakistan's financial crunch rules out any significant increase in it in the near future. In fact, the budgetary allocation to the Ministry of Climate Change was reduced in the 2022-23 budget to Pak Rupees 10 billion compared to Pak Rupees 14 billion in the previous financial year. Pakistan's Water and Power Development Authority launched 10-year green bonds in 2021 and raised \$ 500 million to support hydropower generation and was reported to be considering launching additional green bonds. Consideration is done for resort to Nature Performance Bonds, Carbon Pricing Instrument and Blue Carbon. Pakistan is also encouraging involvement of the private sector in implementing its climate goals. A Public Private Partnership Authority was established in 2017 to facilitate federal implementing agencies in undertaking infrastructure projects on a public-private partnership basis. Pakistan's receipt of concessional international climate financing has been relatively low, but it has received significant climate-related financing from multilateral development banks, which amounted to about \$ 6.4 billion from 2015 to 2020. A large share of World Bank lending to Pakistan (44 per cent in FY21) and 50 per cent of the portfolio of International Finance Corporation has been climate linked.[16] However, the above sources of funding fall far short of Pakistan's needs.

According to a World Bank report,[17] a major problem with Pakistan's environmental and climate mitigating programme is lack of consistency and continuity within the policy space. Although climate-change issues have indeed featured in Pakistan's overall development policies since the 2012 National Development Strategy, specific actions or implementation steps have been lacking. The Government's ownership of climate change policy and responsibilities for action has been fragmented and shifted between different institutions and levels. The institutions that were meant to be established under the 2017 Climate Change Act did not come into existence due, inter alia, to technical capacity and lack of financial resources. The government has been trying to remedy these shortcomings since the establishment of the Ministry of Climate Change in August 2017.

Pakistan's Climate Change Related International Obligations and International Stance

Pakistan ratified the Kyoto Protocol for operationalisation of UNFCCC in 2004 and the Paris Agreement in 2016 and accepted the Doha Amendment to the Kyoto Protocol, thus accepting the mandatory goals prescribed therein. In its Nationally Determined Contributions (NDCs) submitted in 2015, Pakistan expressed its intention to reduce up to 20 per cent of its 2030 projected GHG emissions subject to availability of international grants to meet the abatement costs of around $ 40 billion.

Pakistan adopted the UN Sustainable Development Goals (SDG) to act as the national development framework in 2016. It established a National SDG framework in 2018, which included goals, inter alia, concerning Clean water and Sanitation, Affordable Clean Energy and Climate Action.

In its updated Nationally Determined Contributions 2021,[18] Pakistan has committed to voluntary contribution of overall 50 per cent reduction of its projected emissions by 2030 (15 per cent unconditional and 35 per cent conditional) and has stated that the initiatives taken by the Government of Pakistan resulted in reduction of 8.7 per cent emissions between 2016 and 2018. Other key commitments are: Ten Billion Tree Tsunami; renewable energy 60 per cent by 2030 including hydropower; moratorium on new coal power plants;

boosting the use of electric vehicles; flood risk mitigation and enhanced water recharge; and enhancing protected areas cover from 12 per cent to 15 per cent by 2023.

Making Pakistan's national statement at the COP 27 climate conference in Egypt against the backdrop of the devastating floods of 2022, Prime Minister Shehbaz Sharif said that Pakistan needed additional funding, not debt, to rebuild a resilient and adaptive infrastructure in the face of climate change. He added that the current financing gap was too high to sustain any real recovery needs of those on the frontline of climate catastrophe and called for prioritising the Global Goal on Adaptation both in terms of financing and timelines. Some other key proposals made by him were: 'loss and damage' should be part of the core agenda of COP 27; clearly defining climate finance as new, additional and sustained resources with a transparent mechanism to meet the needs of developing and vulnerable countries with the required speed and scale; creation of a Global Climate Risk Index for all parties of UNFCCC, where projects from the most vulnerable countries could be prioritised and given speedy approvals; and a transformational shift in the flow of capacities, finances and technology to reverse the pyramid of climate capital.[19]

Floods in Pakistan

Climate change has caused the frequency and severity of extreme natural events to rise sharply in Pakistan. Heat waves, drought and floods are its stark manifestations. Droughts have been common. A drought during 1998-2001 impacted over three million people across Pakistan, displaced thousands and hundreds died of thirst and starvation. A flood in 1991-92 had a severe adverse impact on agriculture and significantly lowered the growth rate of the country. Pakistan has faced around a dozen small and big floods in the last 20 years, including the devastating floods of 2010 and 2022. The massive flood of 2022 was preceded by a severe heat wave, which saw temperatures rise continuously above 45 degrees Centigrade, resulting in crop losses, power outages and forest fires.

The flooding of the Indus River in late July and August 2010 caused one of the worst humanitarian disasters in Pakistan. It affected approximately 20 million people over large parts of Pakistan, destroyed homes, crops and infrastructure and left millions vulnerable to malnutrition and waterborne diseases. Estimates of persons killed ranged from 1,200 to 2,200, approximately 1.6 million houses were damaged or destroyed and 14 million people rendered homeless. The

Government of Pakistan claimed that a total loss of over 40 billion dollars had been caused.[20]

In 2022, Pakistan experienced unusually heavy downpour in the monsoon season, which was described as the wettest since 1961 by the Pakistan Meteorological Department. Torrential rains, said to be 10 times heavier than usual, caused the Indus River to overflow, impacting a large part of the country. In southern Sindh and Balochistan, rainfall was reported to be 500 per cent above average by the end of August. According to a UNDP report,[21], total damages were expected to exceed $ 14.9 billion, and total economic losses to reach about $ 15.2 billion. Estimated needs for rehabilitation and reconstruction were over $ 16 billion, not counting new investments to strengthen Pakistan's adaptation to climate change. Housing; agriculture and livestock; and transport and communications suffered the most significant damage. Sindh bore about 70 per cent of the total damage, followed by Balochistan, Khyber-Pakhtunkhwa and Punjab. The floods affected 33 million people, more than 1,700 lost their lives and millions were displaced. Loss as a direct impact of the floods was projected to potentially push 8 to 9 million people below the poverty line.

Causes of Fierce Floods An increase in the frequency and ferocity of floods is among the several consequences of climate change, examined above in this essay, that have been compounded by mismanagement and lack of planning over the years. Unusually heavy rains leading to floods are directly linked to rise in temperatures. It is axiomatic that warmer atmosphere holds more moisture and causes heavy downpours. A team of German researchers found that for every degree Celsius of warming, monsoon rainfalls will likely increase by about 5 per cent and opined that a more chaotic monsoon season poses a threat to the socio-economic well-being of people in the Indian subcontinent.[22] Extensive deforestation increases the speed of rain runoff, adding to the damage.

Global warming also causes glacial ice to melt faster. The northern region – Khyber-Pakhtunkhwa and the illegally occupied 'Gilgit-Baltistan' is said to contain more glacial ice than anywhere in the world other than the polar regions. As per the UNDP, rapid melting of glaciers in the above region has created more than 3,000 lakes, and around 33 are at the risk of sudden bursting, which could unleash millions of cubic metres of water and debris.[23] In 2022, Pakistan experienced three times the usual number of glacial outbursts.

The Indus and its tributaries on the left bank flow in shallow meandering channels across the vast alluvial plain and have a highly uneven flow through the year, with peak discharge in July-August, which increases the risk of floods in the absence of mitigating measures. Thus, the maximum discharge in the Indus is around 240 times the minimum discharge. As stated earlier, Pakistan has very low water storage capacity to alleviate the impact of heavy discharge in rivers during the peak flow season and use it in the scanty season. Water storage plans have often become the cause of inter-provincial disputes in Pakistan. Thus, the construction of the Kalabagh dam with sizeable storage capacity on the Indus river in the Mianwali district of Punjab has been hanging fire for a long time because of objections of Sindh and Khyber-Pakhtunkhwa.

Conclusion

Pakistan faces serious challenges of sustainability due to continued environmental degradation combined with climate change, which has been giving rise to extreme climate related events, including devastating floods, with increasing frequency and intensity. This has imposed onerous costs on Pakistan's fragile economy and its socio-economic fabric. Rapid population growth and urbanisation; depleting quantity and deteriorating quality of water; deforestation; and worsening quality of air, especially in urban areas are some important elements that have added to the aforementioned challenges. Pakistan has taken initiatives, notably in this century, in the face of mounting environment and climate-related disasters. However, its policy response has lacked consistency and continuity and has been largely fragmented due to shifting of responsibility to different institutions. It is also hampered by lack of capacity and technology; paucity of national financial resources; highly inadequate flow of international financial assistance; unsustainable consumption and production; poverty and inequality; and. above all. Pakistan's broken governance. Therefore, environmental degradation and climate change will continue to figure prominently among the key intractable problems that imperil Pakistan and its stability.

NOTES

1. David Eckstein, Vera Kunzel and Laura Schafer, "Global Climate Risk Index 2021," Briefing Paper, *Germanwatch*, p. 13.
2. Ibid.
3. "The Environment and Climate Change Outlook of Pakistan," UNEP, p. 1.
4. Ibid, p. 2.
5. Ibid, p. 3.
6. Ibid, p. 4.
7. https://data.worldbank.org/indicator/AG.LND.FRST.ZS?locations=PK
8. Hannah Ritchie and Max Roser, *Pakistan: Energy Country Profile*, Our World in Data.

9. "The Environment and Climate Change Outlook of Pakistan," UNEP, p. 5.
10. Ibid., p. 5.
11. "Pakistan Country Climate and Development Report (November 2022)", World Bank, OCHA Services, reliefweb, pp. 6-7.
12. Ibid., p. 17.
13. "The Environment and Climate Change Outlook of Pakistan," UNEP, p. 7.
14. https://mocc.gov.pk/SiteImage/Policy/NCCP%20Report.pdf
15. Government of Pakistan updated Nationally Determined Contributions 2021, https://policy.thinkbluedata.com/sites/default/files/Pakistan%27s%20Updated%20 Nationally %20 Determined%20Contribution%202021.pdf
16. "Pakistan Country Climate and Development Report (November 2022)," World Bank, OCHA Services, reliefweb, p. 23.
17. Ibid., p. 19.
18. "Government of Pakistan Updated Nationally Determined Contributions 2021," https://policy.thinkbluedata.com/sites/default/files/Pakistan%27s%20 Updated %20 Nationally %20 Determined%20Contribution%202021.pdf
19. "Now or never: At COP 27, PM Shehbaz says Pakistan needs funds, not debts," *Dawn*, 8 November 2022.
20. "Pakistan Floods of 2010," Britannica.
21. "Pakistan: flood damages and economic losses over USD 30 billion and reconstruction needs over USD 16 billion," UNDP, 27 October 2022.
22. "Climate change is making Indian monsoon seasons more chaotic," Potsdam Institute for Climate Impact Research, 4 April 2021.
23. "How Pakistan floods are linked to climate change?," *BBC News*, 2 September 2022.

4

Tehreek-e-Taliban Pakistan (TTP): Resurgence and the Danger it Poses to Pakistan

Rahul Bhonsle

Terror: Pakistan's Crisis in Perpetuity

Terrorism and Pakistan have an umbilical relationship as the South Asian country of over 240 million has embraced terror as an instrument of state policy over decades to overcome weakness in other dimensions of national power. Thus, terror has been employed in Afghanistan for seeking influence in the West in what has been frequently referred to as, 'strategic depth,' or overcoming the geographic debility vis-a-vis India. While economy, trade, and development are more appropriate tools, Pakistan egged on by the USA propped up the Mujahideen in the 1980s to undermine the invasion of Kabul by the Soviet Union. When the Soviets left in 1989, Afghanistan fell into political and security chaos of its own making. Pakistan facilitated the growth of the Taliban – the Pashtun radical ethno-religious violent extremist group that took over power in Kabul in 1996. Evicted by the USA in 2001, Pakistan provided sanctuary to the Taliban and al-Qaeda – a duplicity that the USA had to swallow. Two decades later, the Taliban is in power in Kabul again, but a 'triumphant' [sic] Pakistan is facing resurgence of terror in the tribal belt of Khyber Pakhtunkhwa (KPK) by the Tehreek-e-Taliban Pakistan (TTP).

The TTP was formed in 2007 and has a long history of terrorist attacks in Pakistan from the GHQ or army headquarters in 2009, military bases and bombing of the Marriott Hotel in Islamabad in 2008. In 2014, the TTP stormed the Army Public School (APS) in Peshawar, killing at least 150, including 131 students which was a turning point that led the Pakistan Army to launch a series of operations which saw the group's sway declining by 2019.

While a comprehensive National Action Plan for countering terrorism was drawn out by the Pakistan government post 2014, this was never implemented due to the ineptitude in governance – political and military. Episodic management of violence rather than viewing terrorism as a holistic long-term security threat has been the underlying concept adopted by the Pakistani state from time to time. Moreover, the use of a philosophy of terror as a tool for external interventions used under the 'bleeding by a thousand cuts,' strategy against India and for seeking control of strategic depth in Afghanistan implied that elements within the Army and the Inter-Services Intelligence (ISI) retained contact with the marginalised TTP.

In August 2021, when the Afghan Taliban took over as the de facto government in Kabul, the TTP which had gathered considerable strength by then and regrouped saw an opportunity for revival of terrorism in their home base, the tribal belt of Khyber Pakhtunkhwa. The government of the day which was in power led by the Pakistan Tehreek-e-Insaf [PTI] with Prime Minister Imran Khan both in the federal capital in Islamabad and the tribal belt opted for strategy of negotiating with the group.

Instead of building counter-terrorism capability and structures during the period of negotiations, the Pakistan security establishment allowed the TTP to re-establish roots within the people having learned little from experience. Thus, when negotiations were suspended in November 2022, resurgence of terrorist incidents was a given. This marker coincided with the change of command of the Pakistan army and a period of political vacuum per se which has created an impression that the TTP is gaining ground. While the TTP is not as effective as in the past decade, the group remains dangerous given the support that it enjoys from the Afghan Taliban, inheritance of a large cache of weapons left behind by the US forces on departure from that country and a perpetually effete response by the Pakistani state with an ambivalent approach to counter terror. Combined with the political and economic crisis in the country in the past year [2022-2023] the TTP will continue to be a major security challenge to Pakistan in the years ahead. Thus, the varied dimensions of the threat posed by the TTP to the Pakistani state are being examined here.

Trends Indicating TTP Resurgence

Is the TTP resurgence real or is it another hype amidst escalation of challenges faced by the Pakistani state today? An examination of data through several sources indicates resurgence of the TTP through the past three years. As per the South Asia Terrorism Portal, terrorist fatalities were down to 365 in 2019 in Pakistan, while rising to 971 in 2022 a spike of 266 per cent within a period of three years. The Global Terrorism Index (GTI) 2023 evolved by Institute of Peace based in Australia has indicated that Pakistan had an overall score of 8.16 and country ranking of 6/163. The GTI is a composite measure made up of four indicators: incidents, fatalities, injuries, and hostages. Pakistan has moved up three notches in 2023, thus indicating a spike in incidents. To measure the impact of terrorism, a five-year weighted average is applied. Pakistan recorded 298 incidents with 643 fatalities, 802 injuries, and 13 hostages as per the GTI Index of 2022. South Asia Terrorism Portal which records only incidents with fatalities has indicated 365 incidents in 2022 with 971 fatalities.

Specifically, the Pakistan based Centre for Research and Security Studies (CRSS), in its annual report, stated that the country suffered 376 attacks in 2022, the majority of which were claimed by the Tehreek-e-Taliban Pakistan (TTP), Islamic State of Khorasan Province (ISKP) and Balochistan Liberation Army (BLA). The report said KPK experienced an "exponential rise in violence" whereby the fatalities there were higher. There was a rise in fatalities in KPK to nearly "64 per cent of all the fatalities in the country", followed by Balochistan which suffered 26 per cent of terror-related deaths. "Most of the terrorist violence originated from eastern Afghanistan," the report further quoted officials as saying, with "top TTP elements operating from Afghanistan".

On terrorist violence in 2023, CRSS Islamabad recorded the number of deaths at 358, injuries 496 in 219 terrorist attacks and counter-terrorism operations during January-March 2023. The province of Khyber Pakhtunkhwa reported most deaths – 245 (or 68 per cent), followed by Balochistan 64 (18 per cent), and then Sind, Punjab and Islamabad. With a death toll of 111, January recorded the second-highest number of fatalities of security personnel in a single month after July 2014 with 118 fatalities. However, violence-related fatalities of civilians dropped by more than half to 63 in the first quarter compared to 136 a year ago. "Most concerning, the fatalities of security and government officials almost doubled, from 88 in the first quarter of last year to 167 in the first quarter this year," the report said.

The outlawed TTP carried out at least 22 attacks causing 107 fatalities as per the Centre's reports. The South Asia Terrorism Portal based in Delhi recorded 162 fatalities based on data compiled through open source reporting for January 2023. As per the SATP, violence was down to 115 fatalities in February and 94 in March again rising from over 100 to 106 in April.

The nature of attacks by the TTP also changed in 2023. Imtiaz Gul, Executive Director of CRSS, states quoting Ihsanullah Tipu, director of Khorasan Diary that attacks assumed complexity with police stations being targeted and reinforcements ambushed when they rushed in. An attack in Lakki Marwat in March is an instance of this pattern.

Greater capabilities to operate at night using night-vision goggles were also evident giving the terrorists a major advantage in targeting the police who remained blind after darkness. Bannu, Waziristan, Bajaur, and Kurram districts opposite the Afghan provinces of Kunar, Nangarhar, Paktia, and Paktika faced the brunt of the attacks indicating the presence of sanctuaries provided to the TTP by the Afghan Taliban despite denials. Apart from the TTP, the Islamic State, the Hafiz Gul Bahadur group and Baloch groups have also mustered to form a nexus.

Pakistan's defence minister Khwaja Asif placed the strength of the TTP in thousands. "According to my information on TTP militants, between 7,000 and 8,000 of them have been involved in the war against NATO with the Afghan Taliban. In this context, there is a camaraderie between the Afghan and Pakistani Taliban which was also seen in their [Afghan Taliban's] words during our meetings that they are not in a position to oppose them [TTP] but they also want to help Pakistan," he said.

Ideology and Regrouping

The TTP founded in 2007 has developed close links with the Afghan Taliban and al-Qaeda over the years. The TTP ideology is aligned to that of the Afghan Taliban. The TTP hopes to replicate the success of the Afghan Taliban. The US National Counterterrorism Centre (NCTC) highlights the main ideological approach of the TTP thus, "The TTP's stated objectives are the expulsion of Islamabad's influence in the Federally Administered Tribal Areas (FATA) and neighbouring Khyber Pakhtunkhwa Province in Pakistan, the implementation of a strict interpretation of the Sharia throughout Pakistan...TTP leaders also publicly say that the group seeks to establish an Islamic caliphate in Pakistan that would require the overthrow of the Pakistani Government."

The TTP is also demanding restoration of the special status of the seven tribal areas known as Federally Administered Tribal Areas and removal of the Pakistan Army from the belt. Tactical demands include release of prisoners which was agreed to by the Imran Khan-led government only encouraging the group and whetting its appetite for more. The released fighters were allowed to return to the tribal areas and soon commenced extensive soft operations of extortion and threatening the key stakeholders.

After neutralisation but not elimination of the group in 2019, a degree of complacency set in allowing the TTP to regroup. Traditionally terrorist groups in the tribal areas are a divided lot, but in 2020 the process of mergers began, and a centralized structure was formed. After the Taliban takeover of Kabul in August 2021, several TTP cadres were released from prisons boosting the ranks.

Mufti Noor Wali Mehsud, the present leader of the TTP, is an experienced commander having fought with the Afghan Taliban. A hardcore Mehsud, the tribe that is said to be the key ethnic component of the TTP, he has been designated in September 2019 as a Global Terrorist by the USA due to his direct involvement in fatal attacks within Pakistan. Mehsud is said to have facilitated the merger of new factions. The major splinters of the group Jumat ul-Ahrar (JuA) and Hizb ul-Ahrar (HuA) joined together while an al-Qaeda affiliate led by Chowdhary Muneeb-ur-Rehman Jatt, aka Commander Muneeb, was another substantial addition. Twenty-two splinters, small and large, reportedly joined under Mehsud.

During this time the TTP also raised a high-profile media arm, 'Umar Media' run by a five-member media commission – the so called "Information and Broadcasting Ministry" under 'minister' Mufti Ghufran. Umar Media produced a series of audio, video, and text material originally in Urdu and Pashto, reproduced in English, Dari/Persian, and Arabic. These include several video series, a daily radio broadcast, a bi-weekly current affairs podcast, an Urdu magazine, and statements on daily attacks and political issues as per the BBC.

A TTP with approximately 6,000 cadres, with sanctuaries and support by the Afghan Taliban operating a structured media channel was thus a much transformed group than the rump of 2019 when it was fragmented and divided into small splinters.

Resurgence Causatory Factors

Apart from internal regrouping, the rule of the Afghan Taliban in Kabul has been one of the most important factors in the resurgence of the TTP. The Afghan

Taliban facilitated talks between the TTP and the Pakistan government at the instance of Sirajuddin Haqqani, the acting interior minister who is on the UNSC banned list. Pakistan's otherwise wily intelligence establishment – the Inter-Services Intelligence (ISI) fell for the bait. As per Imtiaz Gul, the TTP leadership, including their chief Noor Wali Mehsud, presently enjoy shelter and hospitality in Afghanistan. The reasons for the Afghan Taliban's unwillingness to take action against the fellow Pashtun group in Pakistan can be understandable given a possible larger goal to gain influence over the tribal belt of the eastern neighbour with ethnic similarities. The two TTP and Afghan Taliban have fought the USA in Afghanistan thus having a compact of sorts for many years. Thus, as Pakistan launched counter-terror operations, the TTP leaders moved into Afghanistan.

Bill Roggio, a noted counter-terror expert who directs *the Long War Journal* noted, "The Afghan Taliban sheltered in Pakistan in areas controlled or influenced by the TTP, while the TTP provided manpower to fight the USA, NATO and Afghan forces. The TTP's current emir, Mufti Noor Wali Mehsud, as well as its previous leaders, has sworn allegiance to the Afghan Taliban's top leader". Several Afghan Taliban also joined the TTP possibly those who have links in North and South Waziristan and are not attuned to the administrative tasks under the regime in Kabul which has attempted to turn the fighters into policemen and regular soldiers. Pakistan reportedly has killed a large number of them in the first three months of 2023.

The influx of US weapons has boosted the military capabilities of the TTP militant group as well as ethnic Baloch separatist groups equipped with M16 machine guns and M4 assault rifles, night-vision goggles, and military grade communications. "The fact is that they can see us in the dark while we can't. That gives the terrorists an enormous advantage," a police officer was quoted in a report by the RFE RL.

Pakistan's Outreach to Afghan Taliban

While celebrating the return of the Taliban to Kabul, the Pakistan Army and the ISI failed to appreciate the implications on the security in the region or on their own country. That an extremist group on reaching power would promote its own ilk was forgotten by the ISI which had been a master of exporting terror. The resurgence of the TTP was thus facilitated by the Afghan Taliban and soon the Taliban-Pakistan relationship was under stress. The Taliban has taken a leaf out of Pakistan's book to claim that there are no TTP settlements on its soil.

Pakistan made several attempts to influence the Afghan Taliban against supporting the TTP. Apart from the threat of air attacks on sanctuaries in Afghan territory, ministers and diplomats visited Kabul. Defence Minister Khawaja Asif led a high-power Pakistani delegation – comprising Inter-Services Intelligence (ISI) Director-General Lt-Gen Nadeem Anjum, Foreign Secretary Asad Majeed Khan, Chargé d'Affaires (CdA) to Afghanistan Ubaidur Rehman Nizamani and Pakistan's Special Representative for Afghanistan Mohammad Sadiq for talks with the so-called Islamic Emirate of Afghanistan. "[In the meeting] The [Afghan] Taliban had expressed their determination to deal with this problem and said that they won't allow their land to be used for terrorism as per the Doha Agreement."

Days after the visit to Kabul, Khwaja Asif in a *Voice of America* interview said that there were serious concerns of the TTP using Afghan soil for attacks in Pakistan. "The TTP [Tehreek-e-Taliban Pakistan] is using Afghan soil even today for attacks in our country, especially Khyber Pakhtunkhwa," said Asif.

Even after clear evidence of a resurgence of TTP violence in Pakistan in 2023, with a complex terrorist attack in the Peshawar police lines mosque in January 2023, Acting Afghan Foreign Minister Mawlawi Amir Khan Muttaqi called for revival of talks between Pakistan and the outlawed TTP, denying that the group was using Afghan soil to carry out attacks in the neighbouring country. "As for Pakistan's security concerns, we ask that the government of Pakistan and the TTP sit together and find a solution to these problems on their own," said FM Muttaqi at the Institute of Strategic Studies during his four-day visit to Pakistan in May this year. Mr Muttaqi denied that the TTP was using Afghan soil to carry out attacks in Pakistan. "The Islamic Emirate has fulfilled its responsibility. The IEA (Islamic Emirate of Afghanistan) was able to bring both sides to the table. We hosted the talks between Pakistan and the TTP," he said.

While Pakistani intelligence and military officials have been claiming an India hand behind the resurgence of the TTP, factors outlined above indicate that New Delhi does not have the reach nor would have felt the necessity to play a role by promoting a terrorist group as a quid pro quo to Pakistan's role in Jammu and Kashmir. The domino effect within Pakistan and linkages with the Afghan Taliban are adequate to see the surge of terror in the tribal belt in Pakistan.

Pakistan's Ambiguous Counter-Terror Policy

The rise of the TTP in 2022-23 has also coincided with the political and economic turbulence in Pakistan. During the tenure of the government of the PTI, there were differences between the Prime Minister and the Army leading to lack of sustained counter militancy action. The involvement of the Pakistan Army in politics intensified as a conflict brewed between the then Army Chief General Qamar Jawed Bajwa and Mr. Imran Khan, the then prime minister.

As the number of attacks in Pakistan increased from January 2023 onwards, the Pakistan Democratic Movement [PDM] led by the Pakistan Muslim League Nawaz (PMLN) which had assumed power, held several meetings of the National Security Committee [NSC]. The NSC acts as the principal decision-making organisation on national security. Prime Minister Shehbaz Sharif presided over its 41st meeting, which was attended by the senior civil and military leadership, including Foreign Minister Bilawal Bhutto Zardari, Interior Minister Rana Sanaullah, Information Minister Marriyum Aurangzeb, Finance Minister Ishaq Dar, Chief of Army Staff Gen Asim Munir, Chairman Joint Chiefs of Staff Committee Gen Sahir Shamshad Mirza, Services chiefs and chief ministers. It stated that the operation to eliminate the scourge of terrorism in all its forms from Pakistan would incorporate measures at political, diplomatic, security, economic and social levels.

In a meeting in April, the NSC decided to launch an 'all-out comprehensive operation' to rid the country of the menace of terrorism. "The meeting agreed to launch an all-out comprehensive operation with [the participation of] the entire nation and government to rid the country of the menace of terrorism with renewed vigour and determination," the Prime Minister's office press release said.

Chief of Army Staff Gen Syed Asim Munir propagated a three-pronged plan – deter, dialogue and development – to root out terrorism during a meeting of the parliamentary committee which, he claimed was already underway, after lawmakers expressed serious concerns over the resurgence of terrorist groups. He suggested including all stakeholders in this strategy such as security forces, the legal fraternity, civil society, politicians, social workers, bureaucrats, diplomats and the media.

The 3D strategy had the approval of the Corps Commanders of the Pakistan Army which is the collegiate decision-making body in the country. In the 257th corps commanders conference, presided over by Gen Munir at the GHQ, "Corps commanders resolved to continue the govt-approved campaign, call on rulers to involve the 'whole system' to eradicate the root causes of terrorism," as per a report in *Dawn*. Such a strategy would include intelligence-based operations with, "whole-of-the-nation and whole-of-the-government approach to eradicate the menace of terrorism on [a] long-term basis".

People's Resistance in Tribal Areas

After the 3D strategy outlined by the Army Chief General Asim Munir, Ali Wazir, a parliamentarian from South Waziristan, while speaking in the National Assembly declared that they would not allow any operation in the territory without "trial and conviction of those serving and retired army generals" who had helped these terrorists resettle in these areas. The wider military operation was resisted even by allies of the PDM such as the National Democratic Movement (NDM). "They [government and security forces] have lost public trust. People don't believe them any more even if they launch 100 military operations against militants," MNA Mohsin Dawar, the NDM's chairman, told *Dawn*.

He also indicated that a shift in the government's Afghan policy was required. "The government supports the Afghan Taliban, who support the outlawed Tehreek-e-Taliban Pakistan (TTP)," he claimed. The NDM said that a military operation "without going after the root cause of terrorism, Afghan policy and Project Taliban", meant "going back to the sham operations from 2007 to 2014 and the policy of good Taliban and bad Taliban". Meanwhile, there have been several protests in the tribal areas in South Waziristan where people have come out in the open calling for security and protection of lives and livelihood as attacks have increased over a period.

Prognosis: Grim Portents Ahead

The rise of TTP violence suggests grim portents for Pakistan in the security sphere in the months ahead even as it grapples with complex poly-crises – political, economic and humanitarian. The TTP reorganized and refurbished with the active support of the Afghan Taliban working to repeat the success of the two-decade campaign that led to the eviction of the USA and NATO forces in Afghanistan is expected to pose a major security threat to Pakistan with turbulence in the tribal areas which could spill over to other parts of the country, especially Punjab and Sindh. There is no indication that the Afghan Taliban will retract its support to the TTP, continuing to deny their presence. Nor are there any indications that the TTP has the intention of diluting the ideological objectives of rule by Sharia in the tribal areas expanding to a caliphate in the years ahead. Though the wider goals are not achievable yet the terrorist group has an illusion of its own and will attempt to target the State across provinces.

There are claims mainly by the TTP of an alliance with Baloch insurgent groups. In December 2022 the TTP announced that the group led by Mazar

Baloch had pledged allegiance to the TTP chief, Mufti Noor Wali Mehsud. While there has been no confirmation from the Baloch insurgents, the possibility of a tactical alliance between these groups cannot be ruled out. A widened insurgency extending from Khyber Pakhtunkhwa to Balochistan and sanctuaries in Afghanistan promoted by the Talban will pose a major challenge to Pakistan's security.

The political situation in Pakistan has taken a steep dive even as TTP attacks surged in the first quarter of 2023. Thus, it was not surprising that the PDM government and the Pakistan Army focused on managing the rising protests by the main opposition party, the Pakistan Tehreek-e-Insaf, after failing to launch the much-vaunted comprehensive approach to neutralize the TTP. Thus, the military has so far relied on intelligence-based operations in the Ghulam Khan, Datta Khel, Shawal, Shawa and Spin Wamare areas of North Waziristan and South Waziristan's Azam Warsak, Zar Milan, Angoor Adda, Sar Kand and Ladha.

Such an approach has been decried by experts who have studied the tribal insurgency as Asfandyar Mir who remarked in an article by United States Institute for Peace (USIP) that "Pakistan's response to the TTP's resurgence remains incoherent – and is unlikely to improve in the near-term. After downplaying the TTP's strength as well as the Taliban's influence on and relationship with TTP for several years, Pakistani leaders now seem to be contending with the depth of Taliban support for the TTP. Yet, Pakistani officials still seem to be searching for a deal – ideally a cease-fire arrangement – through the Taliban. But the Taliban's uncompromising commitment to the TTP means that Pakistan has to either ignore the violence or concede to the TTP to maintain a relationship with the Taliban."

He further said, "Another key factor shaping the Pakistani response is the country's deteriorating economy, which is on the brink of a default. That limits Pakistan's military options. Pakistan can carry out raids and undertake defensive actions inside the country, but it doesn't have the resources for a sustained high-intensity campaign."

A resurgent TTP is not a new challenge but one that is regurgitating from the past in different dimensions. The key factor this time around is support that has been provided by the Afghan Taliban to the TTP in terms of sanctuaries – political and diplomatic which will ensure that the challenge is long lasting.

To meet such a threat, an in-principle comprehensive approach has been agreed upon by the political as well as the military leadership of the country.

This appears to be a statement of intent rather than implementation involving all arms of the state. In the long-term Pakistan's military and political leadership has to forsake terror as a state policy for exporting abroad to gain political and security space. Such an understanding within the strategic thinking in Islamabad or Rawalpindi is nowhere in sight. Thus, even if the present challenge from the TTP resurgence is managed, recurrence will be a given.

5

Pakistan's Tryst with Terrorism

G. Parthasarthy

Pakistan has been going through difficult times during the past decade. The country has been confronted with an unprecedented economic crisis for several years now. Its foreign exchange reserves are continuously headed for a collapse, together with a growing national budget deficit, which results in spiralling inflation. With economic disaster around the corner, Pakistan has been continuously looking for financial assistance from institutions like the World Bank, IMF and the Asian Development Bank. It largely manages its balance of payments with massive remittances amounting to around $ 18 billion annually, from its citizens living in the Arab Gulf countries, principally in Saudi Arabia and the UAE. But even its principal benefactors, including institutions ranging from the World Bank and IMF, to the UAE and Saudi Arabia, have reached a stage where their assistance to Pakistan, has become firmly linked to Islamabad agreeing to the tough conditions of fiscal propriety set by the IMF.

The talks and bargaining with the IMF have continued for months, before Pakistan was forced to accept the conditionalities set by the IMF. This included an IMF commitment to step in with a $ 3 billion payment, which was accompanied by payments of $ 2 billion by Saudi Arabia and $ 1 billion by the UAE, both of whom have been long-term friends and benefactors, of Pakistan. But despite this, both Arab states have now evidently realized the Pakistan's economy remains a basket case despite freebies received from them. They have now been compelled to link aid to Islamabad behaving prudently on financial matters, and taking difficult decisions in managing its economy. Nevertheless,

Pakistan is set to remain an economic basket case for the foreseeable future, unless it learns to live frugally, and within its means. The term of the present Pakistan government whose members took their oath on 12 August 2018 is set to end next month. The next Parliamentary elections should normally be held 60 days after the Assembly ends its term. It remains to be seen just how all this will play out, though Prime Minister Shahbaz Sharif envisages elections in November this year.

These developments are taking place amidst chaos in Pakistan. Prevailing sentiments in the country are such, that Imran Khan, who is seen as having been persecuted by the army and the present political dispensation, will decisively win in the coming elections. That would obviously not be to the liking of the present ruling elite, drawn primarily from the Pakistan Muslim League, which is led by the London-based Nawaz Sharif, who faces serious charges in Pakistan, and is reluctant to return home, until the charges are withdrawn. His younger brother, Shahbaz Sharif, is the Prime Minister, and his daughter, Maryam Nawaz, runs the ruling Pakistan Muslim League (PML).

While the Sindhi Asif Zardari, leads the PPP, together with his son, Bilawal Bhutto Zardari as principal partner, neither the Sharifs, nor the Zardaris and the Bhuttos, have a great reputation for financial rectitude. On the other hand, Imran Khan has been publicly acknowledged as being financially clean, though some charges have been brought against his wife. But, corruption has never really been a major issue in Pakistan, whether it is ruled by politicians, cricketers, or the military. Both Musharraf and his successor, General Kayani, have led luxurious lives in London, Dubai and Sydney after they retired. Facing charges in Pakistan, Nawaz Sharif has been living primarily in London for years, though he also has friends in high places in the UAE leadership.

After prolonged discussions, Pakistan was finally forced to agree to stringent conditions of fiscal discipline laid down by the IMF before it received the green signal of approval for others to join in its standby agreement with Pakistan, which provides for $ 3 billion to the cash-strapped country. Saudi Arabia, thereafter, informed the IMF that it was pledging financial support of $ 2 billion to Pakistan. It is clear that even a long-term provider of financial aid to Pakistan, like Saudi Arabia, has reached a situation where it felt it was only prudent to join in an international effort, together with the IMF, to bail out a Pakistan verging on bankruptcy, This would ensure that Pakistan observed a measure of fiscal discipline while dealing with aid funds it received from abroad. International organizations like the World Bank and Asian Development Bank will also chip in with aid, only if Pakistan observes strict fiscal discipline, prescribed by the IMF.

In the meantime, Shehbaz Sharif's government is beset with continuing problems at home. There is presently little doubt that Imran Khan's Tehreek-e-Insaf Party will win hands down in any national elections in the coming months. The term of the present Assembly ends this year on 13 August. The elections, according observers in Pakistan, could be held 60 days after the assembly completes it term. Prime Minister Shehbaz Sharif has spoken of elections in November this year. But, this is where things get murky, as the political situation in Pakistan becomes volatile. There is no love lost between the new Army Chief General Asim Munir and Imran Khan, who had, in his term as Prime Minister, arbitrarily transferred Asim Munir from the post of ISI Chief and replaced him with one of his favourites. There is, therefore, a no-holds barred struggle between Imran Khan and the Army Chief, who certainly would not like to see Imran Khan back in office. There is also no love lost between the USA and Imran Khan, who was seen as having high regard for President Putin. China, of course, knows that whoever is elected to office will respect and bend to its wishes.

Pakistan's main troubles today do not arise from India, but from the actions of its own fellow Pashtuns, affiliated with the Tehreek-e-Taliban Pakistan (TTP), and disgruntled Baloch. This Taliban grouping has long been affiliated with and provided safe havens and support by the Pashtun Taliban cadres in Afghanistan. With the departure of the USA from Afghanistan, the Afghan and Pakistan Taliban now have a strong fraternal relationship. Their ruthless repression of women has made the Pakistani and Afghan Taliban the subject of international condemnation. But one should have no doubt that there is no force within Afghanistan to seriously challenge the Taliban at the present moment. Pakistan made the mistake of trying to control the Taliban and determine their behaviour after the Taliban takeover, in much the same manner that they did when the ISI was arming and training them for use against both the Russians and Americans. The Pakistan Army forgot that the Pashtuns never have yielded to foreign hegemony. The Tehreek-e-Taliban Pakistan may have sought Pakistani government assistance to fight the Americans. But today, they represent a combination of religious fundamentalism and Pashtun nationalism.

While the Pakistan army has predominantly been concentrating on its eastern borders with India, it does face serious problems with both the Taliban on its western borders with Afghanistan, and the Baloch nationalists on its frontiers with Iran. The Tehreek-e-Taliban Pakistan, who were for long buddies of the ISI, are now prepared to take on the Pakistan Army in northwest Pakistan across the Durand Line. Following a recent Taliban attack across the Balochistan-Afghanistan border, 12 Pakistani soldiers were killed with the Pakistan military proclaiming that such attacks were "acts of terrorism," in Pakistan. The Pakistan Army proclaimed: "The Armed Forces of Pakistan have serious concerns on the safe havens, and liberty of action, available to the Tehreek-e-Taliban (Pakistan) in Afghanistan. The Pakistan Army statement added: "It is expected that the Interim Afghan Government would not allow the use of its soil to perpetrate terror against any country, in line with commitments made in the Doha Agreement". This referred to the Agreement signed in Doha, Qatar, in 2020, which formally brought an end to the war the USA fought against the Afghan Taliban, which covertly had the full backing of the ISI.

Strangely, the USA has, for long, been averse to call a spade a spade, when it came to Pakistan-sponsored terrorism. The USA waited for two years after the end of its Afghanistan misadventure before it called a spade a spade when it came down heavily on Pakistan's sponsorship of cross-border terrorism. This belated acknowledgement of Pakistan being a sponsor of terrorism came in the joint statement signed by President Biden and Prime Minister Modi, at the conclusion of Mr. Modi's visit to the USA, on 23 January 2023. The joint statement noted: "The USA and India stand together to counter global terrorism and unequivocally condemn terrorism and violent extremism in all its forms and manifestations. Prime Minister Modi and President Biden reiterated the call for concerted action against all UN-listed terrorist groups including al-Qaeda, ISIS/Dash, Bashkir-e-Taiga, Jaish-e-Mohammed and the Hizb-ul-Mujahideen. They strongly condemned cross-border terrorism, the use of terrorist proxies, and called on Pakistan to take immediate action that no territory under its control was used for launching terrorist attacks. They also called for the perpetrators of the 26/11 Mumbai, and Pathankot attacks, to be brought to justice."

The entire task of dealing with the intensity and viciousness of Pakistan-sponsored cross border terrorism has been one which most countries in the world would have found impossible to confront, and overcome. Both the USA and Russia packed their bags and virtually fled from Afghanistan when dealing with Pakistan-sponsored assistance to the Taliban. India has faced and confronted this problem for over four decades now. The ISI, sponsors of such terrorism and prolonged low-intensity conflict, seem to believe that they can prevail in India, because neither the USA, nor Russia could take the suffering and hardship that terrorism sponsored by Pakistan caused beyond its borders in Afghanistan. Pakistan would evidently like to continue on this path that it has followed for some decades in dealing with India. It would, however, hopefully realize that the costs it has paid for its actions on its borders with India were not in the best interests of its own people. Talks and terrorism cannot go on together, endlessly.

6

Societal Decay: Position of Women and Children

Aarushi Gupta

Pakistan, from the time of its creation, has been an unstable democracy. Over time, fluctuating between civilian and military leadership, Pakistan's government and politics grew more unreliable. Frequent coup d'états by the military, imposition of martial law, corrupted politics, weak civilian governance and civil-military conflict never allowed democracy and society to grow organically into a well-functioning instrument for the people.

Pakistan as a society is an ethnically diverse country within the larger Islamic framework. The formation of Pakistan was in the name of Islam. Thus, Islam invariably drives daily life and social structures at all levels. Pakistan is an agrarian society with large extended families. It is a deeply patriarchal society where the woman's place is traditionally considered secondary to men. The perception of the inferiority of women is ingrained in the larger Pakistani fabric. Such a perception affects the personal and social life of women as well as children. It is integral to navigate the complex position of women and children in Pakistan, as it inevitably dictates the future and well-being of the country.

Situating Women and Children in Pakistan

Women's Contribution to the Economy

Women in Pakistan have a relatively lower level of participation in economic activities. According to the Global Gender Gap Index Report 2022, Pakistan stood at 145 out of 146 countries, only slightly out-performing Afghanistan in this regard. Further, Pakistan was ranked 145 in women's economic participation and opportunity, and at 143 for women's health and survival, 135 for educational attainment and 95 for political empowerment.[1] According to the World Economic Forum (WEF) predictions, it will take approximately 135.6 years to bridge this gender gap worldwide.

Pakistan has one of the lowest female workforces in South Asia and in the world. It accounts for a mere 22.63 per cent, compared to a whopping 84.79 per cent of the male workforce in Pakistan. Women are employed largely in the informal sector. Not surprisingly, 81 per cent of the workforce employed in the informal sector are women. However, their contribution to the USD 2.8 billion informal sector economy accounts for only 65 per cent, indicating a huge wage disparity. In the urban areas, female labour force participation has averaged about 10 per cent for over 20 years.[2]

Apart from the striking reality of gross under-representation of women in the labour force, women consistently face discrimination and disproportionately low incomes. Women in Pakistan earn 34 per cent less than men on an average, according to the ILO's Global Wage Report (GWR) 2019. According to the estimates, women comprise about 90 per cent of the bottom one per cent of the entire labour force in Pakistan. The majority of women work in agriculture, where there is an ample labour supply and low wage levels.

In emerging nations like Pakistan, factors like demography and economic inequality further worsen wage disparities. To meet the growth targets established by Pakistani policymakers, the country's female labour force participation must rise to 45 per cent of the entire labour force. According to recent ILO predictions, if Pakistan can reduce the wage gap between men and women by 25 per cent, the country's economy will expand by about 9 per cent.[3] However, the absence of laws prohibiting workplace harassment, discrimination, and unfair compensation, makes this difficult to achieve.

Wage disparities not only affect women's participation in the workforce but also lead to multidimensional vulnerabilities like poor nutrition, health problems, economic vulnerability, violence against women, social justice, and lack of social protection. According to the Global Gender Gap Index Report 2022, Pakistan was ranked higher than its other scores, at 95/146, for political empowerment. Pakistan has had a female head of government for 4.7 years since its creation. However, women are still disproportionately represented in politics and parliament. Women constitute 48.54 per cent of the total population in Pakistan. However, there are only 20.2 per cent female members of Parliament and 10.7 per cent ministers.[4]

Education of Women in Pakistan

Further, lack of education acts as a significant hurdle in the career aspirations of women in Pakistan. Pakistan has an above-average household size of 6.4 people per household. This puts considerable pressure on the average family in a country with a developing low-income economy.

Pakistan has a literacy rate of 58.9 per cent.[5] However, women have a literacy rate of 48 per cent, and men have 70 per cent. Of the 22.1 million children who are not enrolled in schools, 12 million are girls. Some girls who initially manage to attend school drop out by the age of 14-15. Only 13 per cent of the girls make it to grade 9. Ninety per cent of the girls, therefore, lack post-secondary education that further impacts their job prospects. Subsequently, there are only 18 per cent of women STEM professionals, indicating a vast chasm between the genders in terms of professional training and employability.[6] Pakistan's government spends 6 per cent of its total GDP on education, which is half of what it should.[7]

One major reason girls are not allowed to attend schools is harassment and security in public spaces and transportation. Keeping the regressive cultural backdrop in mind, women are expected to be child-bearers and homemakers, while men are expected to provide security and monetary support to the family. Therefore, the workplaces women engage in do not particularly cater to the needs of women with families, lack accessibility, have rigid working hours and do not provide child-care services. To overcome these hurdles, bare minimum policies to 'empower women' by allowing them to work will not reap many benefits. More inclusive policies need to be formulated, and more women-friendly workspaces need to be created to enable women to work and contribute to their families and the economy of the country.

In accordance with the UN Sustainable Development Goals (SDGs), Pakistan committed to end all marriages under 18 by 2030. The legal age of marriage in Pakistan is 16 years for women and 18 for men. However, the prevalence of child marriages is widespread not just in Pakistan but in the whole of South Asia. According to UNICEF estimates, South Asia has 290 million child brides, constituting over 45 per cent of all child marriages worldwide. According to the Pakistan Demographic and Health Survey, one in three girls is married before the age of 18 in Pakistan.[8] Early marriages also open the way for domestic violence.

According to the National Commission for Human Rights (NCHR), 40 per cent of women in Pakistan experience physical or emotional violence.

Health of Women and Children

Pakistan allows polygamy, but only for Muslim men. Muslim men are allowed to have a maximum of four wives at a time. This has a direct impact on the mental and emotional health of women. Since the man is the sole breadwinner in the family and women are expected to refrain from working, it puts substantial financial pressure on the family in terms of basic necessities, fewer resources, education and health care. It also widens the gap between the genders in the minds of young children, as they grow up in a neglected home with the sole power lying on the man, while women are considered the weaker sex.

This practice has adverse effects on the health of women as well as infants. According to the Pakistan Demographic and Health Survey 2018, the fertility rate stands at 3.6. Further, owing to the poor healthcare infrastructure, lack of skilled staffing, insufficient education, and poor access to healthcare facilities lead to a high rate in the Maternal Mortality Ratio (MMR) and Infant Mortality Ratio (IMR).

The World Health Organisation (WHO) defines MMR as deaths during pregnancy or deaths within 42 days of the termination of pregnancy. Globally, the MMR has been consistently decreasing. However, in a low-income country like Pakistan, it has increased. It reported 186 deaths per 100,000 live births in 2019, which was a 32 per cent jump from 2017. These ratios worsen in rural areas as the healthcare system gets worse and old cultural practices continue to be prevalent. So, while urban areas recorded an MMR of 158 deaths per 100,000 live births, rural areas had an MMR of 199 deaths per 100,000 live births.[9] Further, families are hesitant to take women to a male doctor. To exacerbate the situation even more, in 2019, there were close to 85,000 female doctors who never joined the medical system, despite finishing their degrees.[10]

According to UNICEF, an infant is a child below the age of a year or 12 months. The IMR refers to the number of infant deaths for every 1,000 live births. The global IMR average in 2022 was 26.7 deaths per 1,000 live births, while Pakistan had 56.9 deaths per 1,000 live births. Pakistan also has one of the highest mortality rates for children less than five years of age. The global child mortality rate stood at 37 deaths per 1,000 live births in 2020, while Pakistan recorded 65.2 deaths per 1,000 live births. The stillbirth rate in Pakistan was 53.5 per 1,000 births, as compared to 23.2 per 1,000 births in other areas. The

Neonatal Mortality Rate (NMR) refers to the death of infants born in the first month of their life. Pakistan's average NMR was 49.4 per cent in 2018, compared to the global average of 20.4.[11]

These numbers clearly indicate the poor pregnancy outcomes, lack of awareness and education, lack of health infrastructure and insufficient policy formulation and implementation for the health and well-being of women and children. These numbers can only be attributed to registered or recorded pregnancies. The Edhi Foundation, a Pakistan-based social welfare NGO, found 375 bodies of new-born babies in different parts of Karachi in 2019. According to the organisation, this number has doubled since 2018, and it believes most of the bodies are of girls. This is attributed to the lack of laws governing abortion in Pakistan. Islamic jurisprudence does allow it, but only during four months of the pregnancy, given that it affects the mother's health. It not only affects the health of women and children but also indicates the crime against women and children and their social position in society.[12]

Violence against Women

There is a direct association and correlation between violence against women and women's health. Many forms of physical harm, like physical injuries, permanent disabilities, murders, suicides, unwanted pregnancies, unsafe abortions, female foeticides, etc., can be attributed to violence against women. Pakistan was ranked the fourth most dangerous country for women in 2021[13] and ranked 129/140 countries on the Rule of Law Index of the World Justice Project in 2022.[14] The then prime minister of Pakistan, Imran Khan, had blamed women's clothes for sexual harassment and sexual assault in 2021, saying, "It will have an impact on the men unless they are robots."[15] It is a clear reflection of the regressive and orthodox mindset of the society overall.

The social structure in Pakistan's traditional regions is based more on kinship than the caste system. The most significant social institution is the *biradiri* (patrilineage). In many Pakistani communities, a man's preferred marriage is to his father's brother's daughter, and in many other groups, marriages are generally within the *biradiri*. Endogamy is practised frequently to the extent that would be seen as improper in Western society. Such practices of often forced marriages within the family not only reflect the subordinate position of women in society but also specifically target underage girls.

The legal age of marriage is 16 for women and 18 for men in Pakistan. As per the Pakistan Penal Code, child marriage is an offence which is punishable with a minimum of three years of imprisonment and a Rs. 5 lakh fine. Even though getting married off early is common for both genders in most parts of Pakistan, it is worse for women. Despite the laws protecting children and women, most cases go unreported.

Honour Killing

A father killed his 18-year-old daughter in January 2022 in the village of Vano Ghari after a video of her dancing went viral on social media. Similarly, a 19-year-old newlywed was fatally shot by her father out of honour at the entrance of Karachi city court for getting married of her own free will. In another case, in May 2023, a 20-year-old woman was burnt alive in Punjab Province of Pakistan as she wanted to marry a man of her choice. These are all cases of honour killing and there are innumerable more.

The practice of 'honour killings,' in which a male relative may murder a woman if she is believed to have brought dishonour to the family or *biradiri*, is another indication of women's submissive status in Pakistan. According to the Human Rights Commission of Pakistan, over 470 cases of honour killing were reported in 2021 and an average of 650 honour killings annually was recorded over the past decade. However, human rights groups believe this number to be closer to 1,000. According to Human Rights Watch, women not adhering to social norms, which can be arbitrary in nature, is the most common reason for honour killing.[16] These accepted social behaviours can range from a women's choice of employment, refusal to get married, getting married without her parent's consent, having sexual relations before marriage, getting sexually assaulted and raped, to even as simple as a women's choice of clothing.

Honour killing is justified justice according to many in Pakistani society. There have been various attempts to outlaw this practice. The first attempt was made in 2004 when the Pakistan's National Assembly passed the Honour Killing Act. It made the practice a punishable crime. However, it had a significant and problematic loophole. It had a provision that if the relatives of the victim forgave the convict, in accordance with the Sharia practice of *Diya,* the convict could go free.[17] Since family members perform most honour killings, it was not effective. It was only in 2016 that the National Assembly enacted the Anti-Honour Killing law, closing up the loophole of forgiveness. However, still, most honour killing cases go unreported.

Sexual Assault

According to the Human Rights Commission of Pakistan (HRCP), 5,200 rapes were reported in Pakistan in 2021. These figures might be higher. Since there is a social stigma attached to it, a maximum number of rape cases go unreported. Even with these reported cases, according to SAMAA TV's survey, the conviction rate of these rape cases is just 0.2 per cent. According to the survey, a woman is raped every two hours in Pakistan. It had also estimated that 21,900 women had reported rape from 2017 to 2021.[18]

Cases of sexual violence against women and rape cases are often disregarded and do not even reach the trial stage. In 44 courts of the country, 1,301 cases of women's sexual violence were heard in 2022, and the police filed 2,856 charge sheets.[19] However, only 4 per cent of the cases went to trial. Rapes increase drastically in more rural provinces of Pakistan. According to police records, 414 cases of sexual assault were reported in 2022 in Sindh alone. This was a 200 per cent increase from 2021.[20]

Another prevalent form of sexual violence against women is marital rape. Pakistan defined 'rape' as forced sex outside of marriage in 1979. In 2006, this definition was redefined as sex without a woman's consent. However, there were no provisions specifically for married women. Marital rape is not something that is considered an issue in Pakistan. Therefore, there are hardly any laws or data on the subject. There is limited exposure and awareness of married women on the issue of marital rape. Therefore, Pakistan is one of the 36 countries that has still not outlawed marital rape.[21]

Domestic Violence

Hitting a woman or exerting physical might over a woman in the form of violence in a household is extremely common in Pakistani households. According to the policy brief released by the National Commission for Human Rights of Pakistan and UN Women released in March 2023, 90 per cent of women in Pakistan had reported experiencing domestic violence.[22]. Domestic violence had also greatly increased during the COVID-19 lockdowns. Further, the Demographic and Health Survey of Pakistan 2017-18 reported that 34 per cent of women who had ever been married had experienced spousal physical, sexual, or emotional Violence.[23] Besides, 56 per cent of these women have not sought any help.[24]

Crimes against Children

Children are vulnerable to many forms of violence, exploitation, child labour, abduction and trafficking. According to a report by the Islamabad-based child protection NGO, Sahil, in 2021, of the reported 3,852 cases of child marriage, child sexual abuse (CSA), abduction, and missing children from four provinces, 54 per cent of victims were girls, and 46 per cent were boys.[25]

Birth registration is a fundamental right of all children. However, only 34 per cent of children under the age of five are registered nationally.[26] It is a crucial document for any individual as not only is it legal proof of the child's existence but is critical to estimate a child's age, which can further prevent child labour, child marriage and other forms of violence and injustices.

According to UNICEF, 3.3 million children in Pakistan are engaged in child labour. The number can be substantially higher, owing to the hardships faced by households during the COVID-19 pandemic. In rural areas, the children are engaged in agriculture to get additional income for the family, while children in urban areas are primarily involved in industrial areas or as domestic servants. Such practices affect their growth trajectory not only physically but also mentally. Poor education, poverty, and lack of social security can result in spiking juvenile crimes and adverse social and psychological implications as they work in hazardous, toxic, mentally unsafe and taxing conditions. The ILO had urged Pakistan authorities to comply with the international child and forced labour standards. However, Pakistan has been unable to do so.

Sahil's Six Months Cruel Numbers Report highlighted grim figures for 2022. Over 2,000 child abuse cases were reported in Pakistan in just six months. According to the report, 12 children are sexually abused daily in Pakistan.[27]. The report further elaborated that in the first six months of 2022, 567 boys were the victims of crimes of sodomy/gang sodomy/attempt at sodomy/murder/pornography and abduction while 551 girls were victims of rape/gang rape/attempt to rape/murder/pornography and abduction. It also highlighted the harrowing reality that in 47 per cent of the cases, the abuser was an acquaintance. The Kasur child sexual abuse scandal that shook Pakistan in 2015 is a case in point. Around 280 to 300 children, mostly boys, were sexually abused and recorded and sold in the form of child pornography from 2006 to 2014. These organised crime rings blackmailed and extorted huge amounts of money from relatives of the victims. It turned into a massive scandal as Punjab police and political parties tried to cover up the enormous abuse and human rights violation in the state.

According to UNICEF, there are over 1.5 million street children in Pakistan. This makes them incredibly vulnerable to many forms of exploitation, violence and trafficking. Child abduction, forced marriages and child trafficking, combined with poverty and lack of social security, has a distinct common thread.[28] Owing to financial strain and lack of government intervention, street children are often sucked into the harsh realities of child begging. According to the Protocol to Prevent, Suppress and Punish Trafficking in Persons, children below the legal age are considered as trafficked individuals if they are located from one area to another for exploitation. To make matters worse, child begging is, in fact, categorised as the 'organised crime' of mafias. These giant mafias track down children who later wish to leave and are inhumanely tortured.

A Human Rights Commission of Pakistan's report describes Pakistan as the source, transit and destination country for human trafficking.[29] In February 2022, 151 girls were reported to be abducted from just one place – Sargodha, in Punjab.[30] These are common reports that emerge frequently. These abductions lead to trafficking or forced marriages not just domestically but even to Gulf nations and China. There have been harrowing stories that regularly come of victims of child trafficking from Pakistan to China as forced brides. Until the 2000s, the children trafficked to Gulf countries were used as jockeys for dangerous camel races that killed 50 per cent of all camel jockeys and permanently disabled the other 25 per cent.[31] Many children die in the races, and others face serious physical damage due to a lack of medical attention. In 2002, Pakistan ratified the Prevention and Control of Human Trafficking Ordinance (PACHTO) to ban this inhumane practice. However, it was only with the help of UNICEF in 2005 that the practice could be stopped.

Role of Government and Activists

Pakistan has taken substantial steps by ratifying many international human rights conventions to protect the rights of women and children. It has also come up with multiple laws and legislations that are pro-women in nature in all four provinces, like the National Gender Policy Framework (2022), Anti-Rape (Investigation and Trial) Ordinance (2020) and the Domestic Violence against Women (Prevention and Protection) Act. Pakistan has also amended many of its laws that protect women to remove any loopholes or ineffective legal provisions. However, the practice and implementation of these laws for the protection and empowerment of women could be stronger in Pakistan.

Pakistan is a deeply traditional and ethnically divided country which gets reflected in the justice system as well. Since social norms are greatly favoured in Pakistan, gender bias is also prevalent in the judiciary. Many cases of discrimination and violence go unreported in Pakistan. However, the ones that do reach the courts fail due to weak prosecution. Owing to these biases, the conviction rates of the reported cases are abysmally low. The judiciary and law and order are a reflection of the fundamental and core values of society. Such discrimination clearly underpins a strong undercurrent of repressive societal expectations from women.

Multiple movements, activists, NGOs, and marches have emerged to realign and recalibrate women's position in Pakistani society that is more in tune with the expectations and liberties of 21st-century women. These women and activists speak openly and fearlessly against the injustice and scary state of affairs of women in Pakistan.

One such is the Aurat March that was first held on International Women's Day on 8 March 2018 in Karachi in parallel with the 'Me Too movement' in Pakistan. Since then, it has turned into an annual women's rights demonstration in cities like Karachi, Islamabad, Lahore, Quetta and Peshawar. The theme and the agenda of the march change annually. However, the general running theme is women's empowerment, the end of discrimination and harassment, and accountability for violence against women. These marches have held striking and powerful messages and slogans. Slogans like Mera Jism Meri Marzi (*My body, my choice*) and Ghar ka Kaam, Sab ka Kaam (*Housework is everyone's work*) gained huge traction and popularity and turned into rallying cries of the march.

Aurat March has been conducted annually in Pakistan for the last six years. They ask for nothing more than gender equality and space for women in Pakistani society. However, they have continuously faced a backlash and severe criticism from the upholders of traditional and orthodox values in the country. 'Feminisation of Climate Justice' was the theme of the Aurat March in 2023. The purpose of the theme was to talk about climate justice through the feminist lens. However, not just the people but the Islamabad Police also baton-charged the participants of the march. This action was condemned by multiple women's rights bodies, including the Human Rights Commission of Pakistan and some politicians.

Hina Jilani, a well-known lawyer and a civil society activist, co-founded Pakistan's first all-female legal practice in 1980, along with her sister Asma Jahangir.

She is also one of the founders of the Human Rights Commission of Pakistan and the Women's Action Forum. Women's Action Forum is a cornerstone pressure group advocating fair legislation for women and campaigning against discrimination. Farida Shaheed is a Pakistani sociologist who has received several national and international human rights awards. She works on protecting and promoting cultural rights while supporting women and minorities.

There are many strong feminist icons in Pakistan, like Afiya Shehrbano Zia and Khawar Mumtaz, who have been working for years to put pressure on the government to create more women-sensitive policies and laws. Child activists like Iqbal Masih, a 12-year-old boy advocating against child labour, and Malala Yousafzai, who was shot at the age of 15 to protect her right to education, have profoundly impacted Pakistani society and the world's psyche. These activists work to change the basic mindset of society and for the betterment of women and children.

Conclusion

Since the time of its creation, Pakistan has had all the resources and functional organs to sustain the emerging society in a way that allowed it to grow and evolve organically. However, for multiple reasons, Pakistan instead, turned the other way, neglecting to look at the well-being of a huge chunk of its population based on gender. Governance challenges, unstable political systems, corrupted services and bureaucracy were a few reasons for the gradual decay of Pakistani society over the decades. The clash between Islamic law, public morality and constitutional laws has severely hampered the evolution of women's rights and children's rights. An attempt to control women according to the orthodox practices of the past in the 21st century has only stunted the economic growth and social welfare in the country. The gender divide and disrespect based on gender is a toxic generational cycle that continues through children. Without intentional intervention by the government, the cycle will be almost impossible to break. Creating policies and laws to appease Western countries and not implementing them properly can reap no benefits. There are many activists who see the repression and discrimination and have dedicated their entire life to bringing change for the welfare of society. However, there is only so much they can do to fight the system and society all at once, with limited resources. Pakistan society must come together to change the narrative and make Pakistan safe and secure and with an empowering environment for women and children.

NOTES

1. Global Gender Gap Report, "Insight Report," *World Economic Forum*, July 2022, www3.weforum.org/docs/WEF_GGGR_2022.pdf?_gl=1*1o3avwd*_up*MQ..&gclid=Cj0KCQjwr82iBhCuARIsAO0EAZxWU7ewlFUJao8g8Iwuz1kEceu4ValFiywa-_6uxiO6nb0NTXV5rLQaAoiOEALw_wcB
2. Silvia Redaelli and Noor Rahman, "In Pakistan, women's representation in the workforce remains low," *Blogs.worldbank.org*, 14 June 2021, blogs.worldbank.org/endpovertyinsouthasia/pakistan-womens-representation-workforce-remains-low
3. Maria Faiq Javed, et al., "Gender wage disparity and economic prosperity in Pakistan," *Cogent Economics & Finance*, Vol. 10, No. 1, 22 April 2022, https://doi.org/10.1080/23322039.2022.2067021
4. Rohma Saif, "Women participation in workforce of Pakistan: is it a gender inequality?," *Modern Diplomacy*, 7 December 2022, moderndiplomacy.eu/2022/12/08/women-participation-in-workforce-of-pakistan-is-it-a-gender-inequality/
5. IFRC, "Pakistan 2023 IFRC Network Country Plan (MAAPK002)," *Reliefweb.int*, 19 January 2023, reliefweb.int/report/pakistan/pakistan-2023-ifrc-network-country-plan-maapk002#:~:text=Up%20to%2064%20per%20cent
6. "A journey of education, empowerment and entrepreneurialism," *Veon*, 15 November 2022, www.veon.com/media/media-releases/2022/a-journey-of-education-empowerment-and-entrepreneurialism/#:~:text=The%20female%20literacy%20rate%20in
7. "Malala fund," *Malala.org*, malala.org/countries/pakistan
8. "The price of a child bride," *The Express Tribune*, 11 May 2023, tribune.com.pk/story/2416046/the-price-of-a-child-bride
9. Sean Kaisser Shaeen, et al., "Maternal mortality in Pakistan: challenges, efforts, and recommendations," *Annals of Medicine and Surgery*, Vol. 81, September 2022, p. 104380, https://doi.org/10.1016/j.amsu.2022.104380
10. "Gender disparity in Pak healthcare system contributing to dismal health of women," *ANI*, 24 May 2021, www.aninews.in/news/world/asia/gender-disparity-in-pak-healthcare-system-contributing-to-dismal-health-of-women20210524183443.
11. Zoaib Habib Tharwani, et al., "Infant & child mortality in Pakistan and its determinants: a review," *Inquiry: The Journal of Health Care Organization, Provision, and Financing*, Vol. 60, January 2023, p. 004695802311670, www.ncbi.nlm.nih.gov/pmc/articles/PMC10126599/#:~:text=Several%20factors%20have%20influenced%20these, https://doi.org/10.1177/00469580231167024
12. Imtiaz Ali, "Edhi foundation found 375 bodies of newly born babies in 2019," *Dawn.com*, 5 January 2020, www.dawn.com/news/1526263, accessed on 18 May 2023.
13. "Pakistan ranked fourth among worst countries for women," *Dawn.com*, 29 November 2017, www.dawn.com/news/1373623
14. "WJP Rule of Law Index," *Worldjusticeproject.org*, worldjusticeproject.org/rule-of-law-index/?gclid=CjwKCAjw04yjBhApEiwAJcvNoTtkP4QHLZpfYho0t79AxDbalA3ZRJCMnOe7syEiislBSfjQ2bUjkRoCjPQQAvD_BwE
15. "Women wearing few clothes impact men, unless robots: Pak PM on rising sexual violence," *Hindustan Times*, 21 June 2021, www.hindustantimes.com/world-news/women-wearing-few-clothes-impact-men-unless-robots-pak-pm-on-rising-sexual-violence-101624257728279.html
16. "Honour killings," www.hrw.org, www.hrw.org/tag/honor-killings
17. Mariyam Suleman Anees, "Honour killings: continue unabated in Pakistan," *Thediplomat.com*,

28 July 2022, www.thediplomat.com/2022/07/honor-killings-continue-unabated-in-pakistan/

18. "Pakistan rape case turns harsh spotlight on misogyny, justice system," *Nikkei Asia*, 26 February 2023, asia.nikkei.com/Spotlight/Society/Crime/Pakistan-rape-case-turns-harsh-spotlight-on-misogyny-justice-system
19. "In Pakistan, a woman is raped every 2 hours, convictions only 0.2%: report," *NDTV.com*, 13 October 2022, www.ndtv.com/world-news/in-pakistan-a-woman-is-raped-every-2-hours-convictions-only-0-2-report-3428239
20. Zahid Gishkori, "Sindh sees 200% increase in rape cases; conviction rate less than 1%," *Samaa*, 8 February 2023, www.samaaenglish.tv/news/40027189
21. Kaukab Shairani, "Why Pakistani feminists won't talk about marital rape – DW – 04/12/2022," *Dw.com*, 4 December 2022, www.dw.com/en/why-pakistani-feminists-are-reluctant-to-talk-about-marital-rape/a-61449046
22. NCHR, "Domestic violence policy brief," *National Commission for Human Rights*, March 2023, www.nchr.gov.pk/wp-content/uploads/2023/03/Domestic-Violence-Policy-Brief.pdf
23. "Women look for 'solutions' amid rise in domestic violence in Pakistan," *Times of India*, 3 April 2023, timesofindia.indiatimes.com/world/pakistan/women-look-for-solutions-amid-rise-in-domestic-violence-in-pakistan/articleshow/99315316.cms?from=mdr
24. "Pakistan Demographic and Health Survey 2017-18" (2019, January). Retrieved from https://dhsprogram.com/pubs/pdf/FR354/FR354.pdf
25. "Cruel Numbers – Sahil," *Sahil*, 2021, sahil.org/cruel-numbers/
26. "Child Protection," *Unicef.org*, 2012, www.unicef.org/pakistan/child-protection-0
27. Jahanzaib Yasin, "12 children sexually abused per day in first half of 2022," *The Express Tribune*, 15 September 2022, tribune.com.pk/story/2376831/in-pakistan-12-children-sexually-abused-per-day-in-first-half-of-2022.
28. Ilsa Tariq, "Child beggary in Pakistan," *Pakistan Observer*, 8 May 2023, pakobserver.net/child-beggary-in-pakistan-by-ilsa-tariq/
29. Paddy Dowling, "Pakistan's street children: exploitation, addiction and slavery," *The Independent*, 19 August 2022, www.independent.co.uk/asia/pakistan-children-exploitation-addiction-slavery-b2116108.html
30. Faraz Hasan, "Child trafficking," *The Nation*, 2 January 2023, www.nation.com.pk/02-Jan-2023/child-trafficking
31. "Trafficking in children for use as camel jockeys and engaging in hazardous employment. – PKLJC 41," www.commonlii.org www.commonlii.org/pk/other/PKLJC/reports/41.html#:~:text= Thousands%20of%20young%20children%20from

7

Contours of Pakistan's Strategic Posture

Dr. Shalini Chawla

India-Pakistan relations continue to be strained, with predictable exchanges of statements at regular intervals. While there have been brief phases of stability in the bilateral relationship, by and large, the relations have remained disturbed, and the trust deficit continues to dominate the thinking on both sides of the border. Sustained bilateral tensions have altered the security dynamics in the region. Pakistan's preferred low-cost strategy of using covert war through terrorism as a foreign policy tool and efforts to restrain India's engagement in Afghanistan have largely contributed to Kabul being the hub of terrorist activities.

Although varying degrees of intensity in tensions have been a constant feature between the two nuclear neighbours, relations are at their nadir at the moment with the complete absence of a diplomatic dialogue. The dialogue has not been revived after the Pathankot attack in January 2016. The abrogation of Article 370 by India on 5 August 2019 has intensified the tensions, and there has been massive frustration and anger expressed by the Pakistani leadership.

Some welcome developments have suggested that back-channel talks are active and continue to facilitate some peace initiatives. The ceasefire announced in February 2021 is being observed by both nations (at the time of writing this paper). The Kartarpur Sahib Gurdwara Corridor to Pakistan was reopened in November 2021, facilitating religious tourism from both sides.

There have been crucial developments in the last five years in Indo-Pak relations: India's firm position on a conditional dialogue, India's military retaliation to Pakistan's acts of terror, the abrogation of Article 370, India's rise and expansion of its strategic partnerships, the United States' exit from Afghanistan, Pakistan's reactions to the revocation of Article 370, its political instability, economic crisis, and a deteriorating security situation. It would be useful to look into the developments in the last five years and analyse Pakistan's strategic posture, which has a direct bearing on the dynamics of the India-Pakistan relationship.

Abrogation of Article 370: Crises within Pakistan and Pakistan's Strategic Posture

The abrogation of Article 370 in August 2019 challenged the Pakistani establishment's *identity* built on its decades-old phony claim on the Indian state (now Union Territory) of Jammu and Kashmir. Post-abrogation, Pakistan's frustrated leadership went on an aggressive mode to up the ante and intensify the anti-India strategy on all possible fronts. Pakistan's former Prime Minister Imran Khan displayed an irresponsible posture and used the nuclear threat rather often and blatantly after the change of status of Kashmir. There were multiple tweets by him highlighting the threat of a probable nuclear war between the two nations.

Pakistan-sponsored covert war has been intensified in Kashmir, and the deep state's latest asset *The Resistance Front (TRF)* accommodates Pakistan sponsored terror groups against India under a new banner that could be projected as the group fighting for its rights in Kashmir. Pakistan's propaganda against India has been aggressive, and it has been pursuing all channels, including international organisations and various regional groups, like the Organisation of Islamic Cooperation (OIC), to muster a wider consensus to cater to its strategic objectives against India in Kashmir. With the help of its all-weather ally, China, the issue of Kashmir was repeatedly and unsuccessfully raised at the United Nations Security Council (UNSC).

The abrogation of Article 370 challenged the centrality of the military's positioning and actions. Pakistan's position on Kashmir, which it claimed for decades as an *unfinished agenda of partition,* was questioned. There has been frustration, anger, and helplessness in Pakistan, and varied reactions were seen targeting the Indian leadership. Pakistan's strategic posture post revocation of Article 370 has been focused on building strong narratives and highlighting the Kashmir issue at the international level.

Pakistan has been in the mire of multiple crises for the last two years (at the time of writing this paper). The economic challenges have been alarming with low foreign exchange reserves, high debt burden, and exponential increase in inflation. While economic crisis for Pakistan is not new and Pakistan has been largely dependent on external assistance for its survival, this time, the traditional donors for Pakistan were insistent on Pakistan's adherence to the IMF conditionalities regarding structural reforms as a pre-condition for economic assistance. After months of negotiations and exhaustive rounds of meetings, on 12 July 2023, the International Monetary Fund (IMF) finally approved a 9-month Stand-By Arrangement (SBA) for Pakistan for about $ 3 billion, in order to support the economic stabilization program.[1] Economic assistance from China, Saudi Arabia, and the UAE has provided the economy with breathing space and the sustained change will depend on the fiscal management and Pakistan's spending priorities.

On the political front, Pakistan's political crisis started after Imran Khan's dramatic exit from the Prime Minister's office in April 2022. Khan went on a spree of rallies and held a series of *jalsas* pulling crowds in large numbers. The PTI government dissolved the legislative assemblies in Punjab and Khyber Pakhtunkhwa, demanded early elections, Imran blamed the USA for conspiring against him and facilitating his political exit, hit the opposition parties and most importantly targeted the military establishment. After Imran's exit from the PM's office in April 2022, a series of developments demonstrated the complex power dynamics and deep polarisation within the society and state institutions. The judiciary and the military stood divided between pro- and anti-Imran lobbies.

The arrest of Imran Khan from the Islamabad High Court by the Rangers on 9 May 2023, on charge of corruption in connection with the Al-Qadir Trust case sparked massive protests and violence, leading to deaths, destruction of public property and attacks on military vehicles and installations. The Pakistan army, reacting to the violence by PTI workers, called it a 'black chapter' in the country's history. The use of force and intimidation to curtail the opposition has been part of Pakistan's military culture. Following the 9 May events, a crackdown on PTI workers began leading to more than 5,000 arrests. Action against Imran marked the beginning of efforts by the military to step in finally to take control of affairs in Pakistan. Reportedly, more than 100 people, including wives and children of army officers are facing trial, (at the time of writing this paper).[2] Three senior officers, including a lieutenant-general have been sacked, for not being able to prevent the violent attacks on 9 May on esteemed military institutions/assets.[3] Crucial legal amendments have been done which grant unquestionable power and authority to the military.

While Pakistan struggles to stabilise its economy and find solutions to the political crisis, the security situation in the country has worsened with the TTP escalating its terror attacks in Khyber Pakhtunkhwa and Balochistan after the ceasefire with the government ended in November 2022. There are speculations regarding how the military is planning to deal with the TTP and whether the military will once again launch counter-terrorism operations.

Pakistan's Strategic Posture

Given the strained India-Pakistan relations and defining developments within Pakistan, critical trends in Pakistan's Strategic Posture can be identified.

Highlighting Threat Perceptions

Pakistan has long held the narrative of its (perceived) threat perceptions. From the time of its creation, Pakistan has suffered a deep sense of insecurity owing to its geography, small size, having a (perceived) hegemonic neighbour India and insurgencies within. The narrative of threat perceptions have been sustained to allow the dominance of the military, justify the covert war against India and diversion of substantial national resources towards defence spending.

While the highlighting of the threat perceptions is not new in Pakistan, the difference that one sees now is that there is an effort to drive a revised narrative of India's image. The revised narrative is based on India being run on a Nazi ideology. The effort is also to project that "India is a threat to the existence of Pakistan and to the Muslims of the world". Former Prime Minister Imran Khan made multiple statements on social media and during his trip to the USA, he spoke about the Indian posturing as a threat to the minorities of the world.

Pakistan's Army Chief, in his address at the Independence Day event at the Pakistan Military Academy (PMA) Kakul, reiterated:

> "To our neighbour [India], who has never been able to reconcile with the idea of Pakistan and is a threat to the regional peace and stability….The strategic calculus of our arch rival [India], skewed by its outsized ambition, carrying an illusion of being a great power and blinded by Hindutva driven hyper nationalism, needs serious attention of the world."[4]

Projection of Victimhood

Projection of victimhood has been a strong factor in Pakistan's positioning. Portrayal of victimhood allowed Pakistan to draw enormous financial, military and diplomatic support from the Western world and China. Pakistan's acquisitions of major equipment from the West and China were supported by the victimhood rationale. The projection has been used to legitimise Pakistan's sub-conventional war which it conducted for the last five decades in the Valley and other parts of India (and in Afghanistan). The narrative is also used to rationalise the build-up and expansion of the nuclear arsenal. The narrative has been maintained gradually and strongly after 9/11 when its counter-terrorism willingness and capability was repeatedly questioned by the USA.

The narrative of victimhood has continued with the insistence that Pakistan has been compelled to act and behave aggressively in response to India's actions and positioning in Kashmir. Pakistan has often taken the position that the USA has been responsible for radicalization in Pakistan. At the Council on Foreign Relations, New York, Imran Khan said:

> "Pakistan by joining the USA after 9/11, committed one of the biggest blunders. Seventy thousand Pakistanis died in this. We had some say over a hundred and fifty billion, say two hundred billion – some economists, Pakistanis – two hundred billion lost to the economy. And on top of it, we were blamed for the USA not winning in Afghanistan. I thought it was the worst period for Pakistan."[5]

Internationalise Kashmir

Abrogation of Article 370 by India did challenge Pakistan's decades-old narrative on Kashmir and Pakistan's attempts in recent years have focused on two aspects: One, to keep the momentum of the 'Kashmir issue' at home alive, and continue to drive the message – 'Kashmir Banega Pakistan'; second, to internationalise Kashmir and attract global attention.

Army Chief Asim Munir's address at Kakul did demonstrate this:

> "To my Kashmiri brethren, I would say that Inshallah you will also get free from the clutches of brutal occupation forces, as we got our freedom 76 years ago, through your rightful cause of self-determination and indigenous freedom struggle.... It is for the conscience of international community to realize that Indian excesses in Kashmir have gone unaddressed and right to freedom and self-determination is being denied at the altar of geo-political necessity."[6]

Highlighting Islamophobia

Islamophobia has been a crucial factor in Pakistan's positioning in recent times. Imran Khan's speech at the 74th session of the United Nations General Assembly had several references to Islamophobia:

> "There are 1.3 billion Muslims in the world. Muslims live across all continents. Islamophobia has grown since 9/11 and it is alarming. It is creating divisions.... We failed as the Muslim world to explain that there is no such thing as radical Islam. In Pakistan; we were the eye of the storm and our government coined the term 'enlightened moderation'. The West could not understand what was the problem. They don't look at religion the way we do. And so; in their eyes, Islam was an intolerant religion. It became a watershed".[7]

Talking of Islamophobia does complement Pakistan's projected victimhood and, in its view, strengthens its position amongst the Muslim nations. Pakistan did manage to get robust support from Turkey and Malaysia on the Kashmir narrative.

Nuclear Brinkmanship

Pakistan repeatedly flagged the possibility of a 'nuclear war' post abrogation of Article 370. Prime Minister Imran Khan in his unrelenting tweets had repeatedly highlighted various aspects of the nuclear threat, for example, both India and Pakistan possess nuclear weapons and thus, any crisis in the region is alarming; Pakistan has nuclear weapons and thus, the probability of a nuclear war is high; India's nuclear weapons are a threat to global and regional security, etc.

Pakistan has used the nuclear card in the past spasmodically and this stems from its basic insecurity as a state and its failure to develop its strengths. Islamabad has long tried to balance its domestic vulnerabilities with its nuclear weapons which it treats as the ultimate guarantor of its survivability and security. Its nuclear history and thinking explicitly explains its nuclear behaviour and the brinkmanship we see today.

Pakistan till today does not have an officially announced written doctrine and there is an unofficial code adopted by the Pakistani leadership, based on *Indo-centricity, credible minimum deterrence (now full spectrum deterrence), strategic restraint* and *first use*. Pakistan very conceitedly (rather often) talks about Tactical Nuclear Weapons (TNWs)-NASR, which in its opinion, would deter India from a conventional military response.

Pakistan's nuclear posturing has focused on projection of a low threshold with a *First Use* doctrine. The nuclear threat has been used in the past frequently to deal with the crisis situation. Nuclear weapons for Pakistan serve mainly three objectives:

1. The nuclear weapons and *First Use Doctrine* are meant to neutralize India's conventional superiority and deter India from a conventional response in any form.
2. The weapons are projected as the ultimate guarantee for Pakistan's security and survivability.
3. Pakistan has tried to project its nuclear assets as an instrument of blackmailing.

Pakistan's nuclear posture does reflect some distinct contradictions. It talks about being a restrained and responsible nuclear power but at the same time relies on a *first use* doctrine and boasts about the *TNWs* and *Full Spectrum Deterrence*. It continues to assert that it does not want to start a war with India, highlights the disastrous consequences of a nuclear war but repeatedly flags the threat of nuclear conflict creating war hysteria in the region. It would not be incorrect to state that Pakistan has very *rationally adopted the posture of irrationality*.

Pakistan's nuclear posturing did suffer a blow to some extent with India's airstrikes in Balakot on 26 February 2019 in retaliation to the terror attack in Pulwama claimed by the Jaish-e-Mohammed (JeM) on 14 February 2019. But, it seems that Pakistan's reliance on nuclear weapons to serve its strategic objectives has not been altered. Its reliance on the nuclear deterrence has intensified with constantly growing asymmetries between India and Pakistan over the last two decades. At this point of time, Pakistan's repeatedly flagging of the nuclear threat can be attributed to mainly three factors:

1. Firstly, Pakistan has spent enormous amount of national resources in the build-up of the nuclear arsenal on the pretext that nuclear weapons are the ultimate weapons for the state's survival and security. Pakistan has always prioritised its defence expenditure even though it has been at the cost of the socio-economic development of the country. The leadership at this point wants to justify the enormous nuclear build-up to its own population and ensure them that nuclear weapons will ultimately guard Pakistan's future.
2. Secondly, by using the threat of a nuclear war, the leadership wants to remind India and the international community about the presence of nuclear weapons in the region and the dangers emanating from a potential nuclear war.
3. By flagging the nuclear threat, Pakistan attempts to draw international attention to the Kashmir issue.

Complex Relations with Afghanistan

Although Pakistan felt confident that it will be able to now fulfill its strategic objectives in Afghanistan with the Taliban in power, the reality has been quite different. Pakistan's tensions with the Taliban have grown over two critical issues:

1. *Fencing of the Durand Line*: There have been repeated instances of clashes between the Pakistan military and the Taliban on the Afghanistan-Pakistan border. Pakistan perceived the Taliban victory as a favourable development. However, Pakistan miscalculated the Taliban's position on the border and contrary to its expectations the Taliban have opposed the fence from the time it took over Kabul. Even when the Taliban took control of Afghanistan in the 1990s, they did not accept the Durand Line as the international boundary. The Taliban's position on the border clearly indicates that even though Pakistan estimated that it would be able to work the boundary issue to its advantage, the realities are different.
2. *Tehreek-e-Taliban Pakistan's (TTP) Emboldened Posture:* Ever since the Taliban has taken control of Afghanistan (August 2021), the TTP has accelerated its terror attacks specifically targeting the Pakistan security forces. Surely, the defeat of the democratically elected leadership in Afghanistan is seen as a major ideological victory by the group. Pakistan has been pressuring the Afghan Taliban to control the TTP and persuade them for a ceasefire. There have been some cosmetic measures by the Afghan Taliban but not enough to dissuade the TTP from launching terror attacks on Pakistan's security establishment to bolster its demands.

Leveraging Chinese Support

The China-Pakistan strategic alliance has expanded from a purely military alliance to an economic and diplomatic alliance in the last five decades. China's economic assistance to Pakistan in the form of debt rollovers and deposits has been crucial for Pakistan's financial respite.

China's support to Pakistan has been on four critical fronts strengthening Pakistan's strategic posture vis-à-vis India:

1. China has continued to modernise Pakistan's conventional military capability starting in the 1960s, post the India-Pakistan 1965 war.
2. Pakistan's nuclear arsenal has been expanded with sustained Chinese assistance.

3. The China-Pakistan Economic Corridor (CPEC) has been developed despite India's continued objection to it.
4. China has offered explicit diplomatic support to Pakistan against India. The Chinese position on Kashmir has been primarily pro-Pakistan. New Delhi's efforts to list Pakistan-based terrorists as global terrorists have faced continued resistance from Beijing in the United Nations (UN).

Post the abrogation of Article 370, China's unflinching support to Pakistan has been discernible. Beijing used its position in the UN to call for a closed-door meeting at the Security Council to discuss Kashmir after the revocation of Article 370, defended Islamabad's case at the Financial Action Task Force (FATF) to restrain the blacklisting of Pakistan, and very importantly, has offered to extend military support strengthening Pakistan's position in the wake of rising tensions between India and Pakistan. China has reportedly offered to deploy a certain number of an upgraded version of JH-7A II fighters on the Sino-Pak border. An 'official Chinese-language media report' of 28 September 2019 (translation done by the Centre for China Analysis and Strategy, New Delhi) stated:

> "In the face of the strong Indian Air Force, Pakistan's efforts are clearly not enough. China, on the other hand, could help Pakistan turn the tables by providing a fighter which will have remarkable 'strength multiplication' combat efficiency."

According to the report, against the backdrop of an India-Pak confrontation, the Chinese aircraft (JH-7AII variant) "can not only effectively suppress the air defence system of Indian troops; all the more it can let Pakistani fighters hold superiority in the air confrontation."

Beijing feels that Pakistan's economy is not in a position to deal with the "urgent needs of war" and thus China's offer would "leverage the powerful air combat effectiveness of JH-7 AII for strength multiplication and achieve victory for Pakistan." The JH-7AII variant is reportedly equipped with a more advanced radar and avionics system, enhancing its flight performance. While the details of this move by Beijing are not fully known, the fact is that this indicates that China is clearly thinking in terms of offering direct military support to Pakistan to deal with any scenario of a probable Indo-Pak conflict.

During the 3rd meeting of the CPEC Joint Working Group on International Cooperation and Coordination, China and Pakistan, long-term strategic partners, have decided to jointly welcome Third World countries to join the much-acclaimed CPEC. In the past, Pakistan and China have tried offering Afghanistan, Nepal, Saudi Arabia, and the UAE to join the CPEC. Even though there have been speculations regarding the adverse financial impacts of the CPEC on Pakistan's economy, the viability of some of the CPEC projects, and terror attacks targeting the Chinese workers in Pakistan, the China-Pakistan alliance remains unaffected and the second phase of the CPEC has been announced.

India has expressed its resentment against the recent Sino-Pak decision as the CPEC passes through Pakistan Occupied Kashmir (POK) and New Delhi sees this move as an infringement on 'India's sovereignty and territorial integrity.' New Delhi has opposed the CPEC, which involves the building of massive infrastructure projects on territory illegally occupied by Pakistan.

In recent years, China has intensified its position on Kashmir in support of Pakistan. Beijing continues to display double standards. It wants to invite countries to join the CPEC, and on the other hand, was opposed to India hosting the G-20 meetings in Jammu and Kashmir. Ironically for Beijing, the POK is legitimate enough to invest billions of dollars, engage thousands of Chinese workers and invite other countries to participate in the CPEC, but it claims Jammu and Kashmir to be illegitimate and disputed, which needs to be resolved bilaterally through dialogue.

The most significant aspects of China's diplomatic backing for Pakistan are China's position on Kashmir and its support for Pakistan in the wars against India. This has been a critical part of China's long-term strategy of strengthening Pakistan's strategic position to balance India. Although China's position on Kashmir has remained by and large in support of Pakistan, its overt position on Kashmir has witnessed some interesting deviations in the intensity of support it has extended to Pakistan.

China's position on Kashmir after the abrogation of Article 370 by India in August 2019 has projected its frustration, anger, and support for Pakistan's position on Kashmir. It calls India's decision to 'change the status quo in Kashmir illegal and invalid.'[8] India, on the other hand, holds the position that "the Chinese side has no locus standi whatsoever on this matter (Kashmir) and is advised not to comment on the internal affairs of other nations."[9] On Pakistan's perseverance, China raised the issue of Kashmir in the United Nations Security Council (UNSC) and has repeatedly tried to call meetings of the UNSC to discuss Kashmir. China's recent actions and statements have been aimed at putting Kashmir on the multilateral forums and encouraging larger engagement, even though in its statements it continues to maintain that Kashmir is a bilateral issue.

Beijing is also trying to maintain the pressure on India on the Line of Actual Control (LAC). Even after 18-plus rounds of Corps Commander-level talks between India and China, there are limited to no signs of easing off the tensions and the Chinese strategy has been to "keep the pot simmering" and not in favour of any de-escalation.[10]

Conclusion

Given the state of crisis in Pakistan and India's growing economic power and diplomatic profile, the following trends can be expected in Pakistan's strategic posturing and India-Pakistan relations:

India continues to remain firm on its position on a strictly conditional dialogue with Pakistan. New Delhi maintains the position that no talks can take place until Pakistan-sponsored terrorism continues on Indian territory. New Delhi's military retaliation to Pakistan-sponsored acts of terror (Uri and Balakot) is a clear indication to Pakistan that there will be a cost to its (Pakistan's) acts of terror. On the nuclear front, India has shown a restrained and responsible nuclear posture. It continues to maintain a no-first-use nuclear doctrine with credible deterrence and has refrained from using the threat of nuclear weapons during crises.

Pakistan, on the other hand, has shown no change in its covert war strategy. While the Kashmir Valley has been stable and the terror attacks have decreased significantly due to the heavy military presence, Pakistan's covert actions in Punjab have escalated. Narco-terrorism is the latest addition to Pakistan's covert war strategy in Punjab and Kashmir. Pakistan has been using drones extensively to drop drugs in Kashmir and Punjab. The Valley alone has witnessed a staggering 2,000 per cent increase in cases of heroin abuse in the last five years.[11]

Pakistan continues to highlight Kashmir at international forums to attract global attention. Its political leaders have made a number of statements urging global support on Kashmir and this is likely to intensify (with Chinese support).

There have been frequent statements by civilian leaders in Pakistan expressing keenness for talks with India. But clearly, there seems to be a lack of seriousness on this front. Pakistan has often tried to highlight the reversal of the abrogation of Article 370 as a precondition for any talks/diplomatic exchange with India.

This position is a non-starter, as India's decision and position on Article 370 remain unchanged.

India's growing strategic partnerships and economic development are likely to enhance Pakistan's threat perceptions, which will be dealt with by Islamabad through efforts to internationalise Kashmir, justify weapon modernization, continue propaganda against India, and maintain a narrative of victimhood. Pakistan's narrative on the threat of a nuclear war is likely to lie low for some time, but Pakistan's reliance on nuclear weapons to manage its insecurities is not likely to change. China will continue to support Pakistan on military, economic, and diplomatic fronts, and Pakistan's reliance on Beijing will increase.

It appears that India-Pakistan tensions will keep simmering as India is less likely to have a moderate position and Pakistan has shown no resolve to stop supporting the terror network in the Valley. As a result, the space is shrinking for negotiations/dialogue aimed at stability.

NOTES

1. "IMF Executive Board approves US$3 billion stand-by arrangement for Pakistan," International Monetary Fund, 12 July 2023, https://www.imf.org/en/News/Articles/2023/07/12/pr23261-pakistan-imf-exec-board-approves-us3bil-sba, accessed on 20 July 2023.
2. Derek Cai, "Imran Khan: Pakistan army sacks three officers over May protests," *BBC News*, 27 June 2023, https://www.bbc.com/news/world-south-asia-6601633, accessed on 30 June 2023.
3. Asif Shahzad, "Pakistan army general among three sacked over violence by Imran Khan's party," *Reuters*, 27 June 2023, https://www.reuters.com/world/asia-pacific/pakistan-armys-top-3-officers-sacked-over-attacks-by-ex-pm-khan-supporters-army-2023-06-26/, accessed on 30 June 2023.
4. Laiq Ur Rehman, "No power on earth can undo Pakistan: COAS Asim Munir," *ARY News*, 14 August 2023, https://arynews.tv/no-power-on-earth-can-undo-pakistan-coas-asim-munir/, accessed on 16 August 2023.
5. "A conversation with Prime Minister Imran Khan of Pakistan," Council on Foreign Relations, 23 September 2019, https://www.cfr.org/event/conversation-prime-minister-imran-khan-pakistan-0, accessed on 10 October 2019.
6. Laiq Ur Rehman, n 4.
7. "Full transcript of Prime Minister Imran Khan's speech at the UNGA," *Business Recorder*, 27 September 2019, https://www.brecorder.com/2019/09/27/524851/full-transcript-of-prime-minister-imran-khans-speech-at-the-unga/, accessed on 30 September 2019.
8. Ministry of Foreign Affairs of the People's Republic of China, "Foreign Ministry Spokesperson Wang Wenbin's Regular Press Conference on August 5, 2020," https://www.fmprc.gov.cn/mfa_eng/xwfw_665399/s2510_665401/t1804251.shtml 2020/08/05, accessed on 1 October 2020.
9. Geeta Mohan, "China has no locus standi on Kashmir issue: India on Beijing calling change in J&K illegal," *India Today*, 5 August 2020, https://www.indiatoday.in/india/story/china-

has-no-locus-standi-on-kashmir-issue-india-on-beijing-calling-change-in-j-k-illegal-1708191-2020-08-05, accessed on 10 August 2020.

10. Snehesh Alex Philip, "China's pressure tactics along the LAC continue, aim to keep the pot simmering," *The Print,* 25 July 2022, https://theprint.in/defence/chinas-pressure-tactics-along-lac-continue-aim-to-keep-the-pot-simmering/1054168/, accessed on 29 July 2022.
11. Anvit Srivastava, "Kashmir see 2000% spike in heroin abuse cases in 5 years and Pak injects narco-terror poison," *NEWS 18*, 12 July 2022, accessed on 10 August 2022.

8

Pakistan-US Relations: Rethinking and Resetting Ties

Dr. Shalini Chawla

The relationship between Pakistan and the USA is perhaps one of the most consequential relationships that have traditionally impacted the strategic dimensions of the South Asian region. Given the strategic developments in the region, it is interesting to observe that the two nations never trusted each other's intentions but maintained a strong alliance (in three critical phases). While the USA portrayed Pakistan as a vital ally, Pakistan's narratives regarding the strategic necessity of US military (and financial) assistance to Pakistan changed over time. Pakistan's relationship with Washington started as a purely military alliance in the 1950s, catering to the strategic objectives of both Washington and Pakistan. The USA wanted to build a military bloc against the former USSR, and Pakistan, on the other hand, was looking for options to acquire high-quality modern equipment catering to its threat perceptions vis-à-vis India. The bilateral relationship has gone through high and low phases, and the last decade has seen a strained phase of the relationship. Former US President Donald Trump took a firm position against Pakistan by cutting down the sale of US military equipment and military aid to Pakistan, which has been an essential and perhaps the most desirable component (for Islamabad) of the US-Pak dynamics. Under President Biden, the relationship suffered a further blow with Pakistan's former Prime Minister, Imran Khan's, accusatory position where he held the USA responsible for Pakistan's economic and security woes and finally for his scandalous exit from the PM office.

Pakistan has been in dire need of external assistance to effectuate an economic bailout due to its alarming economic crisis. The International Monetary Fund (IMF) maintained a firm stance and demanded severe structural economic reforms and defence spending cuts from Pakistan. The IMF assistance (which finally came after a long struggle for Pakistan), is crucial for Pakistan owing to three factors: (a) Pakistan's economy needs the economic support and cannot function without loans; (b) IMF loan could facilitate the opening of multiple other international financial channels for Pakistan; and (c) the IMF loan is in some ways symbolic of the US support for Pakistan.

The USA (till now) has refrained from offering any direct economic assistance and has insisted that Pakistan conducts the structural reforms according to the guidelines of the IMF. While the focus of the previous phases of the US-Pakistan partnership has been security, the current phase of the relationship centres more on both the USA and Pakistan attempting to reset ties and redefine common areas of interests based on cooperation in the arena of non-traditional security threats. This is a departure in the US approach from the past, where the acquisition of US equipment by Pakistan had been the defining factor of the US-Pakistan relationship.

US-Pakistan relations: A Rollercoaster Ride?

Pakistan's foreign policy has been primarily driven by its strategic objectives, desire to modernise its military and acquire high technology equipment. Soon after partition, Pakistan had started intimating (to the US) about Pakistan's crucial role in the US strategic dynamics of the Cold War. Jinnah told Bourke-White while talking about his views on relations with Washington, "America needs Pakistan more than Pakistan needs America… Pakistan is the pivot of the world, as we are placed…the frontier on which the future of the world revolves…Russia is not so very far away".[1] This is the sentiment Pakistan conceived with its birth and maintained in its narrative of Pakistan being extremely relevant for the USA due to its strategic geographic location. Bourke-White wrote that the Pakistani officials would tell her, "Surely America will build our army… Surely America will give loans to keep Russia from walking in".[2] In 1947, Jinnah conveyed to Raymond A. Hare of the Division of Middle Eastern and Indian Affairs, and Thomas E. Weil, Second Secretary of the Embassy at New Delhi that, "establishment Pakistan essential to prevent 'Hindu imperialism' spreading into Middle East; Muslim countries would stand together against possible Russian aggression and would look to US for assistance."[3]

Pakistan was keen on an economic and military relationship with the USA. On the other hand, America's interest in providing military aid to Pakistan was driven mainly by two factors:

Firstly, the geographical location of Pakistan abutting the oil-rich Persian Gulf region (where the USA and UK had extensive commercial interests) and the strategic location of the Straits of Hormuz offered Washington easy access to energy resources as well as a monitoring point for the southern Soviet Union and western China. Pakistan's strategically important location, in fact, turned it into a convenient launching pad for the Cold War strategies.[4] Secondly, fear of Soviet expansion into the Middle East.

A mutual defence assistance agreement signed on 19 May 1954, between the USA and Pakistan was the first formal bilateral security commitment between the two countries and provided the legal basis to the US military assistance.[5] Following this, in the same year, US officials presented a secret aide-memoiré boosting the military aid to $ 50 million with specific programme goals. The aid-memoiré committed Washington to equip "4 army infantry and 1.5 armoured divisions, to provide modern aircraft for 6 air force squadrons, and to supply 12 vessels for the navy. The estimated cost of this programme was $ 171 million."[6]

Pakistan entered the Southeast Asia Treaty Organisation (SEATO) in 1955 and the Baghdad Pact, renamed the Central Treaty Organisation (CENTO), after Iraq left the pact in 1956, ostensibly joining the chain erected by the USA around the former Soviet Union and its then military-ideological ally, China, to check the spread of communism.[7] This resulted in a robust inflow of military and economic aid for Pakistan. Being a member of these two security alliances provided Pakistan with a stronger claim on US resources and the USA also benefited from the regular interaction between the Pakistani civilian and military officials and their counterparts from the other member-countries. In this process the USA acquired a larger stake in its Pakistan relationship.[8]

By the year 1957, Pakistan was receiving massive amount of sophisticated military equipment, training, and economic aid. The inflow from Washington included sophisticated Patton main battle tanks, modern artillery, howitzers, F-86 jet fighter squadrons, F-104 Starfighter supersonic interceptors, and air-to-air missiles. A further, qualitative boost came from the military training by the US military teams and also in the US military schools for the Pakistani army.[9] Pakistan has not only acquired high-technology weapons from the USA but has also benefited by the interaction with the American armed forces which has influenced Pakistan military's thinking and strategy. The massive US arms aid to Pakistan in the late 1950s provided it with the incentive to initiate the 1965 war, and demonstrated the philosophy of high-technology weapons providing a competitive advantage against India which, in any case, was saddled at that time with obsolete systems being employed after the Sino-India war in 1962. The US military also aided in setting up intelligence and special operations facilities creating the Special Services Group (SSG) which was used to unsuccessfully try and capture Indian airfields in 1965 war. While Pakistan failed to win the war in 1965, its military nevertheless projected it as a victory, especially in the air, and the thirst for high-technology systems intensified.

The US military assistance was suspended after the India-Pakistan war in 1965 when Pakistan used the US equipment in the war. Pakistan's desperation and its quest for alternative sources of military equipment drove it towards China. For Beijing, Pakistan was (and has been) a low-cost option to balance India and counter the US expansion the region. Needless to say, China's energy requirements have been a critical factor in its alliance with Pakistan. The Soviet occupation of Afghanistan in 1979 offered a strategic opportunity for Pakistan and brought in a renewed US-Pakistan engagement. Pakistan became the front-line state in the US war against the Soviets. General Zia-ul-Haq was well aware of the criticality of Pakistan's support for the USA and he did manage to negotiate substantive aid and the latest military equipment. Some issues were unanimously agreed to between the military leadership and Washington: firstly, Pakistan would not compromise on its nuclear programme; secondly, US interference in Pakistan's internal matters was not acceptable and it was Pakistan's prerogative to solve its internal affairs.[10] Zia negotiated an elaborate military and security-related aid package of $ 3.2 billion. The US military assistance programme included the sale of 40 F-16 Falcon multi-role combat aircraft, attack helicopters, and second-hand destroyers. The second US package, worth, $ 4.02 billion, commenced in 1987 but was suspended due to the US arms embargo in 1990 as Pakistan crossed the 'red lines' to acquire nuclear weapons capability. This phase of the US-Pakistan engagement contributed towards a significant transformation in the Pakistan army's posture and position and very importantly, the ISI emerged as a potent institution commanding not only the military's strategic moves but also playing a decisive role in Pakistan's politics. In the 1980s, the ISI explored and developed new modes of financing the Afghan mujahideen, and the narcotics trade flourished on the Pakistan-Afghanistan border. The US weapons which Pakistan acquired during the 1980s were diverted to equip terrorist elements in the Indian Punjab.

9/11, Global war on Terror and US Military Aid to Pakistan

The 11 September 2001, terrorist attacks in the USA led to a major strategic shift for Pakistan, and Islamabad became a front-line state for Washington and an ally in the global war on terror. The new US-Pakistan relationship helped Pakistan move out of the economic crisis that had built up in the late 1990s. The Paris Club rescheduling agreement signed in December 2001 provided for a comprehensive restructuring of Pakistan's debt, which amounted to US$ 12.5 billion.[11] Immediate assistance efforts from the Bush Administration included the waiving of US sanctions on Pakistan resulting from its 1998 nuclear tests and the 'Democracy Sanctions'.

Pakistan's military modernisation received a major boost as it received substantive military assistance from the USA and its Western allies. Pakistan offered its complete military support to the USA, including the use of its air space and agreed to the use of Pakistani air bases at Jacobabad, Pasni, and Dalbandin by American forces for 'search and rescue' missions. The US presence on Pakistani bases led to substantial US investments for renovating the bases, and in addition, Pakistan was paid for providing security for the bases. The Shahbaz air base Jacobabad, for example, went through extensive construction work to renovate the base, including, the installation of radar equipment. Pakistan was able to obtain US equipment and other support systems, including intelligence, which has been actively operating in the war against terrorism. In September 2003 alone, in order to enhance surveillance capability, the supply of US air traffic control radars as well as associated equipment and services worth $ 110 million was authorized to Pakistan.[12]

In February 2002, Pakistan and the USA signed a defence cooperation agreement, and, Pakistan agreed to American forces using its military equipment for training and other military exercises. Pakistan also agreed to provide other facilities like food, water, medical services, and transportation against payment to the US forces operating in Afghanistan. Taking a step towards institutionalizing the military relationship with Pakistan, the USA, in an important strategic move, designated Pakistan as a 'major non-NATO ally' (MNNA) in March 2004. Previously, only three Muslim countries had been accorded this status – Bahrain, Egypt and Jordan. Australia. Japan, Israel, the Philippines, and South Korea are the non-Muslim countries that fall in this category. The status of the MNNA not only enhanced Pakistan's stature but also enabled it to obtain state-of-the-art military equipment and spares at rock-bottom prices and on a priority basis.

Modern US inventories and also spare parts for the US equipment that were being used in Pakistan were made available to Pakistan. One of the most important advantages of this designation was that Islamabad was able to obtain what is called 'Excess Defence Equipment (EDAs)'. These are weapons and equipment that the USA may not need anymore, and may be transferred at nominal rates to its allies. Pakistan did receive the weaponry that the US forces used during their operations at the Pakistani bases and facilities. Some of the significant equipment which Pakistan received post 2001 included, F-16s, Bell-205/UH-1 Huey-2, P-CUP Orion, AN TPS-77 Air Surveillance Radar and AIM-120C AMRAAM missiles.

Pakistan's defence modernization flourished post 9/11 with US assistance and consistent Chinese imports. Even with the lavish US assistance flowing in (see Table 1) on the pretext of Pakistan's counter-terror operations, President Musharraf aided the resurgence of the Taliban insurgency in Afghanistan while the USA was distracted in Iraq in 2003-2004, and support for the Haqqani network remained active, not allowing the war on terror to show the desired outcome. However, a significant shift in US trust and support was apparent after the killing of Osama bin Laden in Abbottabad (Op Neptune Spear), on 2 May 2011 in a US Navy SEALS raid on his compound. While the USA realised that it had limited options in terms of replacing its strategic reliance on Pakistan due to its heavy military presence in Afghanistan, American military support for Pakistan did see a shift after 2011.[13] President Trump took a firm position on cutting down on military support to Pakistan, asserted the withdrawal from Afghanistan and Pakistan-US relations saw a drastic low. In his first tweet of January 2018, President Donald Trump said, "The United States has foolishly given Pakistan more than $ 33 billion in aid over the last 15 years, and they have given us nothing but lies and deceit, thinking of our leaders as fools. They give safe haven to the terrorists we hunt in Afghanistan, with little help. No more!"[14]

Table 1: Direct Overt US Aid Appropriations for and Military Reimbursements to Pakistan FY2002-FY2024

(rounded to the nearest millions of dollars)

Note: Final obligation and disbursement totals may be lower than program account appropriations

Program or Account	*FY 2002-FY 2017*	*FY 2018*	*FY 2019*	*FY 2020*	*FY 2021*	*FY 2022*	*Program or Account Total*	*FY 2023 (req.)*	*FY 2024 (req.)*
CN	341	–	–	–	–	–	341	a	a
FMF	4,073	–	–	–	–	–	4,073	–	–
IMET	52	–	–	–	4	3	59	4	4
INCLE	949	21	40	21	25	25	1,081	17	17
NADR	182	2	2	1	1	–	188	1	1
PCF/PCCF	2,352	–	–	–	–	–	2,352	–	–
Total Security-Related	7,939[b]	23	42	22	30	28	8,406[b]	22	22
Climate	–	–	–	–	–	–	–	9	37
CSH/GHCS/GHP	295	–	–	3	7	31	336	30	32
ESF/ESDF	8,696[c]	48	62	53[d]	45	50[e]	8,954	54	82
Food Aid[f]	643	–	–	–	–	–	643	–	–
IDA	1,065	36	–	6	3	47	1,157	a	a
MRA	371	4	28	32	2	62	499	a	a
Total Economic- Related	11,356[g]	88	90	94	57	190	11,875[g]	93	151
CSF Reimbursements[g]	14,573[h]	h	h	–	–	–	14,573	–	–
Grand Total	34,190	111	132	116	87	218	34,854	115	173

U.S. Departments of State, Defence, and Agriculture; U.S. Agency for International Development.

Source: Table from K. Alan Kronstadt, *Pakistan and Pakistan-U.S. Relations*, 22 May 2023, CRS Report, R47565, pp. 11-12, https://crsreports.congress.gov/product/pdf/R/R47565/6, accessed on 1 June 2023.

CN: Counternarcotics Funds (Pentagon budget)

CSF: Coalition Support Funds (Pentagon budget)

GHP: Child Survival and Health; Global Health and Child Survival (GHCS) from FY2010; Global Health Programs (GHP) from FY2013

ESF: Economic Support Funds; Economic Support and Development Funds (ESDF) from FY2018

FMF: Foreign Military Financing

IDA: International Disaster Assistance (Pakistani earthquake, flood, and internally displaced persons relief)

IMET: International Military Education and Training

INCLE: International Narcotics Control and Law Enforcement (includes border security)

MRA: Migration and Refugee Assistance (also includes Emergency Refugee and Migration Assistance or ERMA; shows obligations)

NADR: Nonproliferation, Anti-Terrorism, Demining, and Related (the great majority allocated for Pakistan is anti-terrorism assistance)

PCF/PCCF: Pakistan Counterinsurgency Fund/Counterinsurgency Capability Fund (PCF overseen by the Pentagon, PCCF overseen by State)

a. This funding is "requirements-based"; there are no pre-allocation data.
b. Includes $312 million "global train and equip" funds from FY2006 FY2009 authorized by Section 1206 of the National Defense Authorization Act (NDAA) for FY2006, within which $100 million in FY2008 and FY2009 funds was for Pakistan's paramilitary Frontier Corps.
c. Congress authorized Pakistan to use the FY2003 and FY2004 ESF allocations to cancel a total of $1.5 billion in debt to the U.S. government. Also includes $17 million in Human Rights and Democracy Funds from FY2002-FY2007.
d. Includes $7 million in FY2020 COVID supplemental funds.
e. Includes $10 million in supplemental FY2022 ESF under the Additional Ukraine Supplemental Appropriations Act, 2022 (P.L. 117-128).
f. P.L.480 Title I (loans), P.L. 117-328P.L.480 Title II (grants), and Section 416(b) of the Agricultural Act of 1949, as amended (surplus agricultural commodity donations). Food aid totals do not include freight costs.
g. Includes $286 million in Development Assistance appropriated from FY2002-FY2008.
h. CSF was Defense Department funding to reimburse foreign forces for logistical and operational support of U.S-led military operations; it is technically not foreign assistance. Beginning in FY2015, successive NDAAs subjected one-third to one-half of annual CSF to Pakistan to Haqqani Network-related certification requirements that could not be waived by the Administration. The Administration did not issue certifications for FY2015-FY2018. The NDAA for FY2019 revamped the CSF program, authorizing $350 million to support security enhancement activities along Pakistan's western border, subject to certification requirements that have not been met to date. The NDAA for FY2020 disallowed the use of FY2020 funds to reimburse Pakistan.

Resetting Bilateral Engagement

Even though, following Operation Neptune Spear and President Trump's tough position on Pakistan, US assistance to Pakistan decreased considerably, Pakistan remained a critical factor for the USA in Afghanistan. The USA did rely on Pakistan for peace negotiations with the Taliban in Doha. Pakistan took the credit for bringing the Taliban to the negotiating table with the USA and finally getting the Taliban in power, which Islamabad perceived and celebrated as a strategic victory.

In the past four decades, Afghanistan has been the most important factor defining US-Pakistan relations. After the US exit from Afghanistan in August 2021, the dynamics have changed. There has been a new phase of resetting US-Pakistan ties. The following factors have been crucial in this regard:[15]

1. The US interest in Afghanistan has decreased significantly since its exit from the region, and its reliance on Pakistan has shrunk.
2. The USA's increasing tensions with China, Pakistan's closest ally.
3. The USA's increasing focus on the Indo-Pacific strategy to counter China, where Pakistan does not occupy any space. The Biden Administration's

February 2022 Indo-Pacific Strategy, and October 2022 National Security Strategy and National Defence Strategy do not mention Pakistan. The USA has been fully engaged with the Quadrilateral Security Dialogue (or Quad, along with India, Japan, and Australia).

4. Pakistan's increasing reliance on China. Pakistan and the USA have completely divergent opinions on China.

India's strategic and economic rise on the world stage, the expansion of India's diplomatic profile, and its expanding partnership with the US are also critical factors contributing to Washington's posture in the region. After the US withdrawal from Afghanistan, there have been serious concerns in Washington regarding regional security and its impact on Pakistan. US Chairman of the Joint Chiefs General Mark Milley told the Senate Armed Services Committee soon after the fall of the democratic regime in Afghanistan, "We estimated an accelerated withdrawal would increase risks of regional instability, the security of Pakistan and its nuclear arsenals…We need to fully examine the role of Pakistan sanctuary".[16]

In the first public hearing in Congress about Afghanistan after the US withdrawal, the U.S. Secretary of State Antony Blinken said, "Pakistan has a "multiplicity of interests some that are in conflict with ours…It is one that is involved hedging its bets constantly about the future of Afghanistan, it's one that's involved harbouring members of the Taliban...It is one that's also involved in different points of cooperation with us on counter-terrorism…this is one of the things we're going to be looking at in the days, and weeks ahead – the role that Pakistan has played over the last 20 years and also the role we would want to see it play in the coming years and what it will take for it to do that."[17]

The USA has an interest in stabilizing Afghanistan, focusing on human rights (specifically women's rights) and would not wish to allow Kabul to become the hub of terrorist activities. Engagement in counter-terrorism and regional security has been maintained cautiously by the Pentagon.[18] This includes high-level military-to-military engagements and a session of the US-Pakistan Counterterrorism Dialogue in March 2023.[19]

The USA and Pakistan's trade relations have been in Pakistan's favour. The USA has been Pakistan's largest export market and the figures for US imports of Pakistani goods stand at $ 5 billion in 2021.[20] The USA has also remained the leading investor in Pakistan in the last 20 years. According to a US Department of State report, US investment in Pakistan in the recent fiscal year has increased by 50 per cent.[21] Major US investments are focused on 'consumer goods, chemicals, energy, agriculture, business process out-sourcing, transportation, and communications.'[22] The US has indicated its keenness on enhancing economic cooperation with Pakistan.[23] In February 2023, both countries concluded the ninth meeting under the US–Pakistan Trade and Investment Framework (TIFA).[24] Other areas of cooperation highlighted by the USA and Pakistan include extensive people-to-people contacts between the two countries.[25] Climate change is another area of potential cooperation as Pakistan encounters serious environmental challenges, and the summer 2022 floods affected one-third of the country and around 33 million people.

Conclusions

US-Pakistan relations are currently at a relatively neutral level, where ties have not fallen to the lows of the 1990s when Pakistan struggled with US sanctions, but US policymakers have conveyed a firm message to Pakistan that the US Administration is no longer willing to provide the easy military assistance it received in the 1980s and 2000s. For decades, Pakistan has sold the narrative to the West and its traditional donors that it is a state too dangerous to fail. A geo-strategically located nuclear weapon state, with a fastest-growing nuclear arsenal and a raging insurgency on its tribal borders, Pakistan cannot be allowed to fail. This has been the argument driven by Pakistan. However, Pakistan's decreasing relevance on the global stage and its inability to control its security situation within, continued political instability, and consistent economic crisis, which requires a constant flow of external assistance, seem to have altered the dynamics for Pakistan.

The US exit from Afghanistan has reduced Washington's direct interests in Afghanistan, but the USA still desires a stable Afghanistan that does not facilitate a global jihadi terror network. Washington certainly seeks Pakistan's support on this front. The killing of al-Qaeda leader Ayman al-Zawahri in Kabul by US drone strikes in 2022 indicates cooperation on counter-terrorism between Pakistan and the USA. Even though Pakistan has denied its involvement in the operation, the fact remains that the feasibility of an operation of this nature remains questionable without the Pakistan military's cooperation.

Pakistan's nuclear arsenal has been expanding at a rapid pace; it reportedly possesses over 168 warheads and its past record of nuclear proliferation raises questions about the integrity of the nuclear programme. The USA has been concerned about the safety and security of Pakistan's nuclear arsenal, specifically with the deteriorating security situation in the country. The Tehreek-e-Taliban Pakistan (TTP) has been emboldened after the Taliban takeover in Afghanistan. The terror organisation has gathered strength given the reported mergers with smaller/splinter groups and support from Afghanistan. The number of TTP terror attacks targeting the security establishment has gone up significantly in Pakistan. The USA cannot overlook the challenges of a Nuclear Pakistan. President Biden did express concern when he said Pakistan is "one of the most dangerous nations in the world" as it has "nuclear weapons without any cohesion".[26]

There are alterations in the dimensions of the US-Pakistan relationship from a strong military and security-based relationship to a more comprehensive relationship that focuses on the economy, trade, climate change, human rights and counter-terrorism. The relationship is likely to stay neutral unless a major strategic development elevates Pakistan's strategic relevance once again. The USA will continue to engage with Pakistan on non-traditional security issues. On the other hand, while Pakistan welcomes Washington's cooperation on non-security issues, it is keen to revive the security dimension in the relationship. Even though, Pakistan's military modernization has been very significant with Chinese assistance in the last two decades, Islamabad has always welcomed US equipment.

Given the evolving situation of the US-Pakistan relationship and the strained India-Pakistan relationship, the critical question for New Delhi is whether the USA can persuade Pakistan to change its strategic calculus. Pakistan, despite its deep economic crisis and political upheaval, has accelerated its covert operations, such as arms-dropping and drug-dropping through drones in Punjab (in India). Can the changing approach towards Pakistan compel it to rethink its strategy of using terrorism against India (and Afghanistan), which has had a severe blowback? And, very importantly, how will Pakistan revive its strategic relevance?

NOTES

1. Margaret Bourke-White, *Halfway to Freedom: A Report on the New India in the Words and Photographs of Margaret Bourke-White* (New York: Simon & Schuster, 1949), 91-93 as cited in Hussain Haqqani, *Magnificent Delusions: Pakistan, The United States, and an Epic History of Misunderstanding* (New Delhi: Thomson Press India Ltd, 2012), pp. 8-9.
2. Ibid, p. 9.
3. Office of the Historian, *Foreign Relations of the United States, 1947, The British Commonwealth; Europe*, vol. III, 845.00/5–247: Telegram, New Delhi, 2 May 1947, 10 a.m. https://history.state.gov/historicaldocuments/frus1947v03/d96, accessed on 18 May 2023.
4. Pran Chopra, "Pakistan Squanders A Strategic Advantage," in Ajay Darshan Behera and Mathew Joseph (eds.), *Pakistan in a Changing Strategic Context* (New Delhi: Knowledge World, 2004), p. 90.

5. Dennis Kux, *The United States and Pakistan, 1947-2000* (Oxford: Oxford University Press, 2001), p. 67.
6. Ibid, p. 69.
7. Shahid Javed Burki, *Historical Dictionary of Pakistan* (New Delhi: Vision Books, 2003), p. 337.
8. Dennis Kux, n 5, p. 74.
9. Ibid, pp. 86-87.
10. Gen Khalid Mahmud Arif, *Working with Zia: Pakistan's Power Politics 1977-1988* (Karachi: Oxford University Press, 1955), pp. 340-341.
11. "Rescheduling of the Debt of Pakistan," Paris Club, 13 December 2001, https://clubdeparis.org/en/communications/press-release/rescheduling-of-the-debt-of-pakistan-13-12-2001, accessed on 1 June 2023.
12. US Defence Security Cooperation Agency, http:www.dsca.mil
13. See, Susan B. Epstein and K. Alan Kronstadt, *Pakistan: U.S. Foreign Assistance*, 1 July 2013, CRS Report, R41856, https://sgp.fas.org/crs/row/R41856.pdf, accessed on 10 August 2022.
14. President Trump's first tweet of 2018.
15. K. Alan Kronstadt, *Pakistan and Pakistan-U.S. Relations*, 22 May 2023, CRS Report, R47565, p. 1, https://crsreports.congress.gov/product/pdf/R/R47565/6, accessed on 1 June 2023.
16. Anwar Iqbal, "US Generals express concern over Pakistan's nuclear arsenal in wake of Taliban takeover of Afghanistan," *Dawn*, 29 September 2021, https://www.dawn.com/news/1649127/us-generals-express-concern-over-pakistans-nuclear-arsenal-in-wake-of-taliban-takeover-of-afghanistan, accessed on 2 June 2023.
17. Patricia Zengerle and Humeyra Pamuk, "Blinken says U.S. will assess Pakistan ties over Afghanistan's future," *Reuters*, 14 September 2021, https://www.reuters.com/world/asia-pacific/blinken-says-us-will-assess-pakistan-ties-over-afghanistans-future-2021-09-13/, accessed on 1 June 2023.
18. CRS Report, n 15, p. 2.
19. US Embassy and Consulates in Pakistan, "Two day US-Pakistan Counterterrorism dialogue concludes in Pakistan," 7 March 2023, https://pk.usembassy.gov/two-day-u-s-pakistan-counterterrorism-dialogue-concludes-in-islamabad/, as cited in CRS Report, n 15, p. 2.
20. U.S. Department of State, "U.S. Relations with Pakistan," 15 August 2022, https://www.state.gov/u-s-relations-with-pakistan/, accessed on 20 August 2022.
21. Ibid.
22. Ibid.
23. See Elizabeth Horst, "The Future of US-Pakistan Relations," The Wilson Centre, You Tube Video, 27 April 2023, https://www.wilsoncenter.org/event/future-us-pakistan-relations, accessed on 12 May 2023.
24. Office of the United States Trade Representative, "Joint Statement from the 9th US-Pakistan TIFA Council Ministerial," 23 February 2023, https://ustr.gov/about-us/policy-offices/press-office/press-releases/2023/february/joint-statement-9th-us-pakistan-tifa-council-ministerial, accessed on10 June 2023.
25. "The Future of US-Pakistan Relations," n 23.
26. "Nukes without any cohesion, US President Biden terms Pakistan 'one of the most dangerous nations'," *The Indian Express*, 16 October 2022, https://indianexpress.com/article/world/pakistan-nuclear-weapons-most-dangerous-nations-in-the-world-joe-biden-8210160/, accessed on 22 June 2023.

9

Stunted Ties: Russia's Troubled Relations with Pakistan

Amb. D.B. Venkatesh Varma

When Russian Foreign Minister Sergey Lavrov met Pakistan's Foreign Minister Bilawal Bhutto in Goa on 4 May 2023, it was yet another bilateral on the sidelines of a multilateral meeting. It kept up the appearances of a relationship, which both sides know was long stunted but neither side was willing to abandon. Bilawal Bhutto had earlier visited Moscow for a bilateral visit where he met FM Lavrov on 30 January 2023.

Troubled Past

Pakistan has had troubled relations with the Soviet Union since its creation. When he met Ambassador K.P.S. Menon in 1953, Stalin doubted the viability of a state based on religion but with two different linguistic people – a prescient comment two decades before the breakup of Pakistan. Pakistan's willingness to be used by the USA and the United Kingdom as a treaty ally and as a staging point for military containment of the Soviet Union contrasted with India's independent foreign policy. This made a strong impression on Soviet leaders which till today forms one of the pillars of Russian policy towards South Asia.

Amongst the big powers, the Soviet Union and later the Russian Federation invested in an 'India-first' policy earlier than others and has maintained it over several decades. The Soviet Union flirted briefly during the 1960s, and perhaps towards the end of the Cold War period in the late 1980s, of balancing India and Pakistan (including during the Tashkent Conference after the inconclusive 1965 war); it also kept open the option of arms supplies until 1969. When discussions for the Indo-Soviet treaty started that year, the initial Soviet position was to offer a similar one to Pakistan. However, in the months leading up to the conclusion of the 1971 Indo-Soviet Treaty, there was a fundamental shift in Soviet strategic preference towards India that in its essential form continues to this day.

Pakistan's role as a front-line state for the USA against Soviet intervention in Afghanistan in the 1980s cut deep wounds in the Soviet psyche including the fundamentally duplicitous nature of the Pakistani state in fulfilling international commitments. This was apparent in the implementation of the Geneva Accords negotiated to facilitate Soviet withdrawal and thereafter in the treatment meted out to President Najibullah. During the early Yeltsin years, Russian interest in India waned. The descent of Afghanistan into chaos during the civil war and the Taliban takeover was a concern for Russia but its interests were defensive in nature limited to protecting Tajikistan and other Central Asian states from the spill over of Islamic extremism – for which Pakistan was seen as both a source of trouble and an essential interlocutor for managing the threat. This duality in Russian perception has been in existence since then.

India-first Arms Transfers Policy

Under President Putin, Russian policy has accorded priority to India dropping any pretence of equating or balancing relations with Pakistan. Putin's coming to power also coincided with the return of US influence in Pakistan in order to tackle the al-Qaeda and Taliban threat in Afghanistan as part of the US global war on terrorism. Putin was also keen to build on the momentum in Russia's relations with India that he inherited from the later phase of the Yeltsin presidency. This was taken forward by the Declaration on Strategic Partnership that was concluded during Putin's visit to India in October 2000.

Russia's objective has been not to impair relations with India by crossing the red line of substantive arms transfers to Pakistan. The Soviet Union had observed restraint in arms transfers to Pakistan after 1969. In the two decades of the 1990s and the 2000s Russia undertook limited supplies to Pakistan including about 32 Mi-17 transport helicopters between 1996 and 2003 and four Mi-35M combat helicopters in 2015 as well as two additional Mi-17 transport helicopters the same year. Between 2007 and 2020, Russia is reported to have supplied through China about 190 RD 93 engines that were integral to the Chinese-supplied JF-17 combat aircraft to Pakistan.

According to the Stockholm International Peace Research Institute (SIPRI) figures, the total value of arms supplied by Russia to Pakistan up to 2022 was less than USD 770 million. This figure is insignificant compared to the substantial arms supplies that Pakistan has received in the same period from China, the USA and others including France, the UK, and Ukraine. The table below shows that the Soviet Union/Russia transferred between 1950 and 2022 only 1.83 per cent of the total foreign arms transfers to Pakistan as compared to the much larger amount transfers from others.

Sl. No.	*Country*	*Total Transfers to Pakistan 1950-2022*	*Percentage of total arms transfers to Pakistan in the period 1950-2022- 41654 million USD*
1.	China	18,877	45.31%
2.	USA	8,498	20.40%
3.	France	4,183	10%
4.	United Kingdom	2,242	5.3%
5.	Ukraine (1922-2022)	1706	5.3%
6.	Soviet Union/Russia	766	1.83%

Source: SIPRI Arms Transfers Data Base of April 2023. (all figures in million USD).

Further, there is an understanding between President Putin and Prime Minister Modi on Russia refraining from transferring combat related arms and munitions to Pakistan. It was also agreed that both sides would consult confidentially on any proposals that may be of concern to India. Upon India's request, Russia cancelled some contracted items and redirected them to third countries. Russian restraint in arms sales to Pakistan is related more to high-level understandings which have a kept a tight lid on such sales, even though there are strong commercial pressures from the Russian defence industry. The Russian Foreign Ministry is of the view that having a blanket ban undercuts Russian interests in Pakistan by providing India a veto at a time when the USA has a free run in the Indian defence market undercutting Russian interests and leaves Russia with no means to compete with other countries. Some sections of the Russian security agencies also have some sympathy with this view considering their interest in securing Pak cooperation on counter-terrorism issues. Pakistan, for its part, keeps up the pretence of a normal relationship with Russia by submitting ambitious arms shopping lists matching the best that Russia has supplied to India, while aware that its requests have had little success.

Russia is aware of the risks of imperilling its long-standing relations with India by undertaking arms transfers to Pakistan, a smaller market with limited financial resources. Similarly, Russia has not engaged Pakistan on cooperation in civil nuclear or space matters. While the current suspension of any arms transfers from Russia to Pakistan is a major diplomatic gain for India, underwritten by understandings at the summit level, it would be a mistake for India to take future trends for granted. There is sometimes a sense of entitlement in some sections of the Indian strategic community on Russian restraint on arms supplies to Pakistan, even while the same analysts have little to say with reference to US or Chinese arms transfers to Pakistan. In fact, it appears that resumption of arms transfers to Pakistan would be used by these analysts to justify a severance of India's defence relations with Russia and a turn towards the USA, even though there is no logical link between the two.

Afghanistan

After lying low in Afghanistan for more than two decades since the early 1990s, Russia stepped up its diplomatic activity once it sensed that the USA was determined to pull out its forces from that country, particularly during the Trump Administration. This phase began in 2016 but reached an active stage in Russian participation in the Doha discussions. Russia was represented by its Presidential Envoy on Afghanistan Ambassador Zamir Kabulov, who interacted closely with his American counterpart Zalmay Khalilzad. This cooperation was insulated from the tensions of the broader US-Russia relations, relating to arms control, Ukraine, and allegations of Russian interference in US elections and yielded substantive results in the form of the Doha agreements with the Taliban. It is another matter that US military incompetence and Taliban betrayal led to the collapse of the Doha agreements and the Taliban re-capture of Kabul. Russia has since maintained its embassy in Kabul.

Russian interest was to curry favour with the Taliban which it saw as the eventual victor in the Afghan civil war and to facilitate an orderly withdrawal of US forces, which was the stated aim of the USA. It entailed Russia to have an active diplomatic commitment with prospects of substantial influence in Kabul while achieving its long-cherished goal of withdrawal of US forces from the region. In working for these objectives Russia saw more common ground with China and Pakistan, which participated actively, while keeping India out in the 'Troika Plus Pakistan' which ran parallel to the Doha talks and the less frequently held larger grouping – the Moscow Format meetings which included India and other countries. Like the USA, Russia extended lukewarm support for India's inclusion in the Troika Plus talks, but in the face of strong push back from

Pakistan and China, backed down. India's lack of leverage with the Taliban during the crucial phase and its decision to stick with President Ghani, despite signs that his position was increasingly untenable are reasons Russian interlocutors provide for not engaging more actively with India in the run-up to the dramatic events of August 2021. The absence of India naturally provided additional space for Pakistan in its interactions with Russia on Afghanistan. However, this space has been reduced somewhat in recent months as India has opened its own channels with the Taliban and now has a diplomatic presence in Kabul.

The Afghan file has for long not received the full attention of the Kremlin and thus became the preserve of the Russian Ministry of Foreign Affairs (MFA) and some sections of the Security Council which see Pakistan as an unreliable but necessary interlocutor on matters relating to Afghanistan and Central Asia. Russia is also aware of Pakistan playing China's cats paw in the region especially about China's ambitious Belt and Road Initiative (BRI) projects which if successful will delink Central Asia from the old Soviet-era routes and relink with Chinese dominated trade and connectivity links in which Pakistan's China Pakistan Economic corridor (CPEC) is a central element.

Russia has thus far adopted a non-confrontational approach to the BRI with China but has its own concerns about BRI success coming at the expense of its own influence in the region. Russia has so far not endorsed any of the projects connected with the China Pakistan Economic Corridor (CPEC). However, the same cannot be said of the future if there is an overwhelming desire on the part of the Central Asian States to use Pakistan for connectivity purposes and access to the Arabian Sea. India's first line of defence is therefore according alternatives to the Central Asian states through the International North-South Transport Corridor (INSTC,) but has so far not accorded either the policy priority nor the resources to address this geopolitical challenge. India's efforts are also stymied by the fear of Indian companies of US sanctions in using the INSTC. While Pakistan too faces formidable challenges in operationalizing the CPEC, given the stakes involved and the resources that China is prepared to commit, over time the risks of territorial marginalization for India may increase. At present, India and Russia have common interests but if India is not able to access its own neighbourhood, it will be seen as a sign of grave continental weakness and Russia, along with the other Central Asian states, will see the writing on the wall and act accordingly.

Weak Bilateral Relations

Russia has long recognized that Pakistan has traded its internal weakness for borrowed strength from abroad, a pattern that was familiar during the Cold War period with external benefactors such as USA, China, and major Gulf states. Aware that it is not in the same league as these countries having leverage within Pakistani ruling circles through various inducements, Russia's patient wait for an opening came with the decisive turn against the USA by Imran Khan in late 2021 and early 2022. Despite the rising tensions with the West over Ukraine, President Putin hosted Imran Khan on 24 February 2022 – the first Pak PM visit to Moscow in 23 years. (In comparison with India, barring the COVID period, there have been annual bilateral summits without exception since 2000.) The visit did not result in any major breakthroughs. President Putin called Prime Minister Modi to brief him on the visit. FM Lavrov also spoke to the EAM that day. When Imran Khan was forced to resign, the Russian MFA said that it was the result of 'shameless' US interference in the internal affairs of Pakistan. Between US and Chinese influence in Pakistan, Russia would prefer the latter, due to its broader global confrontation with the USA, a point that should not be lost sight of in the context of its approach to the Shehbaz Sharif Government now in power in Islamabad. However, it would be a mistake to conclude that Russia would work with China through Pakistan against India's interests. Besides, the India relationship for Russia is vitally important for a broader balance of power in Asia. But India would need to demonstrate its willingness and capacity to engage actively on Eurasian issues, bilaterally or through the SCO.

While the Pak-Russia bilateral Joint Commission met in January 2023 in Islamabad, Pakistan's economic crisis cast a dark shadow on the prospects for the flagship energy project of constructing a North-South gas pipeline with Russian technical and financial assistance. This project has dragged on for years largely due to Pakistan's inability to raise funds for its share of the project. The current focus of Pakistan is on securing concessional oil supplies from Russia and for food imports; Russia delivered about 60 tonnes of wheat in 2022 and is looking for an additional 700,000 tonnes in 2023.

Pakistan has looked to Russia for importing crude oil at concessional rates. Despite differences in policy on Ukraine, Russia agreed to provide concessional supplies of Ural crude though not at the deep concessional rate that it offered to India. Even then, Pakistan felt it was profitable to import Russian crude up to 100,000 bpd. The first cargo arrived in Pakistan in June 2023 but was disappointing and did not meet Pakistani expectations. Large Russian vessels could not be accommodated in Pakistani ports requiring the transfer of the crude to smaller ships which added to the transportation costs. In addition, Pakistani refineries, which were adapted to refine Middle East crude, found the Russian crude unsuitable unless mixed with other crudes thus further raising the costs. Pakistan also found it difficult to make payments to Russia in Chinese Yuan due to shortage of this currency. Further shipments from Russia may slow down or stop altogether.

Ukraine Conflict

Pakistan has adopted a schizophrenic approach on the Ukraine conflict. On the one hand, it has abstained on UN voting condemning Russia and has been careful in its public statements not to endorse the Western framing of the conflict, but on the other, has extended military assistance to Ukraine through the UK and other NATO countries. These include artillery munitions, projectiles, and primers. Media reports indicate intense pressure from the USA and the UK to fall in line, including in the context of its negotiations with the IMF for a financial assistance package. Ukrainian Foreign Minister Dmytro Kuleba on an official visit to Pakistan on 20-21 July 2023 met his Pakistani counterpart, Bilawal Bhutto Zardari, and called on Pak PM Shehbaz Sharif. The main purpose of the visit was to ensure continued supply of Pak stockpiles of ammunition; in return Ukraine promised to supply Mi-17 helicopters for the Pak Air Force. Ukraine has also been a wheat supplier to Pakistan – it supplied about a million tonnes in 2021. These supplies were now imperilled due to the suspension of the grain deal by Russia.

Pakistan has a well-established defence relationship with Ukraine dating back to the 1990s when it supplied T80 tanks and Mi-17 helicopters. China may also be using Pakistan as a proxy for maintaining contacts with the Ukrainian defence industry, which China has been eyeing for a while. Despite reports of Pak assistance to Ukraine, Russia has so far pulled back its punches, except for minor demarches with Pakistan. It has so far not withheld energy or food exports. This may be explained by a mirror division amongst Russian decision-makers on Pakistan – while there is pervasive suspicion of Pak actions, there are sections, mainly within the Russian MFA who feel that shutting the door on Pakistan completely would be detrimental to Russia's broader regional interests in Afghanistan. There is also the issue of priorities –- Russia would like to prevail in the Ukraine conflict while minimizing the costs to its regional interests elsewhere. Additionally, there is also the thinking that however marginal, relations with Pakistan are necessary for retaining some leverage on India's expanding relations with the USA. This is more at the bureaucratic level rather than a view held by the Kremlin.

Multilateral Fora

Russia has stood firmly with India on issues relating to Kashmir – more than any other permanent member of the UNSC. Russia has been steadfast in its support for bilateral dialogue based on the Shimla Agreement and the Lahore Declaration and on the issue of abrogation of Article 370, Russia has said that India was well within its constitutional right to take that action. In the FATF, Russia supported Indian demarches on the issue of grey listing of Pakistan but only up to a point, knowing that Pakistan was separately doing a deal with the USA and China on this issue. In the SCO, Russia has insisted that Pakistan keep out its bilateral issues with India but on other issues it has found Pakistan siding with Russian and Chinese positions more than India. However, Russia sees India's participation far more significant than that of Pakistan in elevating the global relevance of the SCO. Russia has also respected Indian demarches not to undertake bilateral or multilateral military exercises in Pak occupied Kashmir but has conducted exercises elsewhere in Pakistan

Looking Ahead

According priority to India in the region and in global affairs is now a firmly established objective in Russia's foreign policy, which was reaffirmed in the latest Foreign Policy Concept of the Russian Federation released in March 2023. Russia has exercised restraint in its relations with Pakistan due to Indian sensitivities, including it as part of its understandings at the summit level. This is a positive attribute of our bilateral relations with Russia, which is often taken for granted but one which requires constant nurturing. The changing regional situation, including in Afghanistan and Central Asia, and the growing Chinese role and conflict with the USA, merits close monitoring for the implications they may have for changing the dynamics of Russia's relations with Pakistan. The triangular competition between the USA, China, and Russia would also impact the triangular India-Russia-Pakistan relations. Though it has now largely tilted in India's favour, keeping it that way will require deft diplomatic attention and handling rather than a sense of entitlement and hubris. In the changing regional dynamics, the traditionally low-key relations of Russia with Pakistan may lead to new trends as both countries adjust to the new realities of US-Russia and US-China conflicts. This may create new bedfellows as the instability in Afghanistan, Central Asia and South Asia intersect in Pakistan. India needs to watch these trends carefully, and not take Russian policy in the region for granted.

10

India-Pakistan Relations: Everlasting Enmity or Is there a Way Out?

T.C.A. Raghavan

India-Pakistan relations set themselves in an adversarial mould even as they emerged as independent and sovereign nation-states some seven-plus decades earlier. That mould has solidified over the years and newer issues have cemented themselves on to older points of difference and dispute. The present mould accordingly comprises layers upon layers of insecurities, suspicions, and mistrust. It includes now the full spectrum of issues that comprise the negative aspects in interstate relations – geo-political and strategic rivalry, historical baggage, identity conflict, major territorial disputes, and finally power asymmetries. In the India-Pakistan context, the specifics of this portfolio are well known and it would be tedious to list each element.

Given the intensity and longevity of the India-Pakistan lockjaw, it can easily be ranked with other long-standing international disputes – the Arab-Israeli imbroglio in West Asia or between North and South Korea in NE Asia. There are other examples of bilateral relationships deeply underwritten by bitter historical memory and strategic rivalry such as Japan-China or Japan-South Korea. To our west, the Saudi Arabia-Iran interface, although they are not immediate neighbours, often exhibited till recently features of interstate relations in which older historical fault lines are exacerbated by modern geostrategic rivalry. The current crisis in Europe following the breakdown in Russia-Ukraine relations provides yet another example. While larger geopolitical explanations remain valid and relevant in explaining the war in Ukraine-Russian rivalries such as Russian insecurities vis-a-vis NATO and the USA, the ongoing war also remains as a standing and current example of just how fraught relations between neighbours can get.

None of these examples approximate to all the varied dimensions of the India-Pakistan relationship and the brute intensity it has exhibited for such a long period. In fact, each neighbouring country relationship has its own unique features. But there is some analytical value of seeing a historically bad India-Pakistan relationship as a subset of the larger phenomena of neighbourhood relations.

Neighbourhoods in fact comprise a core feature of any country's diplomacy and pose possibly the most enduring challenge to its foreign policy. Thus, at different points of time, India's relations with its other immediate neighbours have resembled features of the India-Pakistan interface. For instance, with Bangladesh and Myanmar relations have been impacted because of the support that was available to Indian insurgent groups from these countries. Sri Lanka in the 1980s provided an extreme example of how India can get sucked into external civic conflict situations because of ethnic spillovers and overlaps across national boundaries. A whole range of India-Nepal issues have periodically surfaced imparting to it also a volatile character. The China factor similarly looms large in geopolitical terms in each of our neighbourhood relations.

Viewed in this context, the India-Pakistan relationship does not appear so much exceptional as conforming to the general pattern of troubled neighbourhood relations. Yet, notwithstanding all the merits of a comparative picture and analysis, the distinctive features of the India-Pakistan relationship obviously also stand out. Their divisions and territorial disputes, underwritten by deep religious and national identity issues, have had an enduring quality to them. Both are declared nuclear-weapon states but that has not curbed the volatility of their interface. Tensions have on occasion led to kinetic and conflict situations. In each of these the possibility of escalation could never have been ruled out. Perhaps more than anything else there is a narrative quality attached to the other country in both India and Pakistan which takes their relationship in a different orbit almost constantly.

Everlasting Enmity as Doctrine

So, is there a way out? This is a question that has an obvious topicality to it today given the long slump in bilateral relations since 2016. It has, however, often reverberated in each of the past seven decades. The US scholar of India and Pakistan, Stephen Cohen, had posed much the same question by the title of a highly regarded study on the bilateral relationship 'Shooting for a Century'. The question Stephen Cohen thus asked was whether the two were destined to be permanently adversarial states, even after a century of their establishment.[1]

The idea of a permanent state of enmity has both a wide prevalence and also a long provenance in both countries. In India in the 1950s and early 1960s, Krishna Menon was regarded as the most consistent naysayer on any suggestion or initiative to attempt to improve relations with Pakistan. He was a powerful member of the cabinet, first as a minister without portfolio and then as Defence Minister. The then Indian High Commissioner to Pakistan, Rajeshwar Dayal, recalled that Krishna Menon possessed an aversion to Pakistan that verged on the pathological. He, Dayal recounted, "would point a warning finger at me whenever I ran into him in Delhi and say that I was on the wrong track and no good would come of whatever I was trying to do in Pakistan."[2]

Such views have persisted in both countries over each subsequent decade and can be frequently encountered in both countries to the effect that any initiative directed at improving relations is foredoomed to failure. This is a doctrine of 'everlasting enmity' and it has shown durability through all the vicissitudes of India-Pakistan relations.

In both countries, the belief is strong that it is the essential nature of the other state that poses an existential threat to it. Added to this foundational difference are other deep divisions – the two-nation theory versus secular state and Kashmir in particular. To these differences in foundational narratives over the decades, additional layers of strategic disputes have accumulated – terrorism, water, 1971 and the break-up of Pakistan and others.

The evolution of Pakistan's domestic policy has since the Sixties also been a major factor in shaping the narrative of 'everlasting enmity' in India. This argument, in very brief, is that to maintain its commanding position in Pakistan's polity and society, the army needs a constant and enduring adversary in India and the role of the military in Pakistan therefore constitutes a structural impediment to any real change coming about in India-Pakistan relations. In Pakistan too, there has been a convergent narrative since 1947 on the essential fraudulence of Indian secularism, and since the coming of the BJP to power in 2014, the view that Hindu majoritarian India is an existential threat to Pakistan. This has become a self-contained and self-fulfilling prophecy driven analysis. In brief, the thesis of 'everlasting enmity' has deep roots and clearly, from conflicting perspectives, on either side, is a position of substantive content.

How has 'Everlasting Enmity' Worked in Practice?

Clearly the overall texture of the relationship over the past seven decades would prove the doctrine of enmity correct. History in a sense vindicates the naysayers, and to many it has also done so unfailingly. Major initiatives have faltered and failed and a recurring pattern of crisis situations has regularly punctuated the chronology of the relationship.

Yet notwithstanding this history of failure and setbacks what is unusual in India-Pakistan relations is the consistency with which efforts to stabilize, improve and even normalize relations have been made. Equally unusual is that the full spectrum of the political environment of both countries has, at different points of time, embarked on such ventures. For instance, over the past quarter century, all the principal political parties of India and Pakistan have been in government at different stages. In Pakistan, additionally, the Army was directly in charge for significant periods of time. This period too in fact shows the characteristic feature of the India-Pakistan relationship – the predominantly adversarial mould yet with regular contrarian impulses in the form of initiatives to impart some element of positivity.

India-Pakistan: A Quarter Century Chronology

The Positives	*The Negatives*
• Lahore Declaration (February 1999) • Delhi Lahore Bus Service (February 1999) • Agra Summit (July 2001) • Islamabad Summit Declaration (January 2004) • Composite Dialogue Meetings (2004-07) • Kokraphar Munabao Rail Service - Thar Express (February 2006) • Increase in Trade; Pakistan Negative List Announcement (February 2012) • Cross-LoC Travel and Trade • Presence of South Asian Heads of Government at swearing in of New Government (May 2014) • PM Modi visit to Lahore (December 2015) • Kartarpur Saheb Opening (November 2019) • LoC Ceasefire (February 2021)	• Kargil (May-July 1999) • Hijacking IC 814 (December 1999) • Srinagar Assembly Attack (October 2001) • Parliament Attack (December 2001) • Mumbai Suburban Train Blasts (July 2006) • Kabul Embassy Attack (July 2008) • Mumbai Terrorist Attack (November 2008) • LoC Clashes post 2013 and Ceasefire under Stress? • Surgical Strike (September 2016) • Balakot (February, 2019) • J&K Legislative Changes (August 2019) • Diplomatic downsizing; no trade; minimal exchanges.

These details are well known but nevertheless bear repetition if only to qualify the picture of a monochromatic relationship.

In the first decade and a half of this century the battle over the Kargil heights, the hijacking of IC 814, the Mumbai attacks of 27/11/2008 and other numerous terrorist outrages elsewhere, and the skirmishes on the Line of Control (LoC), – all the staples of the India-Pakistan dialectic – and the prevailing mould are self-evident. Yet, initiatives to reverse the negative trends have not been lacking and have shown continuity through the governments of the UPA and the NDA in India and through Military, PPP, PML(N) and PTI governments in Pakistan.

Even post the 2016 slump in bilateral relations, such a trend persists. The decline post 2016 is bookended by the major initiatives of 2014 and 2015 – the invitation to and its acceptance by PM Nawaz Sharif to attend the swearing in of NDA II swearing in and PM Modi's dramatic visit to Lahore in December 2015. Subsequently, the reaffirmation of the LoC ceasefire and the opening of the Kartarpur Sahib corridor provide 'against the grain' evidence of the adversarial mould events and these appear additionally significant since they took place after the August 2019 legislative changes with reference to Jammu and Kashmir.

In brief, an overall adversarial mould but with recurrent and surprising contrarian impulses are evident in the past seven years too which has otherwise been an excessively negative phase of the relationship. This pattern is in fact a characteristic even in the full 75-year chronology and gives to this otherwise conventionally negative neighbourhood relationship a persistent counter trend and counter narrative.

Misunderstanding 'Stabilization Initiatives'

To the naysayers in both countries, these initiatives are instances of eccentric and quixotic behaviour or at best instances of a misguided sense of idealism. These are certainly the judgements that have been visited on the major initiatives that characterize recent India-Pakistan history. In India, such indeed are the assessments from this perspective of major initiatives such as PM Vajpayee's Lahore visit or invitation to General Pervez Musharraf for the Agra summit, PM Manmohan Singh's multiple efforts over the 2004-13 period and in particular the back-channel negotiations or PM Modi's 2014-15 initiatives. Such assessments often base themselves on taking the optics and hyperbole surrounding such initiatives at face value and as representing the substance of the motive of why they were embarked on.

However, the persistence of such initiatives and the traction they have sometimes gathered, admittedly for finite periods, suggests that other explanations are needed. These possibly can be usefully found in the realm of a deeper appreciation of the complexity of neighbourhood relations in general and in South Asia in particular.

Most neighbourhood relationships have ups and downs and go through different phases. In South Asia, if each relationship with India were to be plotted graphically most graphs would show something akin to a sine curve. (A sine curve at its simplest is a curve with constant oscillations). A flat line would be exceptional. Viewed simply in terms of such imaginary curves, India-Pakistan relations would resemble India-Sri Lanka, India-Nepal, or India-Bangladesh given the vicissitudes each relationship has gone through. There would of course be the important difference that the crests and troughs, especially the latter, are far more pronounced in the India-Pakistan case. In many ways, the answer to the question 'Is there a way out?' lies in this – can the crests and troughs be made more moderate, less prone to crises and supercharged situations, in brief, made more manageable?

Seen in this light, the contrarian trend to the predominant adversarial India Pakistan mould acquires a new character. It can be seen as driven not so much by high idealism or even by the desire of a particular set of leaders to go down in history as legendary 'peacemakers'. Perhaps, hard-headed pragmatism and a consciousness of how your own interests are best served are better motives to be extracted from any analysis of motives.

The current situation post 2016 of a sharp and significant downward trend in bilateral relations can also be similarly contextualized and the 'sine curve' kind of oscillating behaviour seen as a closer approximation to reality than a flat line or a graph continuously plunging downwards.

India-Pakistan 2015-2023

July 2015	Ufa India-Pakistan Summit.
December 2015	EAM visits Islamabad; Agreement on Comprehensive Bilateral Dialogue.
December 2015	PM visits Lahore.
January 2016	Pathankot airbase terrorist attack.
September 2016	Uri terrorist attack/surgical strikes.
February 2019	Pulwama terrorist attack.

February 2019	India withdraws MFN; Balakot air strike; Pakistan's response.
August 2019	Legislative changes with reference to J&K; Pakistan suspends trade; informal UNSC meeting on J&K.
November 2019	Kartarpur Saheb opening.
June 2020	Downsizing of diplomatic missions.
February 2021	LoC ceasefire.
March 2022	Handling of mistaken launch of Brahmos missile.

In brief, these contrarian initiatives can be seen as being directed towards not changing the basic nature of the other state or even changing the essentially adversarial nature of the India-Pakistan relationship but rather moderating its oscillations and stabilizing its overall contours. The question posed at the beginning of this essay therefore becomes not so much 'Is there a way out?' as 'Can an adversarial mould be softened and managed'?

Can an Adversarial Mould be Managed and Softened?

The contrarian trends against the doctrine of everlasting enmity have comprised over the years a wide spectrum of activities. These include 'Talks about Talks', 'Confidence Building Measures', 'High-Level Summitry', 'Restraint' even in the face of grave provocation, and on occasion attempts at 'Dispute resolution'. Public enthusiasm, often drummed up but usually spontaneous, provides the hyperbole and collapses all of these different activities under the general rubric of 'peace process'. This hyperbole disguises the extent to which the basic impetus to each such undertaking was a stabilization impulse. It is hardly surprising that with the emergence of both countries as formally declared nuclear-weapon powers, a greater intensity would be evident over the past quarter century in such stabilization efforts even as the basic adversarial mould has remained intact and even strengthened. One can reasonably predict that such efforts will recur in the future also and the current phase of downturn and a virtual freeze in bilateral contact is no more than a phase and is by no means a new status quo or even a new normal.

What gives the adversarial mould as also the contrarian initiatives their enduring character? The reasons for the strength of the adversarial mould are straightforward enough – differences on issues such as Kashmir are foundational. That also means that related issues such as 'Terrorism' for instance acquire even greater conceptual complexity (the freedom fighter vs. terrorist binary). Even with a greater meeting of minds on how to deal with this in practice (difficult enough in any circumstances) the conceptual complexity will always come in the way of longer-term sustainability. In brief, the adversarial mould is not going to erode or disappear anytime soon.

If that is a somewhat depressing prognosis it is also useful to recall that even with strong foundational divergences, stabilization measures have always been attempted and these have often worked for significant periods of time. Thus, pragmatic measures for softening the LoC remained in place for over a decade over 2005-15 notwithstanding major setbacks in other areas of the relationship during this period. Similarly, the reaffirmation of the LoC ceasefire in 2021 or the opening of the Kartarpur Sahib corridor coincided in 2019 with one of the worst slumps in the history of the relationship. In a longer time frame, the different versions of the 'Composite Dialogue' process extending to the 'Resumed Dialogue' and the 'Comprehensive Bilateral Dialogue' can be seen as evolution of the same core of stabilization being remodelled and regrouped to address recurrent crisis.

What underwrites these efforts is not the hyperbole that surrounds or greets such initiatives from different constituencies in both countries but rather a discernible pragmatism. Such pragmatism is rooted in the consciousness of the deep divides that exist and that no ready-made solution is available in the foreseeable future to resolve differences. Can such differences be managed and contained therefore becomes the central issue. Such management and containment strategies and measures will always be limited in scope and time as recurrence of crisis may be unavoidable. The expectation however is that stabilization measures are helpful and increase the possibilities that crisis situations will not spill over into unchartered domains.

To conclude, neighbourhood situations are inherently dynamic and in any of them it is unrealistic to expect a stable or static situation for a prolonged period. Each country-specific toolkit therefore requires constant modification, updating, and even overhaul. At the same time, notwithstanding every effort to have a balanced and appropriate policy set in place, situations will inevitably arise that defy quick resolution and bilateral relations will come under strain.

If these general considerations apply to all bilateral relationships in South Asia where India is concerned, they apply with even greater force for Pakistan. Assessing the 'way out' therefore means being conscious of the nature of neighbourhood complexities. Expectations about a final resolution of all disputes and a constantly stable relationship thereafter are unrealistic. Realism demands seeking interim even temporary improvisations and carefully constructed regimens of stability while not being blind to their temporal nature. There is then no alternative to the hard, constant, and sometimes boring, grind of diplomacy. That is the only way out!

NOTES

1. Stephen Cohen, *Shooting for a Century: Finding Answers to the India-Pakistan Conundrum* (Noida: Harper Collins, 2013).
2. Rajeshwar Dayal, *A Life in Our Times* (New Delhi: Orient Longman, 1998), p. 282.

11

Pakistan's Afghan Dilemma: To Engage or Confront the Taliban

Ajay Bisaria

With the Taliban completing two years of its latest spell of ruling Afghanistan, Pakistan faces a wrenching dilemma: whether to continue engaging the Kabul regime, or risk estrangement by responding robustly to the terrorism challenge from the Tehreek-e-Taliban Pakistan (TTP). Both Pakistan and Afghanistan currently feel short-changed by their security relationship. For Pakistan, the Taliban is soft on the TTP; for the Taliban, Pakistan's attacks on the group within Afghan territory are unacceptable. Notwithstanding these security concerns, the structural reality of Afghan dependence on Pakistan remains, as does Pakistan's perceived strategic imperative to control the Kabul regime. Lurking in the background is the traditional suspicion between the Punjabis and the Pashtuns.

Despite Pakistan's advocacy, global recognition of the Taliban regime – or the defreezing of its financial resources – remains an elusive goal. The Taliban should take solace in the fact that no kinetic operation has been launched so far by external powers to drive its forces out of Kabul. But a smaller military challenge to the Kabul regime remains; it comes from the Panjshir Valley holdouts of the previous US-backed regime (including resistance leaders like Ahmed Masood and former Vice-President Amrullah Saleh), as also from elements of the Islamic State: ISIS and IS-Khorasan Province. Fortunately for the Taliban, the Western world's attention has shifted away from Kabul; it is far too preoccupied with Russian actions in Europe and with China's global threat, particularly in the Indo-Pacific. The co-option of China in the Afghan theatre – and converging interests in extending the China-Pakistan Economic Corridor (CPEC) to Afghanistan – marks a significant shift in Pakistan's management of the Afghan situation following the withdrawal of US forces.

Taliban 3.0

The hope that Taliban 3.0 would become a puppet regime, seeking instructions from the Pakistan army, and delivering on key Pakistani political and strategic interests, has been belied. Pakistan's *bete noir*, the TTP, continues to have close links and sympathies within the ruling Afghan Taliban. The latest version of the Taliban may be less of a global threat than its previous avatars (Taliban, 1.0 ran the country under severe *Sharia* law conditions from 1996 to 2001 while Taliban 2.0 was the insurgency that tried to dislodge the US presence after 9/11 from 2002 to 2021; and Taliban 3.0 formed the Afghan government after the hasty US exit of August 2021[1]) but it has not delivered as Pakistan hoped on key security concerns. Pakistan's core objectives were to secure from the Taliban: (a) credible assurances it would not allow TTP safe havens in Afghan territory; (b) a sustained respect for the Durand Line; and (c) steps to remove India's influence from Afghanistan to eliminate the threat to Pakistan's 'strategic depth'. Since August 2021, none of these objectives have been fully realised; the Taliban proved to be less pliant than Pakistan expected.

Pakistan had rejoiced in the arrival of the Taliban regime in Kabul in August 2021. Then prime minister Imran Khan suggested that Afghanistan had broken the 'shackles of slavery'.[2] And then DG ISI Faiz Hameed had visited Afghanistan soon after the departure of US forces, to have tea with the Taliban, in a public assertion of ownership of the regime. However, the Taliban soon insisted on a measure of 'strategic autonomy' from Pakistan, to have its own version of an India policy and one of dealing with its TTP brethren. Pakistan, on its part, deferring to global sentiment, did not recognise the Taliban as it had done with extraordinary alacrity in 1996.

Beyond its political and security concerns, Pakistan is a key stakeholder in the stability of its western neighbour, thanks to the close to four million Afghans it already hosts in different cities. As it faces an economic meltdown, Pakistan, lacks the appetite for an influx of large numbers of Afghans breaching the Durand Line to escape chaos in their country.

Against that backdrop, where does Afghanistan stand nearly two years after the Taliban victory of 15 August 2021? It indeed faces one of the world's worst humanitarian, hunger and economic crises, but mercifully not the bloody civil war the world feared. While Afghanistan did not see a re-run of the chaos of the Nineties, the composition of the Taliban government became a source of global concern, as it included several UN-designated terrorists. Malnutrition and starvation remain a reality, even though the ground situation is not entirely clear. Women, children, and minorities are particularly badly affected, after enjoying a measure of freedom and respect in the two decades of US-backed regimes. Despite global pressure, the Taliban decreed that all women should be clad in burqas, accompanied by male chaperones and face restrictions in education. The Taliban clearly lacks the capacity to govern the country, even to the low standards of pre-2021, while it attempts to consolidate its rule and not repeat the mistakes of the 1990s. The Taliban benefit from not facing an insurgency like their predecessors. It killed an estimated 69,000 troops and police between 2001 and 2021 and rendered economic development dangerous or impossible in much of the country.[3]

Politically, the Taliban's search for legitimacy continues, both domestically and externally. Internally, the regime is relatively stable and unchallenged, despite reports of multiple factions pulling in different directions. A marker of the Taliban's lack of political confidence is its inability to hold the traditional *Loya Jirga* in Kabul, an essential rite of passage for any new king or leadership of Afghanistan. What it managed was a congregation of mullahs, which was seen as the Pakistani ISI's proxy for influence over the Taliban.

Internationally, Pakistan has advocated recognition and support for the Taliban regime, arguing in essence that no viable alternative exists. It has also helped the Taliban articulate some assurances to the global community. In a letter drafted to present the Taliban's reasonable face to the world, the Afghan regime's Foreign Minister Amir Khan Muttaqi assured the UN Security Council in April 2023:

> "During the past twenty months, the Afghan government – despite all pressures, sanctions, restrictions, limited facilities and the completely unexpected situation where the ashes of the twenty-year conflict had not yet been extinguished – was able to functionalize and strengthen the governance and policy-making systems, broaden the basis of governance vertically and horizontally, set the country's economic cycle in motion, provide social services transparently, operationalize the country's triplet courts, maintain the rule of law on every member of society without discrimination, and reduce administrative corruption to zero. These trends will continue for more effectiveness and efficiency."[4]

On the dangers of drugs and terrorists emanating from Afghanistan, the Taliban pointedly promised:

> "Today security is ensured across the country and we have/will not allow(ed) any individual or group to use Afghanistan's soil against others. Cultivation of narcotics has been prohibited in Afghanistan while basic programs have been undertaken for the rehabilitation of addicts as well."

On human rights and gender equality, the Taliban entered a clever caveat that 'all countries of the world have their own unique religious and cultural distinctions and face a degree of limitations where change can hopefully occur through consistent constructive partnership. The letter also made a plea to 'address issues such as informal interaction, frozen assets, banking restrictions and impose sanctions at the earliest'.

Despite all the right noises in their search for external legitimacy, diplomatic recognition for the Taliban is still not imminent, unlike in the 1990s. However, the conversation has begun. A former US ambassador to Afghanistan and a former CIA officer argued in May 2023 that the time had come for US recognition of the Taliban since the alternative would imply 'allow Afghanistan's dangerous descent into a hermit kingdom and forsake the insight and means to influence or shape events – would mean more dire consequences for all.'[5]

We seem now to have global acceptance and a regional consensus on the reality of the Taliban regime and even more, on the absence of an alternative. One marker of this pragmatism is the humanitarian aid that is being funnelled into Afghanistan. Aid routed through the government gives the Taliban some measure of legitimacy, since about two-fifths of the GDP is made up of foreign aid; and over three-fourths of public spending, including for women's education and health, comes from donors. Human rights and women's rights in Afghanistan are important conversations that foreign offices of donor nations normally have with their Parliaments, but interests have trumped values for the moment.

While Pakistan tries to lobby the West to deal with the Taliban, the central dilemma before the world is how to help the Afghan people without legitimising the Taliban regime. The leverage on the Taliban the West holds is of economic aid and political recognition, but these instruments need to be deployed to meet the strategic objective of countering the terrorism threat and the humanitarian one of providing succour to the Afghan people. The unspoken global compact with the Taliban appears to be that as long as they do not export terrorism, refugees and drugs, the world is willing to let in aid and accept the reality of the

Taliban regime. Or, at least, external powers do not for the moment have the appetite to displace them by force, given the experience of 20 years, and global distractions like the war in Ukraine and a new Cold War with China.

In a sense, Pakistan has not changed its policy towards Afghanistan from the 1970s. It has consistently mentored the Afghan mujahideen and all three editions of the Taliban. The USA and the West, on the other hand, have made several U-turns in their approach. From 1979 to 1989, Pakistan was critical to the mujahideen challenge to the Soviet occupation, which was more Zia's war than Reagan's or 'Charlie Wilson's war.'[6] From 1996, the Mujahideen regime was brazenly run by Rawalpindi. In the two decades of US occupation of the country from 2001, Pakistan continued its covert support of the Taliban insurgency, despite assuring the US-led coalition of partnership, and even as the TTP turned against it.

Pakistan continues to exercise significant control over most leaders of the Taliban 3.0 through three means: through the networks of clerics or mullahs, who have deep connections on both sides of the Durand Line; through the families of the Taliban still in Pakistan; and through the funds going across the Durand Line from various channels in Quetta and Peshawar, for the Taliban. The one lesson Pakistan's generals have learnt from the past is that they cannot afford to lose control over the Taliban.

While Pakistan's policy makers see the TTP as the primary challenge to their approach to Afghanistan, they also try to deal with the influence of global players like the USA, China, and India.

The TTP Factor

The terrorist challenge emerging from the TTP remains an existential security concern for Pakistan. In April 2022, soon after the PDM government headed by Shehbaz Sharif came to power, Pakistan launched attacks on the TTP within Afghan territory, killing several civilians. The Taliban summoned the Pakistani envoy for a scolding. The Taliban defence minister, Mullah Yaqoob, threatened retaliation. Pakistan's policy on TTP militants remained confused, altering between kinetic action and calls for dialogue with the TTP, setting what many observers thought was a bad example for the Baloch and Pashtun separatist movements at a time when Pakistan was in the middle of a major economic and political crisis. Pakistan's engagement with the Taliban regime gave primacy to the terrorism issue, with its talking points ironically matching the decades-old ones India uses for Pakistan: to not let territory in their control be used as safe havens by terrorists to attack their eastern neighbour.

The TTP upped the challenge even as Pakistan's army was weakened and preoccupied by internal political upheaval, groping for direction in 2022 during the transition months from army chief Bajwa to his successor, Asim Munir. Soon after Munir was appointed COAS in December 2022, deadly terrorist assaults blew up police lines in Peshawar (January 2023) and Lahore (February 2023). General Munir is believed to have declared that he would be harder on the TTP than his predecessor. While attitudes towards the TTP had shifted radically in Pakistan's security establishment since 2014, following the slaughter of over 130 students in Peshawar, Imran Khan's arrival softened the posture and gave political engagement precedence. With the TTP's increased entrenchment in Khyber Pakhtunkhwa's FATA region, Pakistan's security forces are stretched dealing with this threat. Pakistan's determination to confront the TTP with force has grown stronger, with this security problem even used as a justification to postpone provincial and federal elections.

Pakistan's media revealed intelligence reports that leaders of the ruling PDM (but not Imran Khan of the PTI), were being targeted by the TTP. In May 2023, a media report emerged that the names of PML-N's Maryam Nawaz and Interior Minister Rana Sanaullah were on a hit-list as part of plans to launch attacks on leaders of the armed forces, intelligence agencies, and politicians. Behind the plans were the TTP and its faction, the Jamaat-ul-Ahraar (JuA), which was also planning to target government officials. The TTP has been targeting both the ruling PDM and the army. When Pakistan saw countrywide arson after the arrest of PTI leader Imran Khan on 9 May 2023, a TTP commander, Sarbakaf Mohmand, praised the anti-army rioters.

The TTP's violent attacks have been mounting. Pakistan's Centre for Research and Security Studies assessed that more than 850 people were killed or injured in militant attacks and counter-terrorism operations in the first quarter of 2023 – a figure that was half the number killed or wounded people in 2022.[7]

The US Factor

Pakistan's *Dawn* argued in May 2023 that 'Pakistan failed in its Afghanistan policy, but so did the Americans and Afghans'. It identified the causes of American failure as 'lack of knowledge of Afghanistan's history and culture, poor war aims, the Iraq war distraction, frequent changes of strategy and commanding generals, inept Afghan partners, the dual authority of the Kabul government and the USA whose interests did not always match, and, last but not least, electoral politics in Washington. Finally, America lost the appetite for failure and simply walked out'. Afghanistan, said the paper, was 'a political challenge with a military dimension – and not a military challenge with a political dimension'. What Pakistan needed was a tightrope walk 'to make the best of a bad situation and help Afghanistan by facilitating its international engagement aimed at neither strengthening nor weakening the Taliban, nor a regime change, all of which are bad options.'[8] Pakistan thus continued to blame the USA for the Afghan situation, while advocating US and global engagement with the Taliban.

Pakistan's geostrategic value for the USA diminished after August 2021, with the withdrawal of NATO forces from Afghanistan, but the US-China strategic competition has ensured that Pakistan retained some residual relevance. While US strategic attention was focused on Ukraine, it was also engaged in another cold war with China and felt driven to engage Pakistan to prevent it from disappearing completely in the Chinese embrace. It also needed to retain some 'over the horizon' capabilities to keep an eye on and counter terror within Afghanistan.

The case for accepting the Taliban's rise was building for over a decade. Sometime around 2008, the US administration had had determined that Pakistan was critical to bringing stability to Afghanistan and that mainstreaming Taliban into the Afghan polity was key to the political future of Afghanistan. This soon became a wider consensus, globally and regionally, even though India held a different view. The US belief in this assessment was not shaken by the discovery of the al-Qaeda mastermind of 9/11, Osama bin Laden, in Pakistan in 2011. The Taliban was further legitimised with permission to create a Doha office in 2013 as effectively as an international foreign ministry of the Taliban.

From 2017, President Trump accelerated the process of looking for a hybrid power structure, deploying the evergreen special envoy, Zalmay Khalilzad. But Trump gave vent to his frustration in his January 1 tweet of 2018, when he called out Pakistan's 'lies and deceit' in its double game in supporting both US forces and Taliban terrorists who attacked them. By 2019, the US policy of demanding Pakistan 'do more' on Afghanistan changed to become a plea to 'please do more', with the USA suddenly bereft of options. The Biden Administration continued Trump's policy of diplomatic moves towards a power-sharing hybrid structure in Afghanistan, but was more focused on an early exit.

Due to a series of errors and accidents, a full Taliban regime greeted the world in August 2021. Within a year of the US exit, Shehbaz Sharif's PDM government in Pakistan, or more accurately, the Pakistan army, tried to continue being relevant to the USA as a credible interlocutor with the Taliban.

On 31 July 2022, a drone attack killed al-Qaeda chief Ayman al-Zawahiri, demonstrating a new US–Pakistan security arrangement in Afghanistan. Zawahiri, who had a $ 25 million bounty on his head, had coordinated the 9/11 attacks that killed nearly 3,000 people. President Biden claimed he ordered the strike after months of planning and the USA accused the Taliban of breaking the Doha deal by harbouring Zawahiri. A Taliban spokesman fumed that the strike was a 'violation of international principles'. Credible reports suggested that it was Pakistan that had provided operational intelligence on the wanted terrorist in Kabul, as well as the staging point for the drone that killed him. The killing of the top al-Qaeda leader boosted Pakistan's credibility in terms of its counter-terror promises, as also US domestic assurances that it could still manage its interests in Afghanistan without boots or diplomatic shoes on the ground.

The China Factor

According to classified documents[9] disclosed in 2023, Pakistan and some other nations have been discreetly distancing themselves from the USA on major global issues. Two Pakistani memos, obtained by *The Washington Post* and other US media sites, caution policymakers not to irritate China in order to retain ties with the USA. One of the documents signed by Minister of State for Foreign Affairs Hina Rabbani Khar assesses that Pakistan can "no longer try to maintain a middle ground between China and the USA." The internal communication distributed to official recipients in Pakistan in March 2023, titled 'Pakistan's Difficult Choices,' warned Islamabad against appearing to appease the West. It warned that Pakistan's urge to protect its relationship with the USA would ultimately forgo the full benefits of the country's 'real strategic' engagement with China. As Pakistan finds more reason to join the Chinese camp, it also sees more reason to co-opt China deeper into Afghanistan, where it can raise its geostrategic value by serving as the Chinese intermediary with the Taliban regime.

Qin Gang, China's Foreign Minister, and his counterparts from Russia, Iran, Pakistan, Tajikistan, Turkmenistan, and Uzbekistan met in Samarkand in April 2023 for a conference of Afghanistan's neighbours. The gathering coincided with the publication of a position paper by Beijing on its Afghan policy, titled 'China's Position on the Afghan Issue.' The paper provided a compelling case for Beijing's cooperation with the Taliban. Its Afghanistan approach also signalled China's rebranding effort: from a country bent on disrupting the current world order to one heavily invested in addressing 'international hot button issues' objectively, with 'no motivations to further its vested interests', in contrast to the USA.[10]

In the Chinese view, Afghanistan was 'transitioning from a period of turbulence under a United States-backed government to relative stability under the Taliban'. The paper pins the blame for the crisis on the West's failure in fulfilling its commitments and its decision to intervene militarily to enforce its conception of democracy without taking into account the distinct characteristics of Afghanistan. The paper criticises the USA for imposing unilateral sanctions and for unjustly blocking Afghanistan's foreign reserves. It demands a reversal of these actions.

China's Afghanistan activism is part of a wider global posture. Since 2023, China has taken attempts to cement its image as a power upholding global governance and offering a 'moderate and pluralistic environment' for discourse. The Global Security Initiative concept paper and Ukraine peace proposal released before the Afghanistan position paper indicate Beijing's desire to change its image and consolidate its role as a mediator. Beijing's apparent success in getting Iran and Saudi Arabia to negotiate and European leaders' trips reinforced its self-image of a growing power with a positive global outreach.

While the Taliban hailed the Chinese paper and its 'long-term political assistance', China's success in Afghanistan will be determined by what it can provide the Taliban. China's lofty language about Afghanistan-China ties is yet to be translated into a larger footprint on the ground.

A trilateral meeting in Islamabad in May 2023 was yet another affirmation that Afghanistan's neighbours see no alternative to engaging with the 'de facto government' in Kabul. Pakistan managed to secure special UN exemption from sanctions to allow Taliban Foreign Minister Muttaqi to travel to Islamabad to engage both Pakistan and China.

While counter-terrorism and trade featured on the official agenda, the underlying signal was of conferring legitimacy to the Taliban in return for assurances that they would not offer safe havens to terrorist groups directed at Pakistan or China. The Taliban was also co-opted in principle into the China-led economic corridor (CPEC), a key instrument of Chinese influence. The previous Afghan regime had resisted this move, perhaps concerned that this would make Afghanistan a theatre of contestation between the USA and China.

All three foreign ministers 'pledged to enhance counter-terrorism cooperation'. While for Pakistan, the presence of the TTP in Afghanistan remains a major concern, China is also wary of militants using Afghanistan as a safe haven. Its foreign ministry, referring to the Uighur militant group, observed that 'ETIM forces in Afghanistan pose a severe threat to the security of China'.

The Chinese Foreign Minister reminded the Afghan delegation at the trilateral meeting to "embrace inclusive governance and moderate policies," while Pakistan's Foreign Minister Bhutto said his message to the Afghan side was "help us help you." Later in the month, Bhutto reiterated emphatically that Afghanistan should prioritise Pakistani security concerns. He said that at his last discussion with Muttaqi, he told his Taliban colleague that the sole 'sticky point' in Pakistan-Afghanistan bilateral relations were terrorist groups such as the TTP, BLA, and Majeed Brigade. Bhutto admitted that the Taliban had a 'capacity issue' because NATO trainers had withdrawn and the Afghans did not have a standing army. He said that while he "empathised with the Taliban on capacity issues," Pakistan could not "tolerate the interim government's lack of will" to combat numerous terrorist groups operating from Afghan land. Clearly, the Pakistan army has been pressing Bhutto to enlist the Taliban's unambiguous support in tackling the TTP.

The India Factor

One driver for Pakistan's quest for strategic depth in Afghanistan has been its paranoia about India joining hands with Afghan forces in a pincer to squeeze Pakistan. This fear was not entirely abandoned with the exit of the US forces and the arrival of the Taliban in 2021. India's technical mission in Afghanistan, kick-started from June 2022, is something Pakistan continues to watch closely. Also, the reservoir of goodwill India built among the Afghan people with generous development aid worries Pakistan. It would be keen to keep Indian influence out of Afghanistan or at least retain a veto on the Taliban's India policy.

On its part, India continued to have a pragmatic Afghan policy, working towards a regional and international consensus on prodding the Taliban towards the formation of a truly inclusive and representative government; combating terrorism and drug trafficking; and preserving the rights of women, children, and minorities. India shares the fundamental dilemma facing regional and global powers: how to engage with the Afghan people while not legitimising the regime and sending a message to the Taliban on India's priorities.

On the terrorism concern, while India subscribes to the collective approach articulated by UNSCR 2593, demanding that Afghan territory not be used for sheltering, training, planning or financing terrorist acts, India has an additional priority: to make efforts to ensure that Afghanistan does not become a safe haven, not just for terrorist organisations like the ISIS – Khorasan and al-Qaeda, but also for the India-focussed ones like Jaish-e-Mohammed, and Lashkar-e-Taiba.

Pashtunistan?

By mid-2023, Pakistan's army chief Asim Munir appeared to double down on the army's stated security objective to mercilessly counter the challenge of the TTP with overwhelming force, as it had done against domestic militancy in the past, with joint military operations *Zarb-e-Azb* (2014) and *Radd-ul-Fasaad* (2017). For instance, a brutal operation in May 2023 evoked an angry statement from the TTP that the Pakistani military had attacked them in South Waziristan 'burning and killing' children, using jet fighters and drones along with land operations. This aggressive security posture was seen as a break from former army chief Bajwa's stop-start approach of attempting to engage the TTP in dialogue.

With the brief arrest of former Prime Minister Imran Khan on 9 May 2023, and the ensuing acts of arson against military property, the army exaggerated the seriousness of the assault to use it as an excuse to also double down on Imran Khan's PTI to neutralise it. With its penchant for hyperbole, the army's proxy media said that the PTI had done more damage in 20 hours than the TTP had done in 20 years. Perhaps relishing the irony, the Taliban's Ministry of Foreign Affairs issued a statement on 13 May, calling for political stability in Pakistan in the interest of 'the entire region', hoping for 'tolerance and understanding from the parties involved'. The Afghan Ministry also 'issued necessary instructions to its representatives regarding the safety of Afghans living in Pakistan'. This seemed sweet revenge for the Taliban for Pakistan's bullying and condescension. A media commentator lamented that when Afghanistan 'lectures the Pakistani state and its people on political stability', Pakistan moves from being a failed state, to a 'humiliated state in the eyes of the world.'[11]

As Pakistan's poly-crisis exacerbated in 2023, with multiple failures on the economic, political, security and ecological fronts, the country also groped externally for solutions. From 'iron brother' China, it looked primarily for economic assistance in the face of a standoff with the IMF, but also for a broader strategic partnership, including in its Afghan policy. Pakistan's new paradigm of privileging Chinese influence over US presence in Afghanistan marks a significant shift in its Afghan policy, deriving from its larger geopolitical compulsions.

Among the gloomy scenarios being discussed as Pakistan's crisis deepened, was a breakup of the country into several components, with provinces in the periphery – Balochistan and KPK – declaring independence. One of the scenarios observers gamed was a possible creation of Pashtunistan, merging the Pashtun areas of KPK and Baluchistan into Afghanistan. However, such an endgame was not imminent, as the army attempted to consolidate its control over the polity and security of the realm to ensure that the TTP did not cash in on Pakistan's multi-dimensional misfortunes.

NOTES

1. Gautam Mukhopadhyay, *Pakistan Insights* (ed.), Tilak Devasher (New Delhi: VIF), pp. 21-22.
2. https://www.independent.co.uk/asia/south-asia/taliban-pakistan-imran-khan-afghanistan-b1903821.html
3. *The Economist*, May 2023.
4. Muttaqi, letter to UNSC.
5. Javid Ahmad and Douglas, *Foreign Policy* (London, May 2023).
6. Charlie Wilson was a Democratic US Representative portrayed in a Hollywood film as leading the US Congress into supporting a CIA covert operation, which during the Carter and Reagan administrations supplied military equipment to the Afghan Mujahideen during the Soviet-Afghan War in the 1980s.
7. *The News*, Pakistan.
8. *The Dawn*, Pakistan.
9. Anwar Iqbal, *Dawn,* 1 May 2023, https://www.dawn.com/news/1750266/pakistan-walking-diplomatic-tightrope-between-us-rivals
10. A position paper on "Afghanistan signalling China's image recrafting," ORF, 10 May 2023.
11. Faisal Siddiqi, "People, sword, pen," *Dawn*, 27 May 2023.

12

Pakistan-China Relations: Whither China Pakistan Economic Corridor (CPEC)?

Amb. Jayant Prasad

Pakistan's former Minister of State for Foreign Affairs, Hina Rabbani Khar, penned an internal memorandum in March 2023 suggesting that Pakistan can "no longer try to maintain a middle ground between China and the USA," and must make a strategic decision to prioritise its relationship with Beijing.[1] Pakistan has long relied on its close and strategic relations with China to counterbalance India, develop its nuclear weapons and, in more recent years, for obtaining development finance. Its borrowings from Chinese funding agencies outpace the loans taken from the World Bank and the International Monetary Fund. Pakistani leaders describe Sino-Pakistan relations as higher than the Himalayas, deeper than the oceans, and sweeter than honey.[2] For China, this privileged association with Pakistan is a way to keep India busy in South Asia.

With the downturn in India-China relations in the late 1950s, Pakistan seized on the opportunity to have China as insurance for its foreign and security policy. Its 'all-weather' friendship with China became a function of the state of India-China relations, despite China and Pakistan diverging ideologically from each other. There are, indeed, no two countries in the world that could be so dissimilar. In opposing India, however, the two countries found common ground. On 20 October 1962, the day the Chinese forces launched their attacks all along the India-China frontier, Pakistan's Foreign Secretary told the Chinese Ambassador in Pakistan that India needed to be taught a 'lesson' and expressed the hope that "China will severely punish India."[3]

The fissures between India and China coincided with China and Pakistan opening negotiations with each other on their frontier. Pakistan's President, Ayub Khan, wanted to prepare a memorandum to approach China for boundary negotiations in December 1959 and ordered the Gilgit Scouts meanwhile to seal the border with Xinjiang.[4] In less than three years, there was significant Chinese accommodation and the Sino-Pakistan boundary talks commenced precisely a week before China's 1962 attack. China and Pakistan signed the Agreement on the Delimitation and Demarcation of Sinkiang on the Kashmir Border within five months.[5] It had a sweetener from China: a $ 60 million interest-free loan, with repayment over 20 years and a 10-year grace period.[6]

India had reason to be bitter at the Sino-Pakistan agreement on their frontiers, as Pakistan surrendered over 5,000 kilometres of de-jure Indian territory to China. Nehru felt that Pakistan had no business to hand over western Ladakh to China as the Jammu and Kashmir issue was still unsettled between India and Pakistan.[7] China's position was that since Pakistan had proposed negotiating border issues with China, China had to respond to it, especially as it was a fact on the ground that there was a de-facto border between China and Pakistan.[8] The Boundary Agreement covered the alignment of the entire boundary line between China's Sinkiang and "the contiguous areas the defence of which is under the actual control of Pakistan." It further stipulated that upon the settlement of the Kashmir dispute between India and Pakistan, "the sovereign authority concerned will open negotiations with the Government of the PRC on the boundary, to sign 'a formal border treaty' to replace the Agreement.[9]

Changed Chinese Position on Jammu and Kashmir

Post-1962, China's stand on the dispute between India and Pakistan on Jammu and Kashmir shifted. China openly supported Pakistan's position on Kashmir at the time of the 1965 India-Pakistan War. China then spoke up for 'self-determination' in Kashmir. When Indian forces pushed towards Lahore, China accused India of aggression and described India's action as 'perfidious on the Kashmir question.' Accusing India of sanguinary suppression' of the people of Kashmir, the Chinese statement read that it is entirely proper' that the people of Kashmir should rise in resistance.[10] The gloves came off in an editorial that followed in *The People's Daily*, which attributed exclusive blame to India for the armed clashes. The newspaper suggested the Indian claim to Kashmir being an integral part of the Indian Union exposed India's 'expansionist ambitions.' India was engaged in suppressing the 'legitimate aspirations' of the Kashmiri people for national self-determination, in a bid to maintain its 'colonial rule' in the Indian occupied sector of Kashmir.[11] "So long as India still commits aggression against Pakistan," wrote China's Ministry of Foreign Affairs in a protest note, "so long as she deprives the people of Kashmir of their right to self-determination, China will not cease to support Pakistan against Indian aggression or support the people of Kashmir in their just struggle for their right to self-determination."[12] This note was sent well over 24 hours after hostilities had ceased between India and Pakistan. Within days, a further Chinese note stated that its government "gives all-out support to the people of Kashmir in their struggle for the right of national self-determination."[13] The question remained whether to attribute this position to the fog of war or the quasi-permanent Chinese position on India and Pakistan. The Indian Embassy in Beijing reported that it perceived, for the first time a 'SIGNIFICANT' shift in China's stance on Jammu and Kashmir in 1970 following a *Xinhua* bulletin commenting about India occupying Kashmir and refusing to settle the Kashmir issue.[14]

China promised to assist Pakistan at the time of the India-Pakistan wars of 1965 and 1971. The Chinese put on a show each time to demonstrate solidarity with Pakistan but did not follow through. The memorandum of conversations between Kissinger and the Chinese leaders record Zhou En-lai requesting at the concluding session for Kissinger to tell "President Yahya Khan that if India commits aggression, we will support Pakistan."[15] China did not act the way it spoke. The Chinese action resulted in low-cost diplomatic support to Pakistan and high-cost alienation of Indians – already scarred by the memories of the 1962 war.

China's support for Pakistan's position on Jammu and Kashmir continues to rankle in New Delhi. Pakistan voiced its opposition to the modification of Article 370 and the annulment of Article 35 of the Indian Constitution. China has been the only significant country to have supported the Pakistani position. The Chinese Foreign Minister, Wang Yi, in the United Nations General Assembly, demanded that the Kashmir dispute be settled based on the resolutions of the Security Council and that there should be no unilateral change in the status quo. Reacting sharply, the MEA's spokesperson said that developments relating to the region were "entirely a matter internal" to the country. Speaking of the change in the *status quo*, he made a dig at the "illegal so-called China-Pakistan Economic Corridor (CPEC) in Pakistan-occupied Kashmir", thus underlining India's objection to CPEC.[16] The official Indian stand on China-Pakistan relations is that India is aware of the Chinese military assistance to Pakistan and Chinese aid to developing 'the so-called' CPEC projects, some of which fall within Pakistan Occupied Kashmir (POK). India continues to reiterate its position that Pakistan has been in illegal occupation of parts of the Indian state of Jammu & Kashmir since 1947 and has conveyed to China, including at the highest level, its concerns about their activities in POK and asked them to cease them.[17]

China-Pakistan Economic Corridor (CPEC)

Pakistan was on an unabated downward spiral, especially since the last decade of the 20th century. The CPEC (with an investment tag of $ 62 billion of an estimated $ 1.7 trillion for the Belt and Road Initiative (BRI), described by President Xi Jinping as a 'project of the century' that comprises both the Silk Road Economic Belt and the Maritime Silk Road – in 2014 China announced a $ 45.66 billion energy and infrastructure package for Pakistan) was designed to catapult it forward. The CPEC is BRI's flagship project. China's National Development Reform Commission (NDRC) quotes a Chinese media source designating the CPEC as "truly the most important BRI project anywhere in the world."[18] It is the BRI's sole bilateral connectivity corridor and Pakistan is the only country where the land and sea connection with China converges. The CPEC was attractive for Pakistan, given China's capacity to fund and build. Its main emphasis is on power plants (involving an outlay of $ 33 billion), highways (upgrading the Karakoram Highway and refurbishing the Karachi-Peshawar highway and building a new highway from Kotri, Sind, to Attock, Punjab), re-laying the Karachi-Peshawar and Kotri-Attock railway lines, a new railway (following the alignment of the Karakoram Highway and extending to over the Kunjareb Pass), metro lines (the Lahore metro, slated for completion in 2017, began commercial operations in 2020), ports (Gwadar – that can receive ships with 70,000 tonnes displacement + 2,282-acre free-trade area), and pipelines. The Early Harvest Projects (EHP) included 22 of the 120 projects envisaged under the CPEC, with a focus on four areas; energy, infrastructure, Gwadar Port development, and special economic zones. The next steps at Gwadar are the impending completion of an international airport and floating LNG facilities, based on Iranian supplies. US sanctions have slowed the construction of the Iran-Pakistan pipeline. The Gwadar deep-sea port connecting Kashgar, Xinjiang, is viewed in Pakistan as the jewel in the CPEC's crown. China's Overseas Ports Holding Corporation holds a 43-year lease to manage the port.

The Karakoram Highway (China-Pakistan Friendship Highway), completed in 1986, cost the lives of about a thousand Chinese and Pakistani workers. The

January 2010 flooding and landslides inundated a part of the Karakoram Highway, with the Hunza River extending over the Karakoram Highway for 22 kilometres forming a gigantic lake, at some points 100 metres deep. The re-laid Karakoram Highway, completed in 2015 at a cost of $ 275 million, circumvented that stretch. The Karakoram Highway is unstable both ecologically and geopolitically. It runs through fragile Himalayan passes and Gilgit-Baltistan, an area disputed between India and Pakistan.

The CPEC has been superimposed on the strong strategic and military tie-up between China and Pakistan that the two countries have cultivated since the early 1960s. To pretend that the CPEC is entirely about geo-economics defies credulity. "On the so-called China-Pakistan Economic Corridor," India's External Affairs Minister, S. Jaishankar, said recently that connectivity "cannot violate the sovereignty and territorial integrity."[19] India remains firmly opposed to the CPEC and BRI for this reason. In their meeting on 3 May 2023, in Islamabad, the foreign ministers of Pakistan, China, and Afghanistan reaffirmed their commitment to trilateral cooperation under the Belt and Road Initiative (BRI) and jointly extend the China-Pakistan Economic Corridor (CPEC) to Afghanistan.[20] India is equally opposed to the bid to extend the CPEC to third countries.[21]

CPEC's Problems

While the CPEC has brought benefits to Pakistan in terms of increased energy security and attracting Chinese loans and investment, it is not free from troublesome issues, some of which are as follows.

The growth in Pakistan's indebtedness: In an on-record briefing on the CPEC, the then Chairman of Pakistan's Senate Foreign Relations Committee, Mushahid Hussain, affirmed that the project would not result in a 'debt trap' and that the first repayment to China for the loans contracted, due in 2022 and valued at $ 1.5 billion, would be easily met.[22] That has not been the case. Before the CPEC, Pakistan owed less than 10 per cent of its external debt to China. Now it is 30 per cent.[23] Given Pakistan's foreign exchange crunch, some in Pakistan hoped that the amount owed might be converted into grants or, at the very least, relief provided by China by rolling over the loans (China has responded by providing a modest rollover of repayments). The Chinese financial institutions have extended loans for benefit and not for philanthropy. The Chinese debt is three times the IMF debt and higher than loans from the World Bank and the Asian Development Bank. There are concerns about the circular debt created by the repayment obligations, compounded by the Pakistan government having guaranteed returns to the investors on a cost-plus basis. According to one Pakistani academic, "'circular debt' – a term he uses for the energy sector's overall debt profile – is up from $ 7.2 billion in 2018 to $ 15.8 billion in 2021, and is projected to hit $ 26.3 billion by 2025. The capacity payment to power companies had also swelled from $ 4.4 billion to $ 5.9 billion and is going to increase to $ 9.8 billion in the next couple of years."[24] The anxiety to ensure uninterrupted electricity supply resulted in huge overcapacity. The off-take of electricity is less than the available supply in the winter months. The capacity payments are due from the Pakistan government irrespective of consumption, creating an unsustainable financial obligation.

The terms of the Chinese debt are opaque. Most of Pakistan's borrowings from China are from commercial banks and the agreements are confidential. Sartaj Aziz once implied that CPEC loans from the Chinese government would have a two per cent interest spread over 20 to 25 years.[25] In contrast, the Yen 300 billion Japanese loan to India for the Mumbai-Ahmedabad High-Speed Rail attracts an interest of 0.1 per cent over 50 years, with a grace period of 15 years. Pakistan's National Economic Council approved the much-awaited Mainline-1 refurbishment at the estimated cost of $ 9.85 billion under the CPEC.[26] Its original estimated cost was about $ 7 billion. Nearly 85-90 per cent of the funding, mostly loans, is funded by China.[27]

Security: On 18 July 2018, China launched two surveillance satellites to monitor the progress of CPEC projects. It is said that these were more for monitoring security threats to the projects. According to Pakistan's official account, by February 2019, 19,387 Chinese personnel were in Pakistan executing CPEC projects.[28] Unofficial figures are many times higher. A bus carrying Chinese engineers from the Dasu Hydropower Project in Kohistan was attacked in July 2021, killing 13, including nine Chinese engineers. Over a dozen attacks on Chinese nationals in Pakistan have occurred in the past seven years. The government of Pakistan has promised China foolproof security for Chinese personnel in the wake of the fatal attack on Chinese teachers outside Karachi University's Confucius Centre in April 2022. Security continues to be a concern for China and Pakistan has reportedly created a special committee and a 10,000-man special security force to protect CPEC projects and Chinese personnel.[29] The armed guards impede normal civilian activities and are a source of considerable annoyance.

Corruption and high costs: The Pakistan government appointed a nine-member inter-agency committee to enquire into the losses in Pakistan's energy sector. After eight months of investigation, the committee presented a unanimous 278-page report entitled 'Committee for Power Sector Audit, Circular Debt Prevention, and Future Roadmap.' The committee found standard operating procedures concerning power purchase agreements with independent power producers (IPPs) and fixation of power tariffs and guaranteed profits had not been adhered to. The committee discovered that IPPs were earning a 50-70 per cent annual profit instead of the standard 15 per cent, leading to a huge drag on the exchequer and recommended collecting Rs. 100 billion from the owners of power plants and renegotiating the capacity payment agreements.[30]

The audit report on the accounts of the Power Division in Pakistan's Auditor-General's Office for 2021-22 presents a detailed account of misappropriation, procurement and contractual irregularities, violations of SOPs and other defects resulting in a recommendation for a recovery of Pakistani Rs. 848,899.94 million.[31] The 4,000 MW Matiari to Lahore ±660 KV high-voltage direct current transmission line project executed by the China Electric Power Equipment and Technology Company and the State Grid Corporation of China and funded by a loan from the China Development Bank is said to have cost significantly more than comparable grid projects in India. The $ 2.2 billion project suffered from cost overruns and was mired in disputes.[32]

Low actual disbursements and investments: Over half of the stipulated time for the CPEC has elapsed but the ballpark figure of loans and investments from China to Pakistan hovers around $ 25 billion. Neither Pakistan's Planning Commission nor China's National Development Reform Commission (NDRC) coordinating CPEC projects provide updated disbursement figures. Of the 120 projects identified, less than half are complete.[33]

Overpromises and exaggerated expectations: The CPEC was supposed to be a game changer for Pakistan, transforming it economically, ending power and water shortages, facilitating transportation, and increasing industrialisation and employment. The results have been disappointing so far. Despite this, in Pakistan, expectations remain high. In early May 2023, Pakistani vernacular papers reported on the planned construction of a 1,860-kilometre "mega railway project worth $ 58 billion" connecting Balochistan with Xinjiang via Karachi, Lahore and Islamabad.[34] The NDRC makes no mention of this project. Pakistan expected that the CPEC would make Pakistan a production hub for exports to the Gulf,

West Asia, and Africa. There has been little growth, industry relocation, and the creation of employment.

Political vicissitudes and instability in Pakistan: Since the recent change of government in Pakistan, there have been repeated reports in the Pakistani newspapers about "the lack of commitment to CPEC" by Imran Khan's government.[35] The inter-ministerial and inter-agency CPEC Authority constituted by Prime Minister Imran Khan to streamline the implementation of CPEC projects was dissolved in August 2022, presumably on the ground that it slowed progress rather than speeded it. Prime Minister, Shehbaz Sharif alleges that Imran Khan deliberately and consistently subverted the CPEC.

Subversion of sustainable development goals: Pakistan's Ministry of Planning, Development, & Special Initiatives lists under its projects progress update, 21 energy projects under the CPEC – 20 power projects and one high-voltage direct current (HVDC) transmission line project. Coal-fired plants account for 8,220 MW out of a total production target of 12,584.7 MW, or 65.31 per cent. Hydro was projected at 3,414.7 MW, solar power at 600 MW and wind power at 350 MW.[36] The proportion of non-fossil fuelled power plants covered by CPEC is substantially lower than plants covered by multilateral funding institutions or other major bilateral donors.

Public disaffection in Pakistan: At the root of the souring of the public mood about the CPEC has been its being overladen by strategic considerations rather than developmental ones. Pakistani leaders promoted the CPEC as furthering employment, connectivity, investments, and infrastructure building. The largest province of Pakistan, Balochistan, has been apportioned less than 10 per cent of CPEC funding. Chinese experts, engineers and workers have been executing CPEC projects instead of generating local employment. There have been protests in Pakistan, especially in Gwadar, about the absence of the CPEC's benefits to the people. The Pakistani media has repeatedly commented on the absence of the 'all-inclusive' development and reported protests by thousands of people from all over the region about the lack of basic facilities in their area. Their situation is made worse by increasing unemployment

Moreover, they complain, these woes are acutely worsened by the active hindering by the security forces of their mobility...."[37] These protests in Gwadar, spearheaded by Gwadar Ko Haq Do Tehreek (Give Rights to the Gwadar Movement) leader, Maulana Hidayatur Rehman, persisted for a long time. The protestors, according to reports, "threatened to block CPEC projects," and the

Pakistani government responded by banning gatherings of five or more people and arresting Rehman in January this year.[38]

Moreover, the Agreement on The Long-Term Plan for China-Pakistan Economic Corridor (2017-2030) concluded on 21 November 2017, is opaque on its 'Investment and Financing Mechanism and Supporting Mechanism.' None of the mechanisms have been spelt out. It is well-established that China's external assistance has a low component of grants and a high proportion of commercial loans, which carry significantly higher rates of interest compared to lending by multilateral financing institutions like the World Bank and the Asian Development Bank.

The CPEC has not brought the benefits expected by Pakistan's leaders. Pakistan's Gross Domestic Product (GDP) growth rates are in secular decline. The contrast between the growth rates in the 1960s (1961-1970) and since the implementation of the CPEC (from 2015 onward) is vivid. From 5.9 per cent in 1961, the GDP growth rate went up to 11.35 per cent in 1970. The figures in recent years show a decline, from 4.73 per cent in 2015 to 6.49 per cent in 2021, with negative growth in 2020.[39] For the current financial year (FY) the projections are even lower. The World Bank estimates that the real GDP per capita was 2.2 per cent over 2020-22 and will contract to 0.4 per cent in 2023.[40] The Asian Development Bank's forecast for 2023 is higher by 0.2 per cent.[41] The International Monetary Fund's World Economic Outlook has forecast the 2023 Pakistan growth at 0.5 per cent.[42] The CPEC has not delivered on its promises.

NOTES

1. The memorandum was part of the recently available Pentagon documents leaked by a US military service member, known as the Discord Server Leaks, https://www.pakistantoday.com.pk/2023/04/30/khar-urges-to-avoid-us-appeasement-prioritise-china-in-leaked-memo/, accessed on 3 May 2023.
2. "Pakistan-China relations higher than Himalayas, deeper than oceans," Fawad (Pakistan's Minister for Information and Broadcasting, Chaudhary Fawad Hussain, said this on the eve of Prime Minister, Imran Khan's visit to Beijing in February 2022, https://www.radio.gov.pk/03-02-2022/pakistan-china-relations-higher-than-himalayas-deeper-than-oceans-fawad see also https://www.economist.com/asia/2017/09/09/massive-chinese-investment-is-a-boon-for-pakistan, accessed on 3 May 2023.
3. Cable from the Chinese Embassy in Pakistan, "Minutes of the conversation between the Chinese Ambassador Ding Guy and Pakistan's Foreign Affairs Secretary on the Sino-Indian border clash," *Wilson Centre Digital Archives*, https://digitalarchive.wilsoncenter.org/document/114763, accessed on 28 April 2019.
4. Manzoor Khan Afridi and Abdul Zahoor Khan, "Pak-China boundary agreement: factors and Indian reactions," *International Journal of Social Science Studies,* Vol. 4, No. 2, February

2016, https://www.researchgate.net/publication/285207412_Pak-China_Boundary_Agreement_Factors_and_Indian_Reactions, accessed on 3 May 2023.

5. 2 March 1963.
6. Mansoor Akbar Kundi, “US Pakistan’s relations under Khan 1958-69: impact on South Asia,” *South Asian Studies*, Vol. 24, No. 2, July-December 2009, p. 200, http://pu.edu.pk/images/journal/csas/PDF/2-Mansoor%20Kundi.pdf, accessed on 23 September 2019.
7. In his last important interview with the American journalist Arnold Michaelis, Nehru worried about the ‘grave difficulty’ caused by Pakistan’s virtual alliance with China. The interview aired in the USA on 18 May 1964. From the Doordarshan Archives, https://www.youtube.com/watch?time_continue=1657&v=zlTfXWFQYGQ, accessed on 14 May 2023.
8. “Memorandum of conversation: Deputy Foreign Minister Geng Biao and Director Zhang Wenji with Parthasarathy, 19 July 1961,” Wilson Centre Digital Archive, https://digitalarchive.wilsoncenter.org/document/121757, accessed on 30 April 2019.
9. Article VI of the Agreement. For its text see ASB, op. cit., Vol. V, pp. 4272-76.
10. Statement by the Chinese Government, Beijing, 7 September 1965, ibid., Vol. V, p. 4575.
11. *The People’s Daily*, 11 September 1965, ibid., Vol. V, pp. 4580-81.
12. Note from the Ministry of Foreign Affairs, Beijing, to the Embassy of India in China, 16 September 1965, ibid., Vol. V, p. 4623.
13. Ibid., 19 September 1965, ibid., Vol. V, pp. 4598-4601.
14. Cable from the Indian Embassy, Beijing, to the Ministry of External Affairs, 27 April 1970, ASB, op. cit., Vol. V, p. 4809. The cable noted that the reference to Kashmir was “a specifically new point.”
15. Memorandum of conversations of the final sessions with the Chinese, from Winston Lord, addressed to Kissinger, 12 August 1971, The White House, reproduced at the National Archives, https://nsarchive2.gwu.edu/NSAEBB/NSAEBB66/ch-36.pdf, accessed on 3 September 2019.
16. Statement made by the official spokesperson of the Ministry of External Affairs, New Delhi, 8 September 2019, https://mea.gov.in/response-to-queries.htm?dtl/31881/Official_spokesperson's_response_to_a_query_regarding_a_reference_made_by_Chinese_Foreign_Minister_to_ Jammu_ amd_Kashmir_and_Ladakh, accessed on 29 September 2019.
17. Response by India’s Minister of State for External Affairs to a Lok Sabha question on 23 November 2016, https://mea.gov.in/lok-sabha.htm?dtl/27658/question+no1200+ chinapak+relation, accessed on 29 September 2019.
18. https://en.ndrc.gov.cn/news/mediarusources/202107/t20210713_1290302.html, accessed on 14 May 2023.
19. Media Briefing, 5 May 2023, https://mea.gov.in/media-briefings.htm?dtl/36535/Transcript+of+Media+Briefing+by+the+Presidency+on+SCO+Council+of+Foreign+ Ministers+May+05+2023 accessed on 8 May 2023. Other, independent accounts of the CPEC indicate increasing talk in Pakistan about China’s ‘debt-trap diplomacy.’ See https://www.usip.org/publications/2021/05/pakistans-growing-problem-its-china-economic-corridor, accessed on 13 May 2023.
20. https://www.axios.com/2023/05/09/afghanistan-joins-chinas-infrastructure-plan-as-beijing-pushes-interests and https://www.dawn.com/news/1751728 accessed, on 14 May 2023.
21. Statement by India’s Minister of State for External Affairs, https://economictimes.indiatimes.com/news/india/inherently-illegal-unacceptable-india-on-move-to-extend-cpec/articleshow/93378548.cms
22. Mushahid Hussain, “Can the China-Pakistan Economic Corridor bring prosperity?,” 6 February 2019, IISS, London, https://www.iiss.org/events/2019/02/china-pakistan-

economic-corridor/, accessed on 5 May 2023.
23. "IMF's 2022 report estimated that 30% of Pakistan's foreign debt is owed to China," https://www.newswire.com.pk/2022/09/04/imf-6/, accessed on 8 May 2023.
24. Farrukh Saleem, *Asia Times,* 30 May 2021, https://asiatimes.com/2021/05/pakistan-begs-china-for-power-debt-forgiveness/, accessed on 8 May 2023).
25. Khurram Hussain, "CPEC cost build-up," *Dawn*, 15 December 2016, https://www.dawn.com/news/1302328, accessed on 17 May 2023.
26. https://www.thenews.com.pk/print/1005534-ecnec-okays-9-85bn-ml-1-project-under-cpec
27. https://thefrontierpost.com/ptis-incompetence-doubles-cost-of-ml1-dar/. See also https://tribune.com.pk/story/2258237/cpecs-strategic-ml-1-project-gets-final-nod, accessed on 17 May 2023.
28. Mushahid Hussain, n 22.
29. https://www.iiss.org/online-analysis/online-analysis//2019/09/sasia-pakistan-protects-chinese-investments, accessed on 14 May 2023.
30. https://profit.pakistantoday.com.pk/2020/04/11/govt-asked-to-recover-rs100bn-from-corrupt-ipps/ See also https://www.statecraft.co.in/article/pakistan-unearths-625-million-loss-from-cpec-due-to-chinese-corruption, accessed on 13 May 2023.
31. https://agp.gov.pk/SiteImage/Policy/Final%20Draft%20Audit%20Report%202021-22%20(D.G.%20Audit%20Power,%20Lahore).pdf, accessed on 16 May 2023.
32. https://www.aninews.in/news/world/asia/chinese-transmission-threatens-to-move-pak-company-to-international-arbitration-court20210211210446/ and https://www.dawn.com/news/1669731, accessed on 16 May 2023.
33. https://www.wsj.com/articles/chinas-belt-and-road-initiative-puts-a-squeeze-on-pakistan-11554289201, accessed on 8 May 2023.
34. Editorial, "Major improvement in Pak-China trade and tourism," *Ummat,* 4 May 2023, https://ummat.net/epaper/news.php?date=2023/05/04/&p=idr1.gif accessed on 5 May 2023.
35. https://epaper.dawn.com/?page=14_11_2022_003, accessed on 7 May 2023.
36. https://cpec.gov.pk/progress-update, accessed on 6 May 2023.
37. Editorial, *Dawn*, 3 October 2021, https://www.dawn.com/news/1649856, accessed on 8 May 2023.
38. https://epaper.dawn.com/?page=14_11_2022_005, https://epaper.dawn.com/DetailImage.php?StoryImage=16_01_2023_001_006; https://www.dawn.com/news/1728969, and https://www.dawn.com/news/1662256 all, accessed on 8 May 2023.
39. Figures based on World Bank data, https://www.macrotrends.net/countries/PAK/pakistan/gdp-growth-rate. See also https://data.worldbank.org/indicator/NY.GDP.MKTP.KD.ZG?locations=PK, accessed on 5 May 2023.
40. https://www.worldbank.org/en/country/pakistan/overview, accessed on 5 May 2023.
41. https://www.adb.org/countries/pakistan/economy accessed, on 5 May 2023.
42. https://www.imf.org/external/datamapper/profile/PAK, accessed on 5 May 2023.

13

Developments in Pakistan: Should India be Worried?

Lt-Gen Syed Ata Hasnain (retd.)

I like to label Pakistan as 'the Survivor State'. It somehow survives every catastrophe within and bounces back all over again before going down under. This makes assessment of its nuisance potential of being a wily, crafty and untrustworthy neighbour extremely challenging. The threats flow always and every time; it's a question of how serious they are in the short-, medium- and long-term.

Pakistan has for long been heading towards a situation where it could be perceived as a failed state, or at least a state under immense strain. Everything that goes into the efficient functioning of a nation appears under stress. The economy, internal stability and security, political leadership and foreign affairs, all seem to drive the nation towards an abyss.

Ever since the fall of the Imran Khan government it's been a southward journey with no positive indicators in any domain. To get a measure of how seriously the failure of Pakistan in different domains makes a difference to India's overall interests it's good to briefly examine the factors emanating from the following domains:

- Economy
- Leadership potential
- The Pakistan Army and its interests and capability
- The obsession with Islam, Kashmir and Afghanistan

- The internal security
- Strategic relationships as part of foreign policy

Nations with a propensity to pursue the path of hara-kiri need a deep study of their psyche. From the exercise of joining the dots of the past it is evident that Pakistan's problems are five, as follows:

- The undue focus it gave to the military security domain thus misbalancing its planning process in the allocation of resources and, more importantly, attention towards the well-being of its people.
- The lack of attention to economic planning, especially its food program and manufacturing. 'Cutting the nose to spite the face' was so evident from the decisions taken not to involve in serious trade with India or allow India access to the Central Asian Republics or Eurasia through its territory.
- The inability to bring modern education to the fore and discourage radical ideological belief.
- The refusal to address the necessity for a social transformation among its poorly educated masses thus allowing itself to be overtaken by obscurantist ideological beliefs. A mistaken perception that through this route it could lead the Islamic world.
- The obsession with conflict and the belief that sub-conventional means would deliver the desired results especially in dealing with its more powerful neighbour, India.

All the above have a contributory role to play in the flow of the recent run of events in Pakistan and the effect. How this impinges on India's interests and on Indo-Pak relations is analysed under different headings below.

Economy

Pakistan has never been able to replicate the initial promise it displayed in the Sixties when its citizens, while visiting India, were the cynosure of all eyes. The fantasy items they brought for their friends and relatives made us feel as if Pakistan was El Dorado. After 1971, Pakistan had to go to the IMF 23 times for economic bailouts. The country has been in a perpetual balance-of-payments crisis for many years and the state of its current economy is sufficiently worrisome. Plans of debt servicing and regeneration of the economy beyond do not ever seem to be the priority. Living from loan to loan and building up a cascading debt without any plans of expanding exports is the catastrophic policy Pakistan has pursued for many years. India suffered the ignominy of its forex reserves touching rock bottom at one billion US$ in 1991, but the active consensus-based political approach to changing its economic policies led to a turnaround without which India would have been in serious trouble. Pakistan unfortunately does not have the good fortune of national interest being the uppermost consideration of its political and military leadership, for whom self-gratification is the focus. According to Moeed Yusuf, former NSA under the Imran Khan government, the Pakistan economy for much too long was built upon the security model. The Pakistani leadership was satisfied with resources coming in on the basis of the geopolitical and geostrategic importance that Pakistan posed at any given time. He failed to say how shallow the thinking of the leadership was, that a national economy could be built on the basis of a nation remaining strategically significant forever. He was, however, courageous enough to say that Pakistan first needed to admit its past mistakes. Who is going to experiment with change in an election year? Yet without change, Pakistan will need to find someone with political gravitas and high leadership qualities to admit past mistakes, throw the electoral husting to the winds and take some courageous actions to restore even a semblance of the economy and in fact that of basic governance. If Pakistan is going to get driven by considerations such as those which effectively removed one of its best economic brains from the scene, then no one can come to its assistance. Atif Mian, the well-known Pakistani economist and Economic Advisor to Imran Khan, was removed from the appointment very early in his tenure in 2018; Pakistan's suicidal radical extremists demanded his removal because he followed the Ahmadiyya faith which is banned in Pakistan since Ahmadiyyas do not endorse the finality of the Holy Prophet of Islam.

The creaking Pakistan infrastructure is collapsing with the recent nationwide power outage extending almost 24 hours in some areas. Recovery without infrastructure that supports growth will remain a major challenge. After an elongated set of negotiations on the implementation of various measures that the IMF desired to overcome the political nature of Pakistan's economic expenditure and investment, the IMF finally granted a $ 3 bn bailout. "The arrangement comes at a challenging economic juncture for Pakistan. A difficult external environment, devastating floods, and policy missteps have led to large fiscal and external deficits, rising inflation, and eroded reserve buffers" in the fiscal year 2023, the IMF said in a statement. China has rolled over a $ 2 bn loan and the Saudis have deposited $ 2 bn in Pakistan's central bank to help overcome the problem at least temporarily.

A legitimate question many ask is why the Pakistan Army and Ministry of Defence could not release some funds from the $ 26 bn business empire that they run. A parallel narcotics and arms trade which goes across to Afghanistan and beyond sustains those involved and some others who are well off. Welfare for society, even in times of crisis, is sorely missing. While Imran Khan did not do anything of substance for the economy, and was involved in cases of personal corruption, it is the Pakistan Army which is at the receiving end of the ire of the public. It has lost much of the sheen normally associated with it.

An efficient and honest leadership is what Pakistan misses direly. It forces the public to make frank statements of comparison which recognize the Indian Prime Minister's personal contribution to nation building in every sphere in India.

Leadership Issues and Priorities in Management of Economics

It's a truism that no Pakistan PM has till date completed a mandated five-year term in office. Such is the quality of politics and so far is it removed from commitment and people orientation that Pakistan is perpetually in a state of political instability. The moment an element of independent thinking and compromise in the interests of the Pakistan Army is sensed, the latter undertakes the necessary measures to destabilize the leader and his government. The most important aspect is of course the controls that the Pakistan Army has over foreign affairs and economics. It lacks the ability to prioritize on the basis of real threats such as lack of education, infrastructure, modern agriculture practices, research and development, water management and the like, which are parameters of human progress and welfare. Instead, Pakistan's leadership has turned a blind eye to the money invested in the Pakistan Army capability development. Ayesha Siddiqa writes, "To avoid hard questions from the IMF, Pakistan refuses to be fully transparent about its military spending. Major acquisitions by the armed forces, spending on the public sector development programme, expenditure on the nuclear programme and para-military forces, payments for military pensions, a newly set-up national security division and a few other military expenditures are not reflected in the budget. If these were to be added to it, Pakistan's defence spending would be even higher – at around $ 11 bn more than what it was in 2020-21, at $ 7.5 bn. The Pakistan public has displayed immense patience with its government and its inability to get development going. A strong civil society once existed in Pakistan. It had taken Pakistan President Ayub Khan to task in 1968 leading to his overthrow. Although emaciated to a great extent, the near future will pose an opportunity for its empowerment as climate threats ravage Pakistan's fragile ecology where water deficit and surplus are in sufficiently high measure as to create existential threats.

The unfortunate thing is that while governments and the Pakistan Army are aware of these threats, their time is occupied more by issues such as faith which drives politics perhaps more than in any other nation. A stable and content society could come to terms with compromises with India on issues such as J&K. A restive, turbulent and broadly dissatisfied society can have its sentiments driven far more by radical elements and leaderships. India becomes the entity of hatred allowing the government and the people to be in sync with the Pakistan Army which in turn maintains the equations of power in which it is the dominant force.

Thus, if Pakistan has come to the sorry state it is in, it is nobody's fault but that of its leadership, the Army and its people. Given the serious situation of its internal administration, weak governance, a failing economy and a challenging internal security environment, it is a basket case for implosion. We cannot forget that Pakistan possesses nuclear weapons too and this aspect has to be factored into all scenarios as one of the most important inputs.

It is almost certain that Imran Khan will not be permitted to contest elections; his party may yet get a reprieve; without him it will stand little chance of winning. The Supreme Court has started hedging its bets; a departure from its earlier stance supporting Imran Khan, although this remains in the grey zone.

There is also yet no guarantee that the Pakistan Democratic Movement (PDM) will last. Although stability is desirable for peace, Pakistan's polity is highly unpredictable. The Pakistan People's Party may now like to campaign for the future premiership of Bilawal Bhutto. If the latter has to be a candidate of substance, an aggressive approach towards India will be helpful. His interaction with the Indian media in the June 2023 Goa meeting of the SCO gave no indicators of any changing stance. In fact, it was quite the opposite.

The one aspect which seems a certainty in the landscape of Pakistan's politics and leadership struggle is the fact that Army Chief General Asim Munir is unlikely to assume direct control. The benefits of not being responsible and yet be the dominant force are evident to him and the Generals. The only contingency for a crisis upsetting this assumption is a potential breakdown of the PDM and rancour between the constituents but it appears less likely.

The assessed effect on India arising from this factor also comes from the debt trap that Pakistan is stuck in and its constant kowtowing to China's interests. General Qamar Bajwa, the former Pakistan Army Chief, in the Islamabad Dialogue of the last two years, had reiterated the need to stabilize the relationship with India and aim to resolve the J&K issue. From the position of utter weakness that it finds itself in, no Pakistani government may like to create conditions for dialogue with India. The status quo is therefore likely to continue.

Radical Extremism and Internal Security

The history of radicalism and its birth in Pakistan is well known, although in some measure it existed right from Partition itself. The decision of its earlier leadership to adopt extremist radical ideology as a weapon against India has had a cascading blowback effect. No doubt, Pakistani society was slow in ferment towards radicalization. The political community did not get immediately affected as was evident from the results in elections where the radicals made only marginal impact till 2012. However, over time, the writ of the radicals has increased dramatically and it is now impinging on the political space. Zia-ul-Haq's idea was to employ radical ideology for the purpose of making Pakistan more 'Islamic' than even some of the Islamic states in West Asia, thereby aspiring for leadership status in the Ummah. The second purpose was to take the fight into J&K with pan-Islamic support and wrest it from India through internal turbulence based upon radical networks taking over society. The internal blow back within Pakistan was not anticipated which led to a cascade of events such as the Lal Masjid incident and the assassination of Governor Salman Tasir by a policeman named Mumtaz Qadir who after his execution is the virtual messiah of the anti-blasphemy lobby in Pakistan.

The internal war against the highly radical Tehreek-e-Taliban Pakistan (TTP) was dominated from 2014 to 2018 as part of Operation Zarb-e-Azb but no final victory was ever attempted. Post the US withdrawal from Afghanistan, the TTP is ruling the roost creating a major problem for Pakistan's internal security. It is now being supported even more by the Afghan Taliban as a means of keeping Pakistan on tenterhooks. The TTP is now fast re-emerging; the geopolitical circumstances have changed just as it rightly assessed but much faster than it could have predicted. Within a year of the US withdrawal from Afghanistan, the

Afghan Taliban is correctly assessing that it will need an Armageddon for the US forces to return to a region where its forces fought over 20 years with little strategic outcome. The Afghan Taliban is therefore shaking off the mantle of Pakistan's control over it. It was a creation of Pakistan's ISI and probably envisages a far greater role for itself in the ensuing intra and inter civilizational confrontation against forces that do not profess its extremist radical ideology, in the regional context. It appears that the Afghan Taliban's initial aspiration is to ideologically dominate the Af-Pak region, thereby dictating the internal discourse in Pakistan. That discourse of the early Eighties is what led to the creation of the Taliban movement. Whether today it has changed or not is a debatable point but Pakistan is struggling and realizing the folly of following a policy of promoting such an ideology. The same is deeply embedded in its civil society and is strangulating it from within. The Afghan Taliban is also placing greater pressure on the boundary issue with Pakistan questioning the finality of the Durand Line and its fencing. Its strategy appears to dwell on pressurizing Pakistan by forcing the commitment of its security forces to both border security and internal security related issues. It is fully aware of Pakistan's limitations in being unable to balance its security needs between the three areas of its compulsive focus – Afghanistan (including the border issue), the internal security of Pakistan (to include sectarian, ethnic and ideological threats) and the eastern border with India with special attention towards the Kashmir issue.

The effect of this factor on India is primarily in the long run with the likelihood of the Taliban and the other radical organisations, which have spawned in Pakistan, coming together. The presence of other organizations in Afghanistan, such as the Islamic State, coming together with the Pakistan radical entities, also remains a possibility. As a potentially larger element of a revised and reviewed cycle of global terror, the target will be Pakistan itself followed by an eastward move towards India.

The influence of radical extremists will probably discount any steps towards positive developments on J&K, beyond the current ceasefire. This suits the Pakistan Army too. The Baloch militancy, which Pakistan blames on Indian sponsorship, will no doubt sully Pakistan's internal security challenges even further. However, the intensity is unlikely to be a major factor in Pakistan's attitude towards India.

Foreign Affairs

The international community has reasons to feel concerned, especially because of Pakistan's nuclear weapons which are in a state of tenuous command and control. The USA probably got wind of the deteriorating state of things early enough and changed tack to some extent by backing Pakistan to control the internal situation in Afghanistan and the region in general. The refurbishment package for the F-16s was also linked to this. However, the reality is that the hard money that is required for recovery is not coming Pakistan's way. Without a disciplined approach and strict international oversight, a recovery is yet too far; the first question is that of survival and the manner in which the inevitable violence will manifest.

The feasibility of Pakistan going completely bust with no means of self-administration appears remote. The current arrangements can keep it afloat for some time but in temporary status. An informal economy can keep a nation afloat for some duration; Afghanistan is an example of survival of a nation on a minimalist economy. Nations at war for long durations suffer the same. Pakistan could also reach such a stage and only then the seriousness of its plight may be realized. Ways and means will be found to ensure a plaster and bandage survival. Recently almost $ 600 mn has been earned from the USA for the sale of ammunition to NATO. Ironically, money earned from the USA is being used to pay Russia for cheaper oil. Strategically, Pakistan remains too important a nation for it to be allowed to implode. The USA returned within eight months of withdrawal from Afghanistan to offer Pakistan a $ 450 mn package for the refurbishment of its F-16 fleet.

China has not demonstrated any propensity to go out of its way to assist Pakistan in its hour of need but the strategic relationship remains embedded quite solidly despite the above.

Contingencies and Options for India

Even after temporary stabilization of the economy, at some point if meltdown begins then a late resort to economic assistance, etc., will have little or no effect. From that point onwards, civil war conditions could prevail. India's international border (IB) with Pakistan will need to be sealed in such a situation. In today's security environment allowing displaced persons from Pakistan into our land will be suicidal. We should be prepared for non-tactical skirmishes along the international border with the potential for calibrated upgradation of violence. Human rights could well mire us in international controversy much as it drew Europe into it in 2015-16. It would test our diplomatic capability plus the quasi-military capability of the Indian Army and central border guarding forces to their full. Yet, the chances of that contingency remain remote.

Among the highest priorities in our current consideration should be the need for peace and stability. PM Narendra Modi's intent of putting India on the path of a ten-trillion-dollar economy demands such peace, going into the next ten years. It's the most cerebral and optimum option. It will enable India to develop and build such comprehensive national power that credible deterrence will be possible to be acquired and demonstrated against all adversaries. The temptation to do something, teach an adversary a lesson for his recent waywardness and gain a tactical upper hand may just be temporary. We need permanence in peace and stability.

Should India consider Pakistan's comprehensive weakness of today as an opportunity to weaken it further and let it fracture? There are factors which may argue in favour of such a step. However, we could do well to remember that the Global War on Terror has not yet ended; it's in a state of suspended animation. The establishment of the supremacy of Islam is the intent of the global jihadists. Another theatre of chaos with diverse Islamist forces would be gleeful environment for those who wish to see the spread of militant Islam. A below threshold militancy can take unpredictable shape and erupt differently at different junctures and locations. In other words, instead of the peace and stability which India desires for its growth to a well beyond ten trillion-dollar economy, a prevailing and unpredictable chaos at our doorstep and perhaps even within, isn't something that supports our belief in India's future.

What India really needs is a non-emotive analysis. Much as public opinion demands kinetic steps to destroy Pakistan as a nation, pragmatism points at far smarter ways of victory while maintaining our silent march to such prosperity that we could secure full deterrence through a well budgeted hi-tech set of armed forces. That reminds us of the Deng Xiao Ping model. The first three modernisations of China involved food sufficiency, technological capability and industrial manufacturing. When these were achieved China turned towards the PLA. Till then, the doctrine was 'stable borders'. The modernisation of the PLA gave China the coercive tool it sought and a noticeable change in doctrine has progressed since then. It was all possible because of the continuous high growth rate that China achieved. The overall balance in modernisation programs also lifted 750 million people out of poverty, adding to China's social stability which it has been unable to sustain due to other mismanagement.

Among the options for India there need not be any offensive military manoeuvres or rhetoric which could exacerbate the situation and draw response. A partial defensive deployment along the borders would caution the Pakistan brass against any irrational steps. The same must be conveyed through effective communication strategy from time to time. India's non-provocative and defensive deployment may draw criticism from many quarters within the nation; so be it. No one in the Indian strategic leadership is spoiling for war; our stance has to be defensive with adequate scope for offensive, should Pakistan decide to use the borders and its armed forces to score points from an existential outlook and diversion of internal attention.

Effective communication is the key to the emerging situation. DGMO hotlines are insufficient for such a scenario although initially a thrice-weekly interaction between DGMOs and weekly interaction at the sector and sub-sector level may help in ensuring the continued stability of the ceasefire at the LoC. Pakistan is bound to move its GHQ reserves into the PoJK area the moment there is any indication of Indian reinforcements. It has to be ensured that mistakes do not occur and that the propaganda machinery in the hinterland is effectively countered by Indian narratives. A special hotline between the NSAs will add further credibility to the availability of communications. The CI/CT grid must remain intact even though there may be very few incidents. We do not wish to create openings and give an opportunity. Jihadi elements will wish to see nothing more than an open clash between Indian and Pakistani forces; this has to be prevented.

Since the last time any conventional standoff took place between Indian and Pakistan forces in 1999, the entire domain of information has gained prominence. India will have to see how best it can use the existing means to develop Indian narratives and dominate the media networks, nationally and internationally. The Pakistan media has softened its rhetoric but this is temporary. Our response should cater both for long-term strategic and operational, and the short-term tactical advantage. TRPs of the electronic media and high-profile panel discussions of experts need not become the reference points for policy. The Government has enough experience of its own and sufficient resources for advisory. Its popularity is high and its international image is making waves. There is no need for any populist knee-jerk response but the process of consultation and war gaming with think tanks and within should give us the confidence to handle and see through the challenges emerging on our western borders.

Lastly, the nuclear realm has off late become a talking point. While we accord all forms of rationality to the analyses that we make and discuss, it may well be worth it to discuss the worst case scenarios for better education and deep professional consideration. Let the nuclear domain not become an arena of disadvantage just because we considered it far too sensitive to educate our senior service officers, academia, analysts, intelligence officials and diplomats. To be of deterrence value it must be seen to be well known and war gamed by the decision makers.

14

The Road Ahead

Tilak Devasher

Where will Pakistan be a year from now?

In the previous volume – Pakistan Insights 2021-22 – three trends had been identified as resonating in the year ahead: the precarious economic situation, civil-military relations and the survivability of the Imran Khan government; and developments in Afghanistan that are impacting Pakistan.

All three trends dominated Pakistan during the past year. The economic situation deteriorated with the country teetering on the brink of a default till the IMF bailed it out for the short term. In addition, there was a huge public outcry against massive increases in the price of electricity. Imran Khan was removed as PM through a vote of no-confidence in the National Assembly. Pakistan continues to be faced with the aftereffects of the worst climate-induced floods in the country's history. Though a coalition government led by the PMLN succeeded him, the political crisis has, often with constitutional implications, continued in one form or the other with even the president getting into the act while, despite his incarceration, Imran Khan has continued to dominate the narrative. In addition, there was a judicial crisis and confrontation between the Supreme Court and the Executive due to the partisan attitude of the Chief Justice in favour of Imran Khan. Relations with Afghanistan nosedived after the Taliban government declined to rein in the TTP that upped its attacks across Pakistan leading to a resurgence of terrorist violence with trans-border implications that have revived threats to Pakistan's security. All these crises are likely to continue.

What compounds these multiple crises is the fact that they are being played out against the backdrop of a completely polarised polity and society, where politics is even more bitterly contested than before, where political fragmentation and confrontation has not been amenable to resolution politically. How dangerous the situation had become was apparent in the remarks of the then interior minister, Rana Sanaullah, who said on a TV talk show that Imran Khan had taken the country's politics to a point where only one of the two could remain. Thus, rather than seeing other politicians as mere adversaries, a growing number of people described them as enemies and traitors. The mutual respect needed in a democratic polity thus frayed dangerously.

The second aspect of the situation is that for the last year and a half there was a weak coalition government in power and currently there is a caretaker government with a limited mandate. Though its powers have been enhanced, it is effectively the army that is in charge. By training and temperament, the army is not geared to handle matters of such complexity, though it thinks that it is. Even as the disqualification and imprisonment of former Prime Minister Imran Khan marks the failure of the Army's experiment with a hybrid democracy, it has nevertheless gone back to the drawing board, working out various permutations and combinations.

During the next year, these trends will continue to manifest themselves and possibly even intensify. A lot of attention will also get focussed on the electoral scene. While elections should have been held in November, it is unlikely due to the requirement of delimitation of constituencies after the 2023 census before elections can be held. Tentatively, there is talk about elections being held in February but scepticism continues. Discord in the Supreme Court and confrontation with the executive may get reduced with a new Chief Justice being sworn in.

Over the long-term, Pakistan has been a crisis-prone state that has faced a political and/or an economic crisis periodically. These periodic crises are best described in an editorial in the *Pakistan Times*: "Prompt and drastic measures are necessary to save Pakistan from virtual bankruptcy; but our rulers seem to be content with obtaining foreign gifts to feed the people and relying on heavier doses of foreign aid for maintaining some semblance of continued economic development." The same editorial goes on to say: "For almost a decade now, the political arena has been the safe playground of men cursed with unlimited greed and limited ability. Every year has been a year of crisis, and every season the season of intrigue. It almost seems that the only stable factor in our political life has been a constant instability."[1]

These words could have been written yesterday but actually appeared in a *Pakistan Times* editorial marking the 11th anniversary of Pakistan's creation in 1958. The resemblance with the situation today is remarkable.

Fast forward and compare this to an editorial in *The News* of 1 April 2023: "Today, Pakistan is again at a crossroads, staring into an abyss where the old power structures are leaking away as the new silently look on; where the superior judiciary stands divided; where politicians are baying for each other's blood; and where the people have been left to either rot or run away.... Unfortunately, all stakeholders have lost credibility...the system is collapsing quite rapidly all at once."[2]

The similarity between the situations in 1958 and 2023, sixty-five years apart, is extraordinary.

This provokes the moot question that if Pakistan has survived these crises, won't it survive the present ones too? Having been there before and done that, is there any need to be overly concerned because this too shall pass and, as before, a way would be found out of the situation?

The problem with this rather complacent view is that Pakistan today is entirely different than in the past because the objective conditions have fundamentally changed. (i) The sharp and all-pervasive polarisation in the country is unprecedented despite Pakistan's record of divisive politics; (ii) The overlapping crises – political, economic, security, constitutional, and judicial – are reinforcing each other; and (iii) No resolution of the political crisis, that is the key to resolving the others, is in sight. Moreover, it is unlikely that any one solution would be acceptable to all the stakeholders.

Four other elements of the situation are different and worth noting.

First, the present differs from the past in terms of greater youth activism in politics. Youth activism today is more-broad based and expresses itself in support for the populist politics of Imran Khan. This has obvious electoral implications. Over 44 per cent of the electorate – around 55 million – are young voters between 18 and 35 years of age. If youth activism translates into votes at the ballot box, it could be a game changer that can determine the outcome of the next election. This is all the more so because of the sizeable number of marginal and tightly-fought seats in general elections. In the 2018 elections, 87 seats were won by a margin of less than 1,000 votes, 26 seats by a margin of under 2,000 votes and in

51 constituencies, the winning candidate's margin of victory was under 6,000 votes.[3] Most of these were in Punjab – where general elections are won or lost. The average size of Punjab's national constituencies is around 780,000. So the youth voters could be decisive and no prizes for guessing who the youth support.

Second, social media today is another new factor shaping the political environment. This means traditional methods by which the establishment and political parties controlled or determined the narrative no longer works. While the electronic media is often subjected to government controls, social media cannot be restricted. It has become a mobilising vehicle that taps into and galvanises public sentiment and shapes the narrative.

Third, the military establishment's limits of political influence are also becoming apparent. In the past, it could manipulate 'electables' – politicians who had fairly strong bases of public support in their constituencies – to build up support for or against parties that it wanted. This enabled it to engineer electoral outcomes in their favour. Today, the traditional parties – the PMLN and the PPP – are no match in terms of public popularity, especially among the youth, as the PTI. Hence, without strong political partners, the army will find it difficult to use its old playbook.

Finally, due to steep increases in the prices of fuel and energy, there have been widespread protests across Pakistan. People have resorted to burning electricity bills. There does not appear to be any immediate prospects of a reduction in the high prices. In Gilgit-Baltistan there are major sectarian protests. In KPK and Balochistan, the security situation is grim. Overall, therefore, the situation in Pakistan today is volatile. Compounding matters, no leader, civilian or military, has any vision on what to do and how to tackle the situation.

As a result there is an element of Pakistan entering somewhat uncharted territory and unpredictability making its future uncertain. If not handled carefully by all concerned, the situation could spin out of everyone's control and drive the country towards the edge of the abyss.

NOTES

1. Cited in "Opinion: Pakistan has learnt little from India and India has taken the worst lessons from Pakistan," *The Scroll*, 14 August 2022, https://scroll.in/article/1030362/opinion-pakistan-has-learnt-little-from-india-and-india-has-taken-the-worst-lessons-from-pakistan
2. Editorial, "The centre can't hold," *The News*, 1 April 2023, https://www.thenews.com.pk/print/1056015-the-centre-can-t-hold
3. Maleeha Lodhi, "Electorate's youth bulge," *Dawn*, 27 June 2022, https://www.dawn.com/news/1696964

Index